Front roe

Front Roe

HOW TO BE THE LEADING LADY IN YOUR OWN LIFE

Louise Roe

Running Press
PHILADELPHIA · LONDON

Books published by Running Press are available at special discounts for bulk purchases in the United States by corporations, institutions, and other organizations. For more information, please contact the Special Markets Department at the Perseus Books Group, 2300 Chestnut Street, Suite 200, Philadelphia, PA 19103, or call (800) 810-4145, ext. 5000, or e-mail special. markets@perseusbooks.com.

ISBN 978-0-7624-5666-6
Library of Congress Control Number: 2014954975

E-book ISBN 978-0-7624-5672-7

9   8   7   6   5   4   3
Digit on the right indicates the number of this printing

Edited by Cindy De La Hoz
Designed by Susan Van Horn
Illustrations by Tracy Turnbull
Typography: Filosofia, Gotham, Perla Regular, and Juri Handwriting

Photo Credits: Pages 10, 242 (top left): Lauren Devon
Page 28: Ana Ochoa
Pages 59, 100, 269: Alexandra Piotrowski
Pages 66, 122 (bottom right): Jonas Mohr
Page 292: Ryan Chua

Running Press Book Publishers
2300 Chestnut Street
Philadelphia, PA 19103-4371

Visit us on the web!
www.runningpress.com

To Dad, the writer who gave me a bookmark when
I was ten that read "You can achieve anything
for which you have unlimited enthusiasm,"
and who has championed and supported me
whether I lived at home, or across the Atlantic.

    And to Mum, my best friend, my inspiration, who
always said, "Give them roots and give them wings"...
even though the wings took me a bit too far away
from England.

    I love you both dearly.

contents

Introduction . . . 9

PART ONE:

How to Find Your Style . . . 13

WHY I LOVE FASHION . . . 14

DISCOVERING YOUR VERY OWN STYLE . . . 16

BEFRIEND YOUR BODY . . . 19

WARDROBE REHAB . . . 23

HOW TO SHOP: LOUISE'S STYLE COMMANDMENTS . . . 31

10 WAYS TO LOOK A SIZE SLIMMER . . . 32

PART TWO:

Fashion . . . 35

HOW TO GET DRESSED IN THE MORNING . . . 36

HOW TO DRESS FOR WORK . . . 37

HOW TO DRESS FOR A FIRST DATE . . . 47

HOW TO DRESS FOR A WEDDING . . . 50

HOW TO DRESS FOR A WEDDING: BRIDE EDITION . . . 53

HOW TO FIND YOUR PERFECT JEANS . . . 55

HOW TO TRAVEL IN STYLE...60

HOW TO SHOP FOR SWIMWEAR...63

HOW TO ROCK THE RIGHT SHOES...65

HOW TO UP-STYLE WITH ACCESSORIES...72

HOW TO CULTIVATE YOUR LOVE OF HANDBAGS...81

HOW TO WEAR YOUR SCARVES...86

HOW TO STYLE YOUR HAT...89

HOW TO BUY AND SELL VINTAGE CLOTHES...94

HOW TO SHOP SMART, SPEND LESS, AND SAVE MORE...101

HOW TO FIND THE PERFECT UNDIES...106

HOW TO CARE FOR YOUR GARMENTS...113

PART THREE:

Beauty ...123

BEAUTY DOESN'T HAVE TO BE PAIN...124

SECRETS TO GLOWING, CLEAR SKIN...125

CHOOSING YOUR BEAUTY PRODUCTS...145

HAIR CARE FROM THE INSIDE OUT...157

HOW TO APPLY MAKEUP LIKE A PRO...170

MANIS, PEDIS, AND THE ART OF PAINTED NAILS...205

FINDING YOUR SIGNATURE SCENT...209

PART FOUR:

Lifestyle . . . 217

I'M OBSESSED WITH DECORATING . . . 218

SHOPPING FOR YOUR HOME . . . 219

HOW TO MAKE YOUR BEDROOM A SANCTUARY . . . 220

THE BATHROOM—HOW TO ACHIEVE THE PERFECT LOOK FOR YOUR LOO . . . 232

LOVE YOUR LIVING ROOM . . . 240

CLEANING WITHOUT HARSH CHEMICALS . . . 251

COOKING UP A STORM IN THE KITCHEN . . . 254

HOW TO BE A GLAMOROUS HOSTESS . . . 263

HOW TO FEEL FABULOUS ABOUT YOURSELF ON A SHOESTRING BUDGET . . . 278

THE 10 MOVIES EVERY FASHIONISTA SHOULD WATCH . . . 290

A FINAL WORD . . . AND MORE . . . 293

HOW TO BE KIND TO YOURSELF . . . 294

THOUGHTS TO BE INSPIRED BY . . . 297

Index . . . 299

Acknowledgments . . . 304

Introduction

I am six. Sitting up poker-straight at the table, on my absolute best behavior. It's teatime, it's Christmas Eve, and we're at Granny's house. Dressed in my party frock—saved for special occasions—I look down and wiggle my little black patent shoes, admiring my big taffeta skirt that rustles when I move, and the dark red velvet ribbon fastened around my waist, which makes me feel like a princess. It's a memory clear as quartz, etched in my mind, because for the first time, my clothes are changing the way I feel inside.

Steam rises from the giant antique china teapot as it's poured from what seems like a great height, into my very own china teacup and saucer. Two lumps of sugar follow, balanced precariously on a delicate silver spoon. *Plop, plop.* A dash of milk, from the tiniest china jug I've ever set eyes on. Hand-painted with flowers on the outside, it looks as if it belongs in a doll's house. In the distance sits the Eiffel Tower of candy, my granny's cake stand. Laden-full with cucumber sandwiches (white bread, crusts cut off) and slices of home-made Victoria sponge, the jam and cream oozes from the cake's middle and smiles at me . . . with whipped cream teeth and strawberry jam gums.

My granny was never rich, not at all, but boy was she glamorous. Elegant, ladylike, impeccably mannered, and dressed to the nines at all times, my imagination took flight when she would recant stories of cocktail parties of the 1940s, ladies dripping in sequins, hands covered by lace gloves, with shiny black cigarette holders perched between their fingers. If you couldn't afford stockings back then, you dyed your legs with used tea bags and drew seams up the back of your calves with an eyebrow pencil.

"Did you know, darling," started Granny, her immaculately painted red lips shaping each vowel, "that during the war, *Vogue* magazine was one of the only publications not to be shut down? And red lipstick—it was never, ever rationed. Keeping ladies stylish was deemed *that* important for the country's morale."

Suffice to say, even when bombs were being dropped, women still felt the desire to rock out their

inner Veronica Lakes, and the country understood the importance of that for boosting national spirit.

I was too little to even know what a catwalk was, but at that moment, on clicked my radar for all things glamorous. And it has stayed on ever since. Style isn't something that needs to cost a lot of money; it's more about the effort and imagination you put into it that counts. That was, without a doubt, the first time style became important to me. It was an eye-opener to realize how fashion cannot only change the way you look, but also the way you feel inside and, consequently, the way others perceive you.

Now, after years of working as a journalist within the fashion industry, and as a TV presenter giving people makeovers, I'm bursting with thoughts, tips, and tricks of the trade I want to pass along—some old (like those long forgotten but still vital beauty and fashion secrets my grandmother shared with me) and some new that I've learned through my work in fashion. A lot of people think it's only runway models, celebrities, the very rich, or the very slim that can have great style. Well, I'm here to tell you otherwise.

Keeping up with the constant hamster wheel of new trends, whether beauty or fashion, is exhausting, not to mention financially ridiculous. So how

about finding a style that's more consistent, more inspiring, more personal, more *you*?

Everybody, and I mean everybody, can develop a style of their own, and without breaking the bank. Style is about making clothes work for *you*—your body shape, your lifestyle, your tastes. It's a matter of remembering those flashes of inspiration when you see a photo or a movie that makes you green with envy. It's about savoring a memory, a chapter in a book, a page in a magazine, a chic fashionista on the street, a visit to a gallery—that made you want to recreate a certain look or feeling.

It's time to get your imagination in gear and create an image of what you want to portray to the rest of the world. Once we've got that idea sorted, I'll take you through the key practical elements of developing your own personal style—fashion, beauty, and lifestyle—to help you find yours.

Take a cue from Coco Chanel and start thinking of style not as the new frock you can neither afford nor fit into, but as something you can sprinkle into your everyday life in a myriad of ways, large or small. She wisely once said, "Fashion is not something that exists in dresses only. Fashion is in the sky, in the street, fashion has to do with ideas, the way we live, what is happening."

Part One:

HOW TO FIND YOUR STYLE

WHY I LOVE FASHION

I feel very lucky to get up every morning and look forward to work. My job involves either writing about fashion and giving women tips, or doing the same thing on TV. I get to play dress-up and help girls improve their self-esteem, by showing them new ways to dress their body. Over the past seven years, I have given makeovers to hundreds of women, ranging in age from thirteen to sixty-five. No matter where they're from or what their background is, they all share one misconception: fashion doesn't apply to *them*. They can admire a woman in a great dress, read a fashion magazine and drool, but when it comes to shopping: they hate every minute of it, because they're lost. Needless to say, I am itching to get them through department store doors to show them new shapes and styles to suit their body shape, their taste, and their lifestyle. Some can't wait to try everything on and embrace a whole new image in the mirror; while others are sincerely stubborn, look at me like I'm nuts, and are set in their ways. But I have one rule, and that's to try things on. You can always take them off again and plop them on the "no" pile, but if you don't try that yellow printed dress with a peplum hem on, you'll never know how damn hot you actually look in it. The mirror speaks louder than I do.

To say these shopping sessions are emotional is an understatement. There's no sugarcoating the fact that body image and self-esteem are deep-rooted, psychological, and very personal issues. They are issues that *all* of us have at one point or another in life: so if you're feeling like your confidence levels really should be a lot higher, you're not alone. I certainly had my phase of feeling like I couldn't match up to the polished, slim, designer-clad image of working in the fashion industry. It was tough, and I was extremely hard on myself for a few years when I lived in London. I was my own worst enemy, and it wasn't until I decided to make friends with myself, that I could finally embrace who I was. It was a big weight off my shoulders. And you thought this book was just about high heels! Ha!

These days, I use all that history to help the women I have the privilege of making over. It's never about changing who they are—no way. It's about enhancing what they have, making them see a different side to their character, and celebrating themselves, inside and out. Is fashion the most important thing in the world? Hell no. Is it far more significant than people think, as a means for self-expression, confidence, and power? One hundred percent *yes*.

All I can hope to do in that changing room is show a woman she deserves to feel far more beautiful and confident than she often does. If there's one thing you take away from this book, I'd love it to be a newfound belief in yourself. And if you're already bezzie mates (besties!) with yours truly, then get ready for an awesome shopping spree to transform your wardrobe, beauty cabinet, and home!

DISCOVERING YOUR VERY OWN STYLE

It can be totally confusing walking into a big shop and seeing a myriad of clothing racks—trends and styles leering at you left, right, and center; ON SALE signs trying to lure you their way, bright lights and loud music assaulting your senses. The act of shopping isn't always a calm, happy experience. The key is to walk in knowing what you're looking for and, more importantly, what suits you.

Here's my nerdy little secret: since 2007, I have kept a scrapbook of images and quotations that inspire my love for fashion. Every few months, I cut and glue into collages (yep, just like kindergarten) the magazine rip-outs of looks I love, the Polaroids I take of architecture and artwork, the sketches, and the old ticket stubs of shows I've seen. If I'm ever short on inspiration for an outfit, I flick through it and get so many ideas. It reminds me what my core style is all about, and, for me, that's full of prints, bright shoes, tailored trousers, and fedoras. I'm obsessed with style icons from the late 1960s, like Talitha Getty, and the 1970s, like Ali MacGraw and Lauren Hutton. These women could change from a long, flowy caftan to a white shirt and denim cut-offs, and still ooze glamour. They had an understated sophistication that was so subtle. I love how they didn't feel the need to wear tight or revealing clothes as a way of being sexy.

Before I take a woman shopping, I ask her to scour fashion blogs, magazines, old family albums, art galleries, movies—to get a sense of the look *she* loves. Is it high tops and a beanie—a tomboy look? Or does she love floral tea dresses and little belts—like a 1950s Stepford Wife? Or are leather pencil skirts and red lips her thing? Perhaps she's a sexy femme fatale just waiting to come out of her shell? Has she always liked the floppy hats and flares of a boho retro look, or do bold prints and thick cat eyes appeal, like Twiggy wore in the mod '60s? Anything that makes your eyes light up, whether you think it will suit you or not, is a start.

I'm going to show you over the next few chapters how to make that style work for you and your body. If Audrey Hepburn is your girl crush, I certainly

wouldn't stuff a cigarette holder in your mouth and make you prance around the office in pearls and a beehive, but I would help you buy clothes that nod in her direction. Pearl earrings for example, a black sheath dress and patent ballet flats, could be a modern take on Audrey's look.

It's also crucial to strike a balance between what's out-of-bounds, and what simply makes you step outside of your comfort zone. If baring a midriff or the color purple are two things that make you feel sick, then I wouldn't push you in that direction. But if there is a style or color you love that you've never had the guts to try, now's the time. I will never forget the episode of *Plain Jane* when I was handed a long list by my "Jane" of things she refused to wear. Included were denim, sequins, prints, shorts, hats, oh, and don't let me forget butterflies. Umm, what? I'm not sorry to say I ripped the list right up in front of her, and we had the best shopping spree ever. You've got to have an open mind.

STYLE AS SELF-EXPRESSION

YOUR CLOTHES SHOULD ALWAYS express your personality, but also be eclectic enough to rock whatever mood you're in that day. Simple translation? You need a core group of timeless, reliable pieces that suit you (more on that under Wardrobe Rehab, page 23), but also a bunch of lively, fun accessories to switch things up when you fancy channeling a different facet of your character.

You may not know it, but chances are you've already got a "core style," judging by the items you end up buying time and time again. You keep bringing home garments akin to those you already own (skinny jeans again . . . more printed scarves . . . another blazer?). But this isn't a bad thing; it's a great indicator of what suits you. Wear these signature items proudly, consistently. Now we just need to find the new pieces of your style puzzle.

BEFRIEND YOUR BODY

Once you've done your research, it's time to get naked. For real! An astounding amount of women do not look in the mirror naked even once a day. That means they aren't in touch with their bodies or their body shape. The most powerful knowledge to arm yourself with when you shop is knowing your silhouette. Forget about fabrics, prints, and prices. You should be looking at the cut and shape of a garment. Trust me, you can shave ten pounds off your figure and alter your proportions with the right clothes. This is no diet book. I believe in healthy eating, yes. But I also believe in embracing, enhancing, and streamlining what you've got going on *now*, that curves are beau-

tiful, and I believe in buying for the body you have. Not the one you had at sixteen, not the one you dream you'll have eventually. That girl can buy *her own* clothes. You deserve yours! The French have a perfect phrase for what I'm trying to say: *mettre en valeur*. To paraphrase my own translation, it means, "Rock whatcha got!"

Stand in front of a full-length mirror without clothes on, and look at where your figure goes in and out. Focusing on your shape and proportion (not your size, height, or weight), see which body type on the following pages you relate to most. You might feel you fall into more than one category, in which case feel free to take my style advice for both body types.

TOP HEAVY

Your top half is wider than your lower half, either because your shoulders are broad or you're blessed with big boobs. Top-heavy figures tend to have narrow hips and great legs. LeAnn Rimes, Charlene, princess of Monaco, and Kate Upton are examples.

GOAL: Show off your legs and soften your shoulders and upper body.

LOOK FOR: Bright or printed cropped pants, bright maxi skirts, hipster jeans, and tops with capped or three-quarter-length sleeves. Steer clear of frills around your upper body, off-the-shoulder tops or bandeaus, and boat-neck tops.

HOURGLASS

Lucky you! You're the classic Coke-bottle silhouette that goes in at the waist and out either side of it. Super-feminine and sexy. Think Christina Hendricks, Kim Kardashian, and Sofía Vergara.

GOAL: Show off your beautiful curves by cinching everything at the waist, and elongate the whole feminine figure with a heel.

LOOK FOR: Medium to low necklines that accentuate the bust and balance out the hips. Off-the-shoulder, V-neck, or deep round necks look great on you. Focus on your waist, accentuate it with a thick belt over an A-line dress. And show off that butt and hips in a pencil skirt or high-waisted jeans; it's sexy to be voluptuous. But keep away from shift dresses, boxy jackets, or tunics—or any other shape that is baggy around your waist.

APPLE

Most of your weight accumulates around the middle, so the minute you put weight on, it goes to your belly. The good news is, everyone is jealous of your narrow hips and legs. Reese Witherspoon, Drew Barrymore, and Catherine Zeta-Jones are apples, but you wouldn't know it because they dress themselves cleverly, according to their body shape.

GOAL: Elongate the torso and deflect attention down to your butt and legs, or up to your shoulders and arms.

LOOK FOR: Empire-line tops, where the seam runs just under the bust, allowing the material to skim over and hide your tummy. Loose shirts worn with a few buttons undone and the sleeves rolled, paired with skinny jeans or leather pants is your look. Miniskirts and batwing tops also work. If you want to belt it, go for a hipster option; it will be more flattering than putting one directly around your middle.

PEAR

Your lower body is wider than your upper body. You have a rounded bottom and a smaller waist. Famous pear shapes include Jennifer Lopez, Beyoncé, and Katherine Heigl.

GOAL: Accentuate your waist, your arms, your shoulders, and if you like your butt— your butt!

LOOK FOR: Wrap dresses that draw the eye to your small waist and minimize hips. A boot-cut or flare jean will make your butt look smaller. Buying one size too long and wearing a heel underneath the flare will elongate and slim your whole leg from hip to heel. High waists are your best friend; hipster cuts are not. A pencil skirt looks super sexy on a pear shape. Keep the waist high, your lower half a dark color, and your upper body in a light color. Add heels, preferably with a pointy toe to elongate your legs. Strapless and one-shoulder dresses suit you, too.

COLUMN

You shoot straight up and down, either because you have an athletic figure, a boyish figure, or you're very slender. Either way, the fashion industry makes a lot of looks for your shape! Charlize Theron, Emma Stone, and Kate Hudson rock this figure.

GOAL: You can play up the androgyny with crisp tailoring and flat shoes, or add curves with little tricks. The choice is yours.

LOOK FOR: To create a waist, use a thick belt as a corset. Worn with an A-line skirt, it's possible to achieve an instant hourglass. And for your top half, go for a plunge bra if you want to enhance your chest.

On the other end of the spectrum, you can wear low-cut tops without falling out of them, tailored pants and blazers look slick and chic, and boyfriend jeans look awesome on you with Brogues or Birkenstocks.

WARDROBE REHAB

Before we dive into the fashion section, I want you to plan a wardrobe detox. A closet clear-out gets you super organized, and really ready to shop. It saves you a fortune when you do hit the mall, too, because guess what? We women only wear about a quarter of the clothes we own. A quarter! That's such a waste! So next time you shriek "I have nothing to wear," think again. Chances are you've got plenty, you just need to reorganize and streamline your closet, and most importantly, reacquaint yourself with old faithful pieces that can have new life breathed into them with the right belt or necklace.

Most of our wardrobes are a mix of tops and dresses lost and ignored in a messy bundle on the floor or wedged in the back where you can't see them. An overflowing closet leads to morning chaos and the same old safe daily outfit choices. If you can see everything you own, however, you're more likely to wear a variety of fun looks. A closet blitz also saves you valuable time every morning, because you'll know exactly which items work as an outfit, and where the heck they are.

Set aside a Sunday afternoon and get *everything* out on the bed. Borrow a clothing rail, if possible, for easy viewing, to hang those things you choose to keep and to help style up new looks.

Be Ruthless

DON'T KEEP AN ITEM THAT:

- IS BEYOND REPAIR. I love a vintage skirt with a worn look, but if there's a missing panel, a dodgy zipper, and a tear not on the seam, it's best trashed.

- BELONGS TO AN EX.

- YOU HAVE THREE OF. Unless you're Mariah Carey, with a closet the size of an apartment, you don't need to clog up your shelves with seventeen white tees and eight stripy Bretons. Choose your favorite three of the same item and lose the rest.

- YOU ONLY BOUGHT BECAUSE IT WAS ON SALE—and you don't love it.

- IS ITCHY. Scratchy clothing is my worst nightmare, you spend the whole day wondering when you can rip it off.

- YOU CAN'T WALK IN. I'm talking shoes that are too small, too high, or just the perennial blister-giver.

- IS TOO SMALL. Even if you lost ten pounds, it would still be too small. And just looking at it makes you depressed. Get rid of it! Opening your closet needs to make you smile, so get rid of everything that doesn't!

- IS WAY TOO BIG. Anything more than a size too big, intended to be worn outdoors in the real world, should go (and that's me hinting your baggy college sweatshirt should be for movie nights only!).

- YOU HAVEN'T WORN IN THE LAST TWO YEARS. Because you never will, and deep down you know it.

Take the clothes you're ditching to a charity store (even if a dress is falling apart, they will usually take it and use the fabric) or sell it on eBay or to a consignment store. I often sell my clothes on the stylish websites Pose and Vaunte, the latter of which is for designer pieces. Or why not plan a clothes-swap party? Get the girls over, pop a bottle of wine, and play the game of free shopping. It rules!

But Also Be Creative . . .

BE OBJECTIVE about whether that decade-old little black dress could be updated with some new accessories or by a nip and tuck from the tailor. If you were looking at it in a shop today, would you buy it? What would look great with it? A new red blazer or a printed scarf, perhaps? Think imaginatively. Could you resole a pair of shoes, add a snakeskin belt to your trench, change the buttons on your shirt, *et voilà!* You've got a new, awesome look? Don't be afraid to repair, alter, and customize existing pieces to give them a new life. Adjusting and tweaking your clothes is a great habit to keep. Why play it safe? Have fun with it. Finding your style is about experimenting, and by the way, that includes making mistakes, too.

I never leave my clothes alone. I roll the hems on my jeans or the cuffs on my shirt; I layer a top underneath a sleeveless sweater; I switch the color of my shoelaces. Even wearing your shirt buttoned all the way to the top gives it a completely different, more androgynous look than when the buttons are open and low, exposing the tiniest bit of lace camisole underneath. Not wearing your clothes the same conventional way as the girl in the campaign or on the runway is what true style is all about. The smallest nip and tuck and you've avoided the fashion-victim label and evolved a personal style.

Examine Your Basics

A TRENCH COAT, penny loafers, a white shirt, black or blue blazer, well-fitting blue jeans, a tan tote bag, and Chelsea boots will never, ever date. Don't get too detox-happy and be tempted to chuck out any of these items. You *will* wear them again!

Once you've created a "yes" and "no" pile, do the same for your underwear, hosiery, shoes, bags, and coats.

Style It Up

USE THIS VALUABLE TIME to devise a range of new looks, with photos taken for reference. By teaming clothing and accessories, you'll be amazed at the surprising combinations of new and old. How cool do your old ripped jeans look with mom's retro sequin sweater? It also helps you figure out what you need to buy. That patent red clutch looks amazing with your white dress; all that's missing is a skinny red belt. I know many stylists who will Polaroid the entire look, including jewelry and bags, and save those pics in a bedside drawer. It may seem like a lot of work at the time, but trust me, when you've overslept on a Monday morning but have ten ready-made kick-ass outfits to choose from, you'll be thrilled.

Mirror, Mirror on the Wall

HERE'S A TRICK I LEARNED THE HARD WAY: make sure you buy a mirror that's true. Don't do what I did at university and buy the cheapest full-length you can find, because chances are it'll be uneven and will warp your figure, making you look fatter or thinner, or out of proportion. I spent the best part of an entire semester wondering why I looked weird before a girl's night out, and figured it was the tequila. Ha! So don't skimp on a mirror. Pay a little extra and you'll know what you *really* look like.

Be a Neat Freak

LITERALLY—CLEAN YOUR WARDROBE AREA. Hardly any of us bother doing this. But actually, closets need as much care as a fridge. Spritz the walls, remove fluff and dust from the floor, and wipe the shelves and railings.

Now morph into a fashion fanatic and hang everything facing the same way—this makes it much easier to pull pieces out. Use the same types of hangers if possible. For silks and chiffon though, invest in padded hangers. Hang pencil skirts upside down so they keep their shape, and don't layer clothes on hangers. You'll forget what's underneath and never end up wearing it.

Separate winter from summer clothes, and if necessary box up and store the opposing season's stuff to give yourself more space. Color coordinate the rest of your clothes from dark to light. I like to group my dresses, skirts, tops, and trousers, and then color coordinate each section. Take out anything that needs mending, washing, or dry-cleaning.

Keep your tees folded on shelves or inside drawers, and fold knitwear horizontally with the arms across the body. This can be tricky, so try a T-shirt folding

board to help you get the hang of it. You can buy these cheaply from most department stores or make your own from cardboard. Folding your tops properly creates fewer creases, which equals way less ironing. Stack jeans in similar styles.

Use dividers in your socks and underwear drawers, and find matching sets of lingerie easily by hooking your knickers through your bra band and fastening the clasp.

Maximize your storage space with a vertical hanging organizer. These are inexpensive and tend to have deep pockets for shoes, and transparent pockets for smaller items.

A bookcase is a great option for storing, and displaying shoes or bags. In my study I have a bookcase full of color-coordinated clutches, filed like books to keep them in place. I love looking up from my laptop and seeing a rainbow of handbags; it's inspiring to say the least! You can also use sweater dividers for delicate materials like satin (which can snag) and patent (which can discolor).

If your bookcase or shelves are full of clothing you'd rather not show off, hide everything behind a curtain. A weighty fabric in cream or caramel looks simple and clean.

Tack coat hooks onto the wall inside your closet; these are handy for storing delicate items, such as scarves and hats. Soft totes should also be hung up, to prevent them losing their shape. Try not to lie them down. Ladders are a cute way to hang scarves and belts, and help reach the higher shelves, too.

Archive your evening gowns and anything fancy into garment bags. This is really important to help stop moths and dust from ruining the fabric.

And buy shoe racks! These save so much space and help you see more of what you own. Many people love to store heels in shoeboxes, with a photo of the pair stuck to the front. This is a great way to keep shoes safe and organized, but personally it's too much hassle and, when I tried that idea, I didn't wear many of the shoes at the bottom of the pile because it was a pain getting them out.

For expensive shoes, or shoes made from soft material, such as suede or silk, insert a shoe tree to help keep their shape. The same goes for long boots.

To freshen things up, throw some dried lavender into a cotton bag and hang it on a hanger, and add one or two of the scents moths hate, just to prevent them from becoming your new residents. For my top tips on stopping moths, see the How to Care for Your Garments section, page 113.

Fill in the Gaps

FINALLY, FIGURE OUT WHAT'S MISSING from your capsule wardrobe. These are the essential building block items every woman should own, from which we can style up hundreds of fab, and different, looks. Do you have a white button-down shirt, a pencil skirt, a blazer, a little black dress, a great-fitting pair of jeans, and perhaps a leather biker jacket? These classic, timeless six or so pieces are worth investing in. With them, every woman can build upon the shell of a wardrobe with new on-trend accessories, so that her look can be updated cheaply, easily, and frequently. Make a list of any key, timeless items your closet is missing. Then, make a list of trend-lead items that could update your collection. I'm talking bright belts, costume jewelry, a felt fedora, a printed blazer, or a patent pair of heels—zingy, punchy pieces that instantly draw the eye.

HOW TO SHOP:
LOUISE'S STYLE COMMANDMENTS

1. As I've already mentioned, do your homework. Rip out a few magazine pages for inspiration, even watch an Audrey Hepburn movie to get you in a stylish mood, and take a long hard look at your closet. What are you missing? What could you revamp with a cool new belt or necklace? Which pair of shoes is falling apart and truly needs to be replaced?

2. Before you buy a piece, imagine how you would wear it in three different ways, using clothes you already own. Then it will actually get worn.

3. See it, get it. Well, that's my mom's rule, but she's right—if you dillydally too long or leave the store—Murphy's law practically guarantees someone else will grab it.

4. Spend money on classic items, such as a white shirt, blazer, jeans, leather jacket; and go to the cheap stores for an edgy trend that might not tickle your fancy this time next year. Be real: none of us are going to be digging baggy denim overalls for years to come, so you might as well get them for twenty dollars.

5. Try everything on. My sister hates the changing rooms, and buys before she tries. But the amount of pieces I give back to the sales clerk after they just don't work on me shows how much money I could spend on wasted purchases that I didn't try on. It would suck to have brought all of those home and then have to return them. And give yourself a chance in there. Those lights are always unflattering so apply a little makeup, wear flattering underwear, and take a pair of heels. Don't try on a dress with your socks on. We've all done it, but is that how you're going to wear it to the party? Didn't think so.

6.   Never, ever go shopping when it's that time of the month. Bloating combined with a tendency to feel mad or sad does not bode well for a makeover day! I do, however, encourage tipsy shopping. Some of my best dresses were found after a cocktail or two with the girls. Take an honest wing-woman along or if, like me, you like to shop alone, have one on speed dial for your fitting-room selfies.

7.   And my final rule? Break the rules. By that I mean, wear white after Labor Day, mix your prints up, wear a miniskirt if you're sixty-five if it makes you feel good, buy out-of-season because you fell in love with something. Fashion is meant to be experimental, self-expressionist, and most of all—fun.

10 WAYS TO LOOK
A SIZE SLIMMER

1.   Wear something fitted and structured, not baggy and loose. It's a common misconception that floaty clothes will flatter, but they really only serve to add bulk and volume to your silhouette. It's far better to cinch in and draw the eye to your slimmest part, which is usually the waist.

2.   Invest in the right underwear. Spanx and shapewear, minimizer bras can completely change your shape.

3.   Forget about numbers on a hanger or size tag—wear what fits. Stores and brands all vary in their sizing, so don't be obsessed with fitting into a certain digit. Not having a muffin top because you bought a size up, will mean you look much slimmer anyway.

4. Be aware of texture. Skip pleats and ruffles unless you're trying to create curves in a certain area, as these add bulk. Silk might feel great, but it is not your bestie. Satin and silk are unforgiving, showing even the tiniest lump and bump. The same goes for anything shiny or heavily embellished fabrics (like a top with big shimmery sequins or chunky beads all over it). They look pretty on the hanger, but wear with caution.

5. Wear high heels. I know, I know, it's impractical to totter around in stilettos 24/7, but at least buy a pair of wedges to give your figure a lift. Skin-colored shoes lengthen the leg, just "try before you buy" to be sure they flatter your skin tone.

6. Vertical lines, seams, and dark color panels down the outside of a dress or pencil skirt create brilliant optical illusions and shave off pounds.

7. Stand up. Good posture can shave ten pounds off your figure. As my mom says, "Shoulders back, boobies out!"

8. Wear small prints, instead of large. Fine patterns make a surface look even, whereas big flowers or fruit on a fabric will draw the eye to an area and potentially show off lumps and bumps.

9. Put the dark color on your heavier area, and show off your favorite area with a bright tone, a pattern, or a statement piece of sparkly jewelry. You decide where you want people's attention to be directed.

10. Check where your top and pants meet, and make sure it's a straight line. Anything that cuts you off at the widest part of your hips will make you look wider. That's why I'm constantly pushing the women I make over to try a high-waisted pencil skirt. Surprisingly slimming and flattering, the eye is drawn to your tiniest part.

Part Two:

FASHiON

HOW TO GET DRESSED
IN THE MORNING

This sounds simple, but when you're tired and in a rush, putting together a cute outfit in the morning—no matter where you're headed—can easily go wrong. The no-brainer, boring option is to resort to your old jeans and a tee, but what if looking stylish was just as effortless? We all know a girl or two who just seems to nail it every single day. She doesn't look overdressed, she just looks . . . well, *cool.* Sometimes the simplest of ensembles can pack the biggest punch. If something fits you well, suits your style, and is highlighted by one or two bright, key accessories, you're golden. And those are the kinds of outfits that can be thrown on in an instant every day, once you know how. So here's how I get dressed in the morning.

Where am I going? Work, beach, shopping, running errands . . . ? That determines how formal I need to look, how much running around I'll do (so heels might be a no-go), and how warm or cool the temperature might be (for example, if I'm outdoors all day in the winter in London, then a chic trench coat is the main statement of my look and I won't be taking it off: easy).

Next up, I begin my look with the shoe. Don't ask me why—it just helps me figure out the rest. Then, I'll pick the brightest part of my outfit, which could be a printed scarf or a red hat, and pull colors that either match or compliment it, and wear them elsewhere. So for example, I am obsessed with a line of scarves called Theodora & Callum. Each scarf has about six colors woven into it, and I wear them wrapped loosely around my neck on planes, for meetings, or just on a weekend day out. If there's a hint of army green and coral in there, I'll pair it with skinny cargo pants in a similar hue, and patent coral flats.

In terms of color, I like to look neat, even if my silhouette is loose and boho. Always mix up textures: an expensive silk shirt looks amazing worn with a more relaxed denim vest or beaten-up leather motorcycle jacket.

Bite the bullet and try wearing a hat. It gives instant lift and pizazz to your outfit. For summer, I love a cream panama, and for winter, a wide-brim fedora.

Finally, always carry flats in your bag during the day. Your feet will thank you!

HOW TO DRESS FOR WORK

Before I worked in television, which is always a fairly relaxed, informal environment, I was a fashion journalist for magazines like *Elle* and *InStyle* in the U.K. I learned a lot in those few years what companies looked for on a résumé, how much first appearances do matter, and how to make the most of new contacts.

When online TV channels were just beginning to evolve, I saw in the news that *Vogue* was about to start its own video programming. I found a name, worked out the e-mail address configuration (educated guess!), and sent a short but focused message, asking for an interview. Even though there was no job available, I was so sure I could add value to the company, and I figured, what do I have to lose? A reply came back: "Come in for a chat, but there's no job currently available."

I still remember the outfit I wore that day: a gray, fitted wool dress, black tights, a black leather tote, and Miu Miu heels I'd spent every last penny on in the sale. I felt confident in my look, although inside I was shaking like a leaf. But the "chat" went well. I had done my research about the launch, and I tooted my own horn about my experience—enough to be heard, without being annoying.

A week later I was informed they would be making a position for me at Vogue.com! Can you imagine my screams?! I still remember the phone call. I was standing on a train station platform, whooping like a kid in a candy store until people turned around and looked at me like I was *loco*. So that was the start of my career in front of the camera, and I love that I get to combine both my favorite things: writing and presenting. Here are some of the career tips I've picked up along the way.

Clothes Matter

EVEN IF YOU'RE NOT WORKING IN THE FASHION INDUSTRY, your outfit is still crucial. Statistics say that we're judged on our appearance within eight seconds of meeting someone. So if you're going to an interview, make sure you've got a bright coat or cape, a well-fitted dress, pencil skirt, or suit. It's up to you to judge what's appropriate for the specific job, but pressed, fitted clothes, and polished shoes will make a good first impression. Be bold with color, but don't overpower with it, either.

Studies show that orange is one of the best colors to wear to a job interview. It sends messages of happiness, courage, success, enthusiasm, adventure, warmth, and energy. Lucky it happens to be all over the runways and stores, too! Search Instagram or Pinterest for "orange fashion" to find some great ideas on how to add a splash of the tone to your look. Even just an orange belt or handbag will make a statement. Blue is next in line (and looks gorgeous with orange), and gives off feelings of authority, trust, knowledge, responsibility, caring, loyalty, and integrity. So blue and orange is a killer combo!

If the job's in a creative field, wear an accessory that has an interesting story. A vintage handbag found under a pile of junk at a Paris flea market, or your mom's favorite pendant from the 1970s when she lived in Rio (as in my case) can be a good conversation starter, especially if the person you're meeting is into travel, antiques, or fashion. Try to tailor the story to something the firm would find intriguing.

If you're interviewing somewhere very formal, such as a law firm, stick to a tailored suit, and express your inner fashionista with your accessories. Statement jewelry and a bright patent or print bag will look gorgeous with a more demure suit or LBD.

If in doubt, err on the side of more formal. You have to take yourself seriously so that the employer will, too.

Keep hair clean and makeup simple, but still make the effort. I always think it's best to look groomed but not like you're on a night out, so keep makeup natural but flawless, hair blown out, and nails manicured.

If you're one of the many people who has to wear a suit for work, here's how to stand out from the crowd: go for a woolen suit. Wool is by far the best option, and look for 5 or less percent elastin on the label, too, for a little stretch. When trying a suit on, the vents (i.e. the splits at the base of the blazer) should lie flat against your butt. If they're spreading, the jacket is too small. The sleeves should graze your wrist bone. If they're too long, a tailor can easily shorten them. Check the lining. If it puckers, it's the sign of a cheap suit, which will make you look bulky. Move on to the next peg.

Choose a single-breasted jacket, which is slimming on the chest. If you want to emphasize your waist, go for a thicker lapel that tapers toward the waist, and fasten the button. If you prefer a more modern, edgy look, choose a jacket with slim, straight lapels. This creates a straight vertical line and elongates the figure. The quarters of the jacket (the lower part that hits the hemline) should be straight. If it tapers outward, as many jackets do, I find it draws attention to the tummy area. My absolute favorite cut of blazer is akin to the white amazingness Bianca Jagger wore to marry Mick back in 1971. Sharp, slim shoulders; a slightly longer-than-standard length (so it hits just below the hip); and a flat pocket at the waist. It's feminine and sexy, in such an understated way. Perhaps one of the most crucial parts of buying a suit jacket is making sure the shoulders fit. The seam should hit right where your shoulder ends. It is easier to have sleeve and waist alterations than it is to fix shoulders on a suit, so get this right first.

If you opt for trousers (and I'd suggest buying both a skirt and pair of trousers, so you can wear your jacket two ways), then make sure you bring a pair of heels you intend wearing with them to the fitting. Trousers can be hemmed and shortened in a matter of minutes, so it's most important to make sure they fit around the waist and butt. Don't go for boot-cut pants, whatever you do. These look dated. A peg leg, cropped trouser, or tapered pant look far more chic, plus they show off your shoes. If you go for a skirt, I'd advise a pencil skirt that ends just below the knee. It's a very chic shape and length that suits far more body shapes than you'd imagine. Just remember the golden rule with a tight skirt of that length: always pair it with closed-toe heels for work. A-line skirts work well, too, and minimize the size of your waist. Calf-length skirts are less formal but are absolutely gorgeous with heels. Don't wear a miniskirt though: if your office is formal enough to warrant a suit, then a short skirt is going to be deemed inappropriate. Save that for the cocktail bar after hours!

Do Your Homework

SO NOW YOU KNOW what to *wear* for the interview, how about prepping for it in other ways? Well, first and foremost, be extremely careful with social media. Never post anything that could come back to bite you on the butt, and be quick to de-tag yourself in any Facebook pics your friends might put up after a weekend of partying. I was recently at a talk given by a high-powered ad exec. She began by telling the crowd the very first thing she does, before even reading a candidate's résumé, is Google their name. That leads her to Facebook, Twitter, and Instagram. They could be very qualified for the job, she said, but if they're posing drunk with friends or behaving inappropriately, then game over, before it even begins.

Prepare questions of your own. Sure, an interview is predominantly about them asking you questions, but just as things wrap up, the employer will usually ask if you have any questions. Asking the wrong question could cost you the job, but asking the right ones, could put you at the front of the race.

"What is the culture like here?" is a great question, because bosses care that you want to fit in and get on with the rest of their team. "What is the company's plan for the future?" shows a keen interest in the company's growth, and how you would potentially fit in to that. "What are the biggest challenges to this role?" is a great chance to express how you might overcome any challenges or difficulties. Asking a future boss to be transparent shows you like to be realistic and honest from the get-go.

What not to mention? Money. Avoid questions about salary so early on. You should come across as more interested in the role and your career, rather than payday. Once the job is offered, then it's time to negotiate!

Climbing the Corporate Ladder in High Heels

I'M IMPARTING MY CAREER TIPS smack-bang in the fashion section, because—well, this book isn't just about style. It's about confidence, self-esteem, losing your inhibitions, and reaching the furthest goals you ever thought possible. Any nuggets of information I've picked up along my working life that can help you do that, I'm going to share. A female who is prepared mentally, oozing confidence and has great style? She's an unstoppable force, quite frankly. And whether you're already following your chosen career path or still at school, my advice will still help you speak up and move up.

SMASH THE GLASS CEILING

- At work, speak up, reach out, and learn to say no. You will be amazed at how people take you seriously once you start doing those things.

- Smile at the office bully. You've taken the high road.

- Keep to-do lists limited to five items. Otherwise, according to research, our brain gets overwhelmed and stressed out. As a major list-keeper, I can relate to this!

- Apply for that promotion or that new job. One of my favorite, inspiring books, *Lean In* by Sheryl Sandberg, extols the virtues of biting the bullet when it comes to the career ladder: "One reason women avoid stretch assignments and new challenges is that they worry too much about whether they currently have the skills they need for a new role. This can become a self-fulfilling prophecy, since so many abilities are acquired on the job. An internal report at Hewlett-Packard revealed that women only apply for open jobs if they think they meet 100 percent of the criteria listed. Men apply if they think they meet 60 percent of the requirements. This difference has a huge ripple effect. Women need to shift from thinking 'I'm not ready to do that' to thinking 'I want to do that—and I'll learn by doing it.'"

KNOW YOUR WORTH

Nobody goes into a new job feeling 100 percent confident. There will always be new things to learn. But in general, women have a much harder time being able to self-promote than men. So remember you got that job because you earned it, you deserve to be there, and with the passion, drive, and commitment you showed in your interview, you are unstoppable. Don't be afraid to show off what you've mastered.

SPEAK UP

Ask for regular feedback and take it on board, even if it sometimes isn't quite what you want to hear. If you feel undervalued and you've been there for over eighteen months, ask for a raise, and following that, a change to a more senior title. Six months to a year after starting a new job is a perfectly acceptable amount of time to ask for a raise or change of title. Ask for a salary review, and go into that meeting with evidence to prove you've really contributed to the firm.

Speaking of speaking up, it's important to champion those around you, too. Chicks can be cheerleaders or mean girls, and it's important to set a good example to everyone down to the interns. Be generous with praise—even your boss will appreciate the feedback, too. It creates a positive energy in the office.

SET GOALS

I achieve more by writing down what I need to get done; it helps keep me efficient and competent. Physically jotting down what I'd like to accomplish during the next year (and six months in, assessing how it's going), always helps me focus on future plans and aspirations.

LOOK FOR A MENTOR

It usually happens naturally and gradually (don't try to force a mentorship), but in each place I've worked, somebody has naturally become a mentor and long-lasting friend to me. I will never forget the deputy editor of *InStyle* magazine in London, Tasmina Perry, who gave me my first paying job after university and challenged me to up my game when I began writing for the features department a year later. She taught me so much about the fashion industry, always with a smile and a great perspective on life. She's now a bestselling author writing her eighth novel, and we're still great mates. And another, Holly Jacobs at Sony Pictures Television, who not only bought my makeover show, *Plain Jane*, when I first moved to Los Angeles as a green twenty-six year old, but has since become a great friend and mentor, whose support and nuggets of advice have, in turn, led me to help out newer members of the projects I now work on.

NETWORK

Attending that boring after-work workshop or drinks can often lead to bigger things, if you chat away to new people and play it right. Always swap business cards with new contacts, research them online, and follow up with an e-mail the next day. Promptness shows efficiency and may well land you a new project—or, one day, a new job. Share the love, too, take the opportunity to introduce people if you find common ground. It pays to keep good career karma!

MANAGE YOUR BOSS

Well, in the sense that the more you know, the more powerful you can be. To avoid sweating the small talk, find out her favorite hobbies or TV shows, whether she has kids, lives in the city or suburbs. Most people are more than flattered to talk about themselves or shared subject matter. Figure out what makes her tick;

what she expects and even what she *doesn't* expect. Does she like weekly or daily updates? Note what she asks or complains about most, and pre-empt the results or solutions.

"WATCH OUT FOR THE OFFICE BITCH!"

Those were the words my mom uttered to me as she dropped me at the train station before my very first day as an intern at *Elle* magazine in London. She never swears—I couldn't believe it! I hate to say it, but there's usually one devious, insecure Mean Girl in every office. Don't be drawn into bitching sessions with or about her. Steer clear of office politics. It's poisonous. Instead, work hard, banter when you're being involved in a conversation, but otherwise keep your head down, stay late, arrive early, and be as polite as humanly possible to everyone.

DON'T SEND AN ANGRY E-MAIL

We've all done it, but at work it's even more serious than to your boyfriend or best friend. Always take a step back, go for a walk outside, or trip to the water-cooler, before responding to something that's wound you up. Too late? Then call the recipient. Better to chat human to human than to send a groveling e-mail.

HOW TO DRESS FOR A FIRST DATE

If I had to sum this section up in two tips, I'd say dress for the occasion, and be comfortable. I can't stress those ideas enough, and here's why: dates come in many different scenarios. A little red dress and heels are perfect if you're being treated to a swanky dinner and the theater, but what if it's a beach picnic? Paintballing? Tickets to a baseball game? A comedy club? Rom coms have instilled the ideal first date image into our heads as an LBD, high stilettos, and shiny, wavy hair swooshing around our shoulders (thanks, Jennifer Aniston and Reese Witherspoon). But actually, real life is different.

Before opening your closet or hitting the shops, think about a look that's appropriate for where you're going. I much prefer the idea of running around having fun and laughing your head off for a first date. It's a lot more relaxed than a restaurant with white tablecloths. It wasn't a first date, but my all-time favorite Valentine's Day date was spent eschewing the overpriced, overpopulated "romantic" restaurants in favor of a buzzing sports bar. I wore low-slung boyfriend jeans with a fitted white cotton top. We ate chicken nachos, drank tequila (my number one), and played every arcade game from Pac-Man to basketball hoops.

Any scenario which brings out the fun and silliest side of you is, in my opinion, the best place for a first date. If he or she is attracted to you in that zone, they're a keeper!

Okay, back to fashion . . . Don't be afraid to call the establishment or Google Image it to see what it looks like and what the dress code is. If it's a bar or restaurant, focus on your top half and choosing a shirt or top that is really flattering, because most likely you'll be sitting down. If you're off on a hike or somewhere active, remember your entire look will be on show. Make your outfit sporty, or casual, but don't mix the two. Jeans worn with sporty gym sneakers is my pet hate.

My second tip is feeling comfortable. If you buy something new, be sure to road-test it for fit and shape beforehand. A first date is not the time to go to fashion extremes or create a whole new persona.

First off, the outfit could go plain wrong, and secondly, this person chose *you* to date, so why pretend to be someone else?

Try to stay away from anything overly offensive or political. Don't wear a T-shirt with a cheesy slogan on it. Ponder the effect of wearing anything too *avant-garde*. I'm not turning my back on fashion's out-there trends, but there's a reason one of the industry's biggest bloggers called her site "ManRepeller."

Fit is key. Constantly adjusting the corset that took twenty minutes to tie up, or limping awkwardly in heels that are giving you blisters is a nightmare. The best dates are the ones that go on and on unexpectedly to new places across town. If your feet are killing you, you'll be less inclined to impulsively skip from a walk along the river, to cocktails, to a dance floor.

Oh, and eat! Don't wear anything that's so tight you can't enjoy a delicious meal *à deux*. Sharing a toffee pie or a slice of cake dripping with warm chocolate sauce can be pretty sexy. You don't want to skip that just because of your clothes.

How sexy is too sexy?

Understated glamour is spot on: you want to look seductive, but not like you tried too hard. Don't show too much cleavage or leg on the first date, or wear anything too sheer. You want to hint at your best bits, but leave something to keep him coming back for date number two, and three, and four! A dress with a slit in it is gorgeous, or off-the-shoulder sleeves. If your top is low-cut, then I'd pair it with trousers or a longer skirt, rather than with short shorts.

Wear the color red. Statistics show this is the sexiest color a woman can wear; it attracts people to flirt with you and sends a message of passion. One-shoulder dresses or tops are great for a first date. They show off just enough décolletage to spark your date's interest, without being revealing.

Dress to impress, but don't overdo it. Too many accessories and extras can be overwhelming. Of course, you want your date to be pumped that they're out on a date with someone as hot as you, but you never want to look like you spent hours agonizing over what to wear. Forget about labels and trends; guys tend not to care about those things anyway. The right pair of jeans and a white shirt, or leather skinny pants and a thin knit sweater can have huge impact. Keep the look simple and classy, making sure the clothes fit you really well, are in good condition (that means ironed, and no stains), and I have no doubt you will carry yourself with confidence and pride.

Choose your materials carefully. The fabric your clothes are made from send out signals, too. Soft fabrics, such as cashmere and lambswool, are hugable. Silk is sophisticated. Tweed is formal and a little old-fashioned. Denim is relaxed. Studding, beads, and sequins are scratchy, and can be a little unapproachable. Leather and lace are beyond sexy.

Consider a heel. A high heel can be a beautiful finishing touch to a dress. If you're going out to dinner, then take a day or two beforehand and learn to walk in heels if you don't already know (see page 68 for my how-to). Practice makes perfect, and platforms or wedges are the easiest to balance in. Heels make you stand up straighter, they're slimming, and they really make a difference to the silhouette and attitude you give off when entering a room. If you're worried about being taller than your date in heels, try a kitten heel. But if things blossom into a relationship, it's not like you'll magically shrink or give up heels forever (at least I hope not), so come on, don't wear a flat shoe if, in your heart, you're dying to rock that sexy heeled boot.

Hair and Makeup

WHEN IT COMES TO BEAUTY, time and time again men have told me they prefer less makeup, so don't cake it on. One of the biggest turnoffs is red lipstick because it doesn't seem kissable. But please don't get the wrong message here—if you absolutely love red lips and it expresses who you are, then go for it. I'm not saying alter your vibe for another man or woman, I'm just giving you ideas. I'd put money on the bet that Gwen Stefani wore red lips for her first date with Gavin Rossdale and those two have been married for over a decade!

In my experience of setting up couples and having a bunch of straight male friends, guys like a woman who's comfortable in her own skin, looking as natural as possible. Of course, there are little secrets we ladies share to get that "natural" look—such as getting a light spray tan for our "natural" glowing skin, blowing out our hair with surf spray for those "natural" beachy waves (either buy a bottle—Bumble and Bumble makes a great one—or make your own by filling a spritzer with one cup of warm water, two teaspoons of salt, and a teaspoon of hair gel, and shake it well), and adding false lashes (but without coating them in heavy mascara—it's a trick lots of the models use). Ha! The boys are none the wiser.

If you're going out as a result of online dating, keep your hair and makeup relatively similar to the pic on your profile, perhaps with a little extra emphasis on the eye or lip. A thin lip gloss, a winged eyeliner, or cat eye can be very alluring. Overall though, the image that made the person click on you is the look they're hoping to meet in person.

HOW TO DRESS FOR A WEDDING

In your late twenties and early thirties, wedding invitations seem to flood in. My friends all seem to be getting married at once. Last year I went to a whopping ten weddings! And each and every one was completely unique. Different setting, different food, different music, different vibe—and therefore a different kind of outfit was needed each time. Weddings are a minefield for what to wear, but they can also be a fun chance to dress up and try out new looks. So where to start when planning your ensemble? First up, take a look at the invitation. Is it a stiff, expensive card, with embossed gold script written in super formal language? Odds are the wedding will be similarly structured and formal, meaning a dress to the knee or longer, closed-toe heels, and shoulders covered at least for the ceremony. Or, is it relaxed and friendly, asking you to come see your friends get hitched on the beach? Then look for a flowy, casual outfit with flat sandals or a wedge.

Next: when and where is the wedding set? If it's a winter wedding in an old stone church, be sure to bring an elegant but warm coat. And plan on wedges instead of heels if the reception is outside on the grass.

An evening wedding at a country club or restaurant is better suited to a tailored cocktail dress, whereas for a destination wedding somewhere hot—a printed, bright, floaty maxi dress would be ideal.

Of course, the dress code might be clearly stated on the invitation:

DRESS CODES

- BLACK TIE: Go for a long dress if possible, but make it your own with bright accessories: think Carrie Bradshaw chic. Black tie officially means a black tuxedo, complete with black bow tie or a slim black regular tie for him, but if the event isn't crazy formal, he can often get away with a dark suit.

- WHITE TIE: Veronica Lake-style glamour . . . sequins, fabulous heels, cigarette holders, the lot! For him, a black tuxedo (including a blazer with tails) worn with a white vest and either black or white bow tie. I love a man in white tie with a thin dress scarf thrown around his neck. He'll look like he just stepped out of a Ralph Lauren ad. Dress to the nines people, white tie is as formal as it gets.

- SUITS: For you, a cocktail dress, long, short, or knee-length, is perfect. For him, a tuxedo isn't required, but the wedding is formal enough for one to be appropriate. He should go with a dark suit if it's a nighttime wedding.

- SEMIFORMAL: For you, a cocktail dress, or skirt and top. For him, a light or dark suit, depending on the season and time of day.

- CASUAL OR BEACH FORMAL: A bright maxi dress with wedges or flat sandals for you, and a summer suit with deck shoes or Converse—clean, cool Converse—for him.

One golden fashion rule: never, ever wear black or white, or anything too sexy. Not only is sexy inappropriate for a religious ceremony, but upstaging the bride in any way is considered a faux pas. This is her day; let her shine.

Now, I'm English, so I can't talk about wedding etiquette without discussing hats. We Brits love wearing a great hat to a wedding. There are some amusing, and in some cases antiquated, rules about wearing hats to a wedding. I'm a big fan of the medium-size saucer hat, worn on an angle at the side of the head. It's elegant, not too cumbersome, it suits every height and body shape, and is a cooler version of 2013's obsession with fascinators. Nothing says "fabulous wedding outfit" quite like a hat, worn with a beautiful dress. Remember, you're wearing the hat, it's not wearing you. Be confident but choose a style that ultimately you're comfortable in and one that complements your shape and height.

Traditionally, ladies decorate hats on the right-hand side, the opposite to that of men, who always stick to the left. Women's hats are fashion accessories and are part of their ensembles, which means we girls are not required to remove our hats when going indoors. For the guys, it's a different story: they need to remove their hats when going inside, especially in religious buildings. That means no top hats in the church or inside the reception venue, even for photographs. Gentlemen should also remove their hats whenever speaking to a lady, in particular their new mother-in-law. It's a sign of respect that dates back generations. Another old rule: it is considered rude to show the inside lining of your hat, so when taking off, tipping, or doffing your hat, make sure you hold the lining against your torso, so that only the outside is visible.

And take note! The mother of the bride dictates when other ladies may remove their hats and fascinators. Until she removes her hat, other ladies are expected to leave theirs on. The mother of the groom is supposed to pick a wedding hat smaller than the mother of the bride's. This is a set rule across all social situations that dictates guests should never outshine their hosts. If you and your groom are hosting the wedding, then the two moms can opt for equally grand creations.

Don't choose a hat that blocks others' views of the altar, or that blocks other guests in official photos.

But my biggest rule: if you are at a posh wedding full of hats and pomp, don't ever be that person who points out the faux pas of other guests. Weddings should be about fun, not rules!

HOW TO DRESS FOR
A WEDDING: BRIDE EDITION

S peaking of *breaking* the rules, if you are in fact the bride then here are my favorite fashion wedding rules to break:

You don't have to wear white shoes. Yes, they're in fashion, but unless you pick very wisely, you might feel more like a nurse, and the chances of you wearing them again are slim to none. Instead, make your heels an unexpected statement and opt for a metallic. My absolute favorite tones at the time of this writing are rose gold or pewter, but simple yellow gold or silver look fabulous, too, and add a touch of modern glamour.

Explore options other than white for your gown. Your wedding dress should be an expression of your style, so don't feel pressure to conform. Just look at how Gwen Stefani rocked a custom Christian Dior pink dip-dyed dress when she tied the knot in London in 2002, and how Cindy Crawford wore a simple, short silk slip with bare feet on the beach for her wedding back in 1998. Try on dresses with a champagne hue, blush tones, or honestly—any bright color you fancy. Another favorite is cocktail or tea-length if the wedding is casual or particularly urban.

Mix and match your wedding bands. It's a big trend in fashion to mix metals on your hands, and wedding rings should be treated just the same. Think about what's going to work in your everyday life. If you absolutely love emeralds or rubies, then opt for a bright stone. A solitaire diamond is gorgeous, of course, but I'm a big fan of wedding rings and engagement rings with a little individuality, too.

Bridesmaids *can* wear white. It's the bride's choice, and personally, I think bridesmaids and flower girls in white or cream dresses, look beyond elegant down the aisle. I can never forget the scene in *Sex and the City* when Charlotte gets married, and the girls all wear cream dresses as her bridesmaids, but all with a different silhouette. It totally worked. I was obsessed with that episode!

Try tousled, romantic hair. Women often feel they should sport a tight chignon or bun for their wedding day, but I absolutely love a loose finger wave. It's effortless and a nice balance with the formality of the dress. The same goes for makeup. If you don't normally wear much, then tell your makeup artist to create a natural look. Sure, she'll have to apply foundation to create the most flattering light in photos, but it's important that you still look and feel like *you*, when you say "I do."

Go for an unexpected twist. Whether it's a bejeweled ear cuff, a slick of red lipstick, a lavender garland, or an intricate vintage veil, add your personal style to the look, something that people will notice and remember, and that will really pop in photographs.

And remember, you don't have to leave the party! Back in the day, it was tradition that the happy couple was waived off into the distance to set off on their honeymoon, while the wedding guests danced the night away. Nowadays, the bride and groom want to stay and catch up with all the friends who have traveled far and wide just for them. The best wedding I went to recently was in the beautiful countryside of Scotland. Not only did the wedding couple hang out with everyone until the early hours, they even stayed in the same old pub hotel, so we could all have breakfast together. It's a personal decision if you want some alone time with your brand new hubby, but I love the fact that recreating your high school or college days, just for the weekend, is now a perfectly acceptable option.

HOW TO FIND YOUR PERFECT JEANS

Quite honestly, I could write a whole book just about jeans. This item that most of us wear more than any other, can be an absolute nightmare to get right. I've stood in changing rooms trying over twenty pairs on before, and left with nothing. The right pair of jeans should be like a best mate—they'll accompany you to a casual day outing or to a glitzy party. They support you, hug you, and compliment you.

Jeans are, arguably, one of the oldest trends still popular today. Way back in 1873, a tailor just outside Las Vegas had a customer whose trouser pockets kept ripping. The tailor decided to add rivets, and to be on the safe side, he patented the idea with his business partner, Levi Strauss. For almost a century, denim jeans were worn by laborers for the specific purpose of work. Fashion didn't come into play until the 1960s, when the likes of Cher, Jackie O, and Ali MacGraw made bell-bottoms an overnight sensation. From that moment on, jeans became the staple of a mass market closet and a symbol of American fashion. Today, there are 450 million pairs of jeans sold every year in the U.S., and the average consumer owns seven pairs. But I bet you they only wear one or two of those pairs, because they didn't choose right when they shopped. I know I have a few pairs that sit untouched in my closet, but I also have four pairs on rotation that are like a second skin to me, so comfy and flattering.

Shopping for Jeans

MOST DENIM BRANDS have a signature fit. The only way to find which suits you, is to try, try, try, and then try on some more.

Getting into the right pair *should* be a bit of a struggle. If they go on too fast, they're probably too loose. The waistband should feel snug, but not dig in. If you can fit two fingers down the back: perfect. If you can fit a whole hand: go down a size.

Low-rise jeans mean the waistband is a couple of inches below your belly button. They are sexy, but look best on athletic and boyish figures, or those blessed with a flat stomach. Earl Jeans makes great low-rise jeans.

A midrise waistband suits most people, particularly if you're pear-shaped. Look at the brand Paper Denim Cloth. Try sitting and bending over. Do you feel comfortable or are you showing off your knickers to the world?

High-rise jeans hark back to the days of Farrah Fawcett riding a skateboard, and whether skinny or flared, I love this cut. The waistband comes up to or just above your belly button. The shape can really suck you in, and elongates your legs like crazy. MIH, Wrangler, and DL1961 are my faves.

Baggy boyfriend jeans really suit a variety of body types. They look edgy on sporty and slender frames, but also great on pear-shape and hourglass figures. They shouldn't cling. They need to be loose, low-slung with a belt, and I like mine ripped up, with a turn up at the bottom. Gap, Levi's, and Mango make my favorite boyfriend jeans.

Boot-cut jeans are a little outdated, but a wider flare looks awesome. The bell-bottom shape also balances out your silhouette, making your thighs and waist look smaller. I have a great pair of flares from Topshop, and I love MIH for this style.

Skinny jeans are great to create more curves, especially if they're high-waisted. I love Lee skinny jeans.

To flatten your tummy, go for a smooth-closing zip fly, or look for a pair that zips up at the back. Avoid front pockets, as this adds bulk. Look for jeans with a tapered outside seam. This creates the illusion of slimmer thighs. Some denim washes are faded or distressed down the center, and darker at the edges. This is a very slimming technique. Try 7 For All Mankind.

Buy dark jeans snug; they're very slimming. White and bright jeans should be a smidge looser, because they'll reveal every lump and bump, and you'll wash them more. Uniqlo and AG make killer white jeans.

To look taller, iron a crease down the front of stiff, dark blue jeans. Check out J Brand and True Religion.

Avoid hems that drag on the floor. They remind me of going to high school in the 1990s and seeing bedraggled, filthy denim hemlines everywhere. If you do invest in a pair too long for you, reserve them for wearing with high heels. It's a great trick to elongate your legs. Look at the way Victoria Beckham and Rachel Zoe sport bell-bottoms with platforms, to make their legs look sky-high.

Pocket positioning makes *all* the difference to how your butt looks. Large pockets situated low on your behind will minimize your rear. Small pockets slanting down and outward will lift and accentuate a flat butt. If you've got a bootie like Kim Kardashian and want to show it off, small, centered pockets on high-waisted jeans will draw major attention to your bottom.

Denim has a varying degree of "give" in it, everything from jeggings (the mega-stretchy lovechild of leggings and jeans) to structured and rigid. Contrary to what you might think, the more stretch, the less flattering on curves. The stretch will allow bulges here and there, whereas a rigid denim that is the correct size will hold you in and flatter a more voluptuous figure. Skinny or cropped jeans with 1 or 2 percent stretch are the most formal variety, suitable for most workplaces and going out to a formal evening event. I like James Jeans and Genetic Denim, to hold me in.

Styling Your Jeans

THINK OF YOUR JEANS as the neutral foundation for the rest of your outfit. Not to say they won't take center stage, but they're a springboard from which to build up the rest of your style. There's no look you can't create with the right jeans.

For low-key, weekend cool, pair your slouchy boyfriend jeans or ripped skinnies with a simple white button-down, a plaid lumberjack, a tomboy sweat-shirt, or a denim jacket with the sleeves rolled up.

Brightly colored, printed, or white jeans are great for a punchy look. Let the jeans be the star and keep the rest of your vibe minimal: a gray tee, baggy knitted beanie, and leather biker jacket will pull everything together.

For work, cropped, dark jeans without any distressing look elegant and preppy paired with stiletto pumps. Adding a bright, structured bag and a neutral blazer is spot-on for a meeting.

Faded blue jeans in any shape look cozy and seductive with a thick-knit sweater. That's a timeless look I absolutely adore.

Last, but not least, for a glamorous evening look, pair skinnies, flares, high-waisted, or boyfriend jeans with strappy high-heeled sandals and a sparkly top. Each of the cuts I mentioned will give the look a completely different feel. My personal favorite for a girls' night out? Ripped boyfriend jeans, white patent sti-lettoes, and a roll-neck crop top. It's so '90s it could have come straight from *Clueless*. I'm obsessed.

Caring for Your Jeans

DON'T OVERWASH YOUR DENIM. Most jeans only need to be laundered every four or five wears.

Never put your jeans in the dryer or on the radiator. Machine-wash them cold, inside out, then hang them up to air dry.

Store wide-leg jeans by hanging them, to avoid creases. Skinny jeans can be folded; any creases disappear as soon as you put them on.

HOW TO TRAVEL IN STYLE

Jumping on a flight or taking a road trip does *not* give you a free pass to dress like a bum. For some reason, travelers tend to dress one of two ways: super-chic and elegant, or major Sloppy Joe. I'm not saying you have to go all Victoria Beckham, and rock six-inch stilettoes with a leather pencil skirt, but if you're going to have a chance at that upgrade or meet the man of your dreams mid-air, it's time to step up your travel look. And I promise you'll still be comfy. I take a lot of planes and make it my business to snuggle up and sleep as much as possible.

First up: never wear jeans. The thick, structured denim and bulky buttons dig into you when you're trying to snooze—super uncomfy. Jeggings, leggings, or a maxi dress, are perfect. Invest in a waterfall-front cardigan. These are open sweaters with plenty of fabric at the front to wrap around yourself like a blanket. A loose, baggy beanie is a nice way to look cool but keep warm when the temperature drops in the cabin; I never, ever fly without my chunky-knit cream one. I can't deal with heels on a long haul flight. When I land exhausted and jetlagged, with swollen feet, stilettos are the last thing I want to squeeze into. Flat loafers, high tops, or low wedges work well. A lofty printed scarf wrapped loosely over a thin sweater or cotton top instantly gives the look a chic feel—plus a huge scarf can double up as a pillow or blanket! I also take a velvet eye mask stuffed with lavender, ear plugs, and fluffy socks to help me catch some zzz's. Looking after your skin and hair on a long journey is also crucial. Here are my fave travel products.

CABIN FEVER—THE BEST LBBS
(Little Beauty Bottles) I TAKE ON BOARD

- **VICTORIA'S SECRET PINK FRESH & CLEAN BODY MIST, TRAVEL SIZE:** Especially handy if the guy next to you stinks!

- **OJON RARE BLEND OIL:** Apply this before boarding and twist your hair into a knot. The longer the flight, the better your hair will absorb the oils, leaving you with shiny, hydrated locks when you land.

- **MAYBELLINE FIT ME CONCEALER:** Small enough for the plane, thin enough not to clog pores and contains SPF for when you land. I use the shade Sand, but they have a plethora of colors to suit any complexion.

- **THIS WORKS IN TRANSIT FIRST AID:** A little stick containing soothing rosewood and antiseptic petitgrain to sooth blemishes, redness, and disinfect scratches.

- **COWSHED NATURAL ANTIBACTERIAL HAND GEL IN COW SLIP:** A must for any journey, and this one lacks the harsher chemicals contained in some other hand sanitizers.

- **BAREMINERALS DEEP CLEANING FOAM, TRAVEL SIZE:** Good to wash your face with in the airplane lavatory, especially on a long-haul flight.

Packing

WHEN IT COMES TO PACKING, take a couple of hours to try on outfits in advance—or at least place them on the bed head-to-toe. I do this before New York Fashion Week, because otherwise I'd never fit everything in my bag. Yup, it sounds time-consuming, but you'll be so grateful when you get to your business trip or vacation and you haven't forgotten the perfect pair of shoes and earrings to match that maxi dress.

Pack according to a color scheme. Begin with some neutral staples you feel comfortable in and then add two or three brighter tones, so you can carry less and create easy mix-n-match looks. Pack three tops for every bottom. Generally bottoms take up more space, and jeans, formal trousers, or shorts can be recycled into very different looks just by switching your top half. Stuff smaller items like socks and undies into the cups of your bikini and bras, so that they hold their shape. Try rolling clothes instead of folding them—it's proven to keep creasing to a minimum. But don't stress if your favorite shirt arrives crumpled. Not only do most hotels provide an iron, but my favorite trick is to put the shower on hot and hang my garment on the outside of the shower door. The steam has it looking freshly pressed within ten minutes. Don't forget to pack whatever you'll want first at the top. That could be your beach stuff, an evening look, or pj's if you're landing late.

HOW TO SHOP FOR SWIMWEAR

Seeing as we're talking travel, let's move on to beachwear! Choosing swimwear is somewhat terrifying. After all, we are suddenly deciding to wear a more elasticated version of our undies, in public. Scary alert! But there are many tricks you can employ to streamline your figure, keeping your best bits on show, and your worst bits under wraps. If you're feeling worried before a vacation, may I remind you there is only *one* Gisele on earth, and just over 7 billion of the rest of us. So you're not alone in wanting your swimsuit to work for your body.

Try your swimsuit on in-store, keeping your G-string on underneath. Take two sizes in with you to save time. You can't guess which size will work, and this has to fit with precision. Too tight and we're talking muffin tops, too loose and we're talking saggy diaper-butt. Most stores now realize women come in top-heavy or bottom-heavy sizes, so you may need to try different sizes on the top and bottom. I also like to switch up the print and colors between top and bottom. This is a huge trend that started on the world-famous Copaca-

bana Beach in Rio, Brazil, and it looks great. Added to which, a darker, plain color on your bottom will reduce the size, and a fine, bright print on the top, especially with frills, tassels, or a bow, will accentuate the area.

Test to see if the top fits by raising your arms and bending over. Does everything stay in place? Just like a bra, you shouldn't get a double boob, either. The material should be snug, but not dig in.

When it comes to making your butt look great, I'd like to break the myth that the more material covering it, the smaller it will look. Yes, a cute miniskirt or pair of hot pant shaped bottoms will hide the area, but if you're looking at regular panty-shaped bikini bottoms, a narrower Brazilian cut is actually more flattering. I finally succumbed to this notion and bought a pair. It actually makes my bum look smaller and higher. Success!

A string bikini with a side-tie is good for accentuating narrow hips, while a thicker band at the side will narrow wider hips. Strapless and string tops are good for smaller chests, while thicker halter-necks and underwire cups give more support, and a sportier feel. For a feminine touch, look for floral prints, tassels, and cute frills.

One-pieces are a brilliant option. They're so popular right now, because the varying shapes really flatter any figure. A deep V will elongate the torso; side panels cleverly slim your waist; a high-cut above the hip will elongate the leg; a low back is super sexy, and tummy panels or ruching over the stomach will flatten the area.

My favorite swimwear designers are Melissa Odabash and Heidi Klein. They both make sexy silhouettes, and dresses to match their swimwear. Also try Figleaves.com and Victoria's Secret for a wide choice of shapes and sizes.

Swimsuit TLC

LOOKING AFTER YOUR SWIMWEAR IS KEY. Wear old swimsuits in the hot tub, as the high temperature and chemicals weaken spandex and make colors fade. Sitting on rough surfaces, such as cement and unvarnished wood, can pill your suit, leaving bobbles and nicks. Put a towel down first. Avoid the washing machine; instead, wash your suits by hand in cold water, with a mild detergent. After a day on the beach, I often throw mine in the shower with me, but only if the water is cool or lukewarm. Dry your bikini or swimming costume flat (try not to hang it from the taps in the bathroom), in a cool, dry place. A hot dryer will break down the materials. Finally, alternate your suits by at least one full day (an excuse to buy more!). Spandex needs twenty-four hours to retain its shape, so giving it a rest will reduce permanent stretching.

HOW TO ROCK
THE RIGHT SHOES

I'm not gonna lie, this is the part of my book I was most excited to write, because I am shoe-obsessive. A friend recently commented that the high heels in my closet seem to be breeding, and I think she's right. Any color, any shape, any fabric, any designer—as long as they're heels—I'll take 'em!

If I had to lose everything in my wardrobe apart from one item, I'd keep a fabulous pair of heels. They're my favorite part of every outfit—and the first thing I look at on a stylish woman. I can't really explain it—I just love shoes. I agree with the great Christian Dior, who said, "You can never take too much care over the choice of your shoes. Too many women think they are unimportant, but the real proof of an elegant woman is what is on her feet."

Think of it this way: you can rock a threadbare tee with ripped-up cargo pants and messy hair, and if the shoes are cool, the look works. It just doesn't fly the other way around unfortunately. A pair of crappy, scuffed shoes will serve to ruin a beautiful dress or a stylish top.

I never realized it until my bestie pointed it out once, but I plan every outfit starting with my shoes. They're the foundation and the highlight of each look, and, in fact, it makes pulling together the other items a piece of cake. Try it!

"I don't know who invented the high heel, but all women sure owe him a lot," said Marilyn Monroe. Funnily enough, nobody's exactly sure who did. Everyone from the ancient Egyptians to Leonardo da Vinci has been credited with inventing heels. During the eighteenth century, Louis XVI began wearing them in Paris, making them extremely fashionable for both men and women. The trend stayed as long as the royal family did, dying out in spectacular fashion during the French Revolution. On one particularly violent day an angry mob chased the king and his wife, Marie Antoinette, outside the famous château of the Tuileries. As they tried to flee, the queen lost

one of her satin slippers, which was trimmed with ruched ribbon. Like a hideous parody of the Cinderella fairy tale, the shoe was later found, and is now on display at the Carnavalet Museum in Paris. That ended the trend for high heels for quite some time.

But, of course, back it came! The truth is, wearing a beautiful pair of heels can absolutely change your outfit, your posture, your silhouette, your elegance, and state of mind. Designer Roger Vivier, who invented the stiletto, once said, "To be carried by shoes, winged by them, to wear dreams on one's feet, is to begin to give reality to one's dreams."

Think of the iconic scene in Fellini's *La Dolce Vita*, when Anita Ekberg decadently drinks champagne from her shoe in Rome's Trevi Fountain, or think of Dorothy clicking her red glitter heels together in *The Wizard of Oz*, or Carrie Bradshaw drooling over her Manolo Blahniks in *Sex and the City*. Shoes can make you feel sexy, powerful, and stylish.

Shoe to Kill

I ALWAYS SAY, THE EASIEST AND SAFEST way to channel a new trend is on your feet—be it leopard print, sequins, velvet. Give it a shot on your foot first, before investing in a whole outfit, and see how you like it. It's also a very cool style statement to keep your entire ensemble casual, and then go nuts with foot candy.

For example, I often wear a simple white shirt or tank, skinny jeans, and then killer ankle boots for an understated-yet-glamorous look. If you're unsteady walking in heels, opt for wedges or platforms, which make the gradient of your foot much less.

I must also mention: if you're planning on wearing open-toed shoes, get a pedicure, or paint your own toenails, first.

How to Walk in High Heels

POINT AND FLEX YOUR TOES a few times. Slide into the heels, find your balance, and give it a go. Stand up tall, press your shoulder blades together, and lean back a little, so that the weight is equally distributed between the balls of your feet and your heels. The shoes will make you lean forward, but keep pushing yourself upright.

Check yourself out in the mirror, and try to make each step smoother than the last. You should try not to look like someone's poking you up the bottom with a stick. Take small steps (there's no rush!) and get used to the feeling of having your feet at an angle. Practice makes perfect, and there's no better place to practice than in a supermarket. The aisles are long and straight, you have the support of the shopping cart, and your local neighbors will be in awe of this glamorous chick who buys her groceries wearing stilettos!

And remember the golden cheat rule: always carry a pair of ballet flats in your bag. Even for me, there comes a time—a dance floor or catching the last train and having to run—when something is more important than my high heels.

Red Alert

I BELIEVE EVERY WOMAN should own a pair of red shoes. They make me think of the iconic ballet film *The Red Shoes*. They capture your imagination, they give you ridiculous amounts of pleasure, and the color pops an outfit like no other.

If red shoes are too bold for you, then think of a red detail like a zipper or bow—or if you're really splurging, then a red sole. And there's only one place those come from: high heels with a red sole have now become an iconic beacon of chic thanks to Paris-based designer Christian Louboutin, who paints all his soles red. I had the honor of having tea with Monsieur Louboutin once and found out why his shoes are red underneath. I love this story. . . .

When he first started out in shoe design, a young, beautiful assistant of his would arrive in the office every day primped and polished to the nines, matching her glossy scarlet lipstick to her nail polish. One day he asked to borrow the nail varnish, and painted the bottom of one of his shoes, just for fun. He liked the effect. So he had the whole collection that season painted with red soles. Being a somewhat traditional city, the Paris stores were not impressed, and tried to send the shipment back. But it was too late: Christian's loyal and stylish customers had already fallen in love with the look, and demanded the shoes be sold red. And so, his trademark twist was born.

A pair of Christian Louboutins to me is what Manolo Blahniks are to Carrie Bradshaw. Something akin to a fashion deity, to be treasured, adored, and kept for decades. If you take the plunge and buy a pair, let me tell you a tale of woe as a warning! If they need any kind of repair, don't just take them to the nearest cobbler, which I foolishly did with the first pair I ever bought. Trotting in to pick up my newly resoled Loubys, I immediately noticed the nasty black rubber replacement sole on them—and promptly began to cry. I really did shed a tear. I'd saved up more than a month's salary for those puppies, and now they were ruined. I still have them in my closet and wear them once in a while, but it isn't the same. So take care of yours and look online for specialist shoe repairs in your area, which can keep the sole red. It may even mean shipping them somewhere, but I'd recommend it.

Shoe Shopping

ALWAYS TRY ON BOTH SHOES IN THE STORE, because most of us have one foot almost half a size bigger than the other. Try to shop in the afternoon or evening, as your feet swell during the day. And never shop for shoes when you've just got off a flight. My feet swell the size of pumpkins in the air so I'd inevitably buy the wrong size!

There are a gazillion names for different shaped shoes and heels—stack, cone, kitten heel, pin heel, stiletto, pump, wedge, peep-toe, ankle-boot (sometimes referred to as a "shootie"), but don't be baffled by it all. The main thing is you choose the one you like, the one you'll wear, and don't be afraid to ask advice from the sales assistant. That's what they're there for. Shoe trends change like the wind. One minute we wouldn't be seen dead in kitten heels or Birkenstocks and the next they're on the front cover of *Vogue*. So, as much as I love to experiment with new shoe trends, the pair I'll spend my money on is the classic, nude or gold stiletto pump. A simple high heel sandal and knee-high winter boot will never go out of fashion, either.

If a shoe feels a little too tight, remember that suede and leather will give and stretch, but that synthetic fabrics will not. Cobblers can help stretch your shoes if need be, or punch extra holes in a sling-back strap, but never buy an open-toe shoe that is too small. An editor friend of mine once referred to toes poking over the edge of a shoe as hooker toe—and it's stuck in my mind since! If you've bought sturdy leather boots, break them in by laying the leather over the arm of a chair, covering it with brown paper and giving it a few whacks with a hammer. This softens the leather up like butter and avoids you getting nasty blisters. For daintier leather shoes that pinch or feel a little too small, put them in the freezer for a few hours and the leather will soften, molding more easily to your feet.

Shoe TLC

POLISH YOUR LEATHER SHOES as soon as you get them home. Leather needs care, and this helps hydrate it, and prevent scratches.

Scratch the soles of new shoes in a crisscross pattern a couple of times with scissors, to stop you from slipping when you walk on carpet.

If you're wearing heels without tights, sprinkle a little talcum powder inside the shoe first, to stop you from sweating—that's my mom's trick. If you forgot to do that and your shoes get a little stinky, place a couple of cloves in each shoe overnight. They'll smell of Christmas by morning.

Vaseline or a dab of nail polish remover can get rid of stains on shiny patent leather, and gently paint over any scuffs on black leather with a marker pen.

Suede can be rescued if you hold it in the steam of a boiling kettle and then tease it with a dry old toothbrush.

HOW TO UP-STYLE WITH ACCESSORIES

Picture this: you're wearing your old ripped jeans, a cream sweater, and flip-flops. Nothing wrong with the look, but there's nothing special about it, either.

Can I play stylist here for a second? How about we add a caramel-colored fedora with a stiff, wide brim that sits low on your forehead. Now let's stack some gold bangles along your wrist, and add a chunky ring to your index finger, plus a midi ring to your pinkie. Ooh, why not punch things up with a skinny leopard-print belt around those jeans? Now throw a gold, oversize clutch under your arm. And can we switch out the boring flip-flops for a pair of velvet smoking slippers? *Kaboom!* Suddenly you're the coolest chick walking down the street, and it's all because of those finishing touches.

Accessories aren't just a sidekick to your clothes; in my opinion, they're even more important than your clothes. They make a statement, they are eye-catching, they're a way to try out a bold new trend, print, or texture without having to cover your entire body with it. What's more, accessories save you a fortune. Instead of buying a new dress or pair of pants every few months, you can keep up with the trends by buying the right accessories and revamping your look with a few tweaks here and there. You can also get multiple looks out of the same garment.

Get inventive with your combinations. The right pair of earrings and heels can transform a formal office ensemble into cocktail bar attire that Olivia Palermo would be proud of. And P.S. ladies, trying out different bag-shoe-jewelry-scarf-belt combinations is a lot of *fun*. Marc Jacobs put it best once, when he said, "Any opportunity to adorn oneself is human, and accessories are an easy way to do it."

My most prevalent memory of being *adorned*, was at the Cannes Film Festival. I was lucky enough to be working alongside the fabulous jewelry house Chopard and got to pick out some ridiculously expensive diamonds to wear on the red carpet. I chose a rose gold watch, some ruby earrings, and a beautiful diamond necklace. It felt surreal being handed this velvet-lined box from the vault and being allowed to put these enormous, sparkling, rather heavy gems on. As I was getting dressed, there was a knock at my hotel door. *"Bonsoir mademoiselle,"* a Jason Statham look-alike in a suit with an earpiece whispered. *"Je suis votre garde du corps."* My high school French translated that to . . . OMG! . . . "I am your bodyguard." Was I suddenly in a James Bond film? It felt like it. The man hovered near me all night long, which was slightly creepy and slightly awesome, but what an experience!

The icing on your outfit-cake doesn't have to cost a fortune though. Some of my absolute favorite pieces are cheap as chips. I love costume jewelry, secondhand hats, and bargain shoes. In fact, one of my favorite fedoras is one I permanently borrowed from my dad's wardrobe! I wear it with everything. Accessories are what you make of them; they're powerful; they emphasize your personal style; they take a look from nice to *wow*. Don't get trigger-happy and make yourself up like a Christmas tree though, three or four bright accessories are plenty. As Coco Chanel advised, "Before you leave the house, look in the mirror and remove one accessory." But before we get there, let's start putting things *on*. Time to sparkle.

Diamonds Are a Girl's Best Friend

IN MY MIND, the glamour and wonder of diamonds is encapsulated best by three silver screen movie stars: Audrey Hepburn, who nibbled on her Danish while staring longingly at the sparklers in Tiffany's window during the iconic opening scene of *Breakfast at Tiffany's*; Marilyn Monroe, who played the diamond-hungry Lorelei Lee in *Gentlemen Prefer Blondes* and sang "Diamonds Are a Girl's Best Friend" in an immortal production number; and last but not least, Elizabeth Taylor, who owned and wore some of the biggest diamonds in the world. She pretty much dripped in diamonds just for a trip to the supermarket.

Diamonds, however, have a rich history that spans way back before classic Hollywood. The idea of a diamond being given to a lady when a man proposes began almost six hundred years ago, when Archduke Maximilian of Austria gave a diamond to his bride-to-be, Mary of Burgundy. The trend caught on.

And ever wondered why engagement rings are worn on the third finger of the left hand? A few centuries before good old Maximilian, the Egyptians believed that the *vena amoris* (the vein of love) ran directly from the heart, through to the third left finger. Now *that's* romantic!

Diamonds come in an array of cuts, shapes, and most important, varying quality. If you're going to invest, make sure it's got what's known in the jewelry industry as the "Four C's":

CUT

Put simply, the better the cut, the more your diamond will sparkle. Nowadays, lasers cut diamonds with intricate facets, so that light reflects and refracts through the stone, creating a stunning glow and rainbow effect.

Antique diamonds will have been cut by hand. So although the story of who owned them may be fascinating and the ring may look pretty, it will never shine as brightly as a modern diamond.

Cut also refers to shape:

ROUND: The most popular and timeless, often used for a solitaire engagement ring.

PRINCESS: Another classic cut, with square lines, it's a mix between emerald and triangular facets.

MARQUISE: Elegant and elongated, the shape tapers to a point at each end. Marquise rings make your fingers look long and slim.

EMERALD: Often in a rectangular shape, usually cut with parallel-line facets. Shines beautifully.

RADIANT: Another rectangular outline, this is a combination of emerald and round cuts. Looks gorgeous on a bracelet.

CUSHION: Very rare and with a regal feel, the cushion cut resembles a 3-D cushion and doesn't come cheap. Beautiful for earrings.

PEAR: A very feminine shape, like a pear drop. This also serves to elongate the finger, but looks pretty as earrings, too.

OVAL: My favorite shape of diamond. It's an elongated circle, beautiful, ladylike, and rare enough that you won't see many others around.

HEART: A very romantic shape, cut to look like a heart. This can be tricky to keep clean and brilliant, due to awkward facets.

TRILLION: A bold, eye-catching triangle shape which mixes brilliant faceting with a radiant cut.

CLARITY

This refers to the quality. Almost all diamonds have tiny imperfections, and it's important to measure any internal or external flaws that cannot always be seen with the naked eye. The deeper down in the earth that the diamond is mined from, the purer it tends to be. So if you can see any scratches or dots, or if the stone looks oily or milky, it's a no-go. Always buy a diamond with a certificate of validation or a diamond grading report. On the report will be the clarity reading. There is a scale from flawless to visible imperfections, which your jeweler can explain in detail when you pick a stone.

COLOR

Always ask to see your diamond in natural light, and see how it shines. You don't want any brown or yellow tint in a clear diamond; it should glimmer white and bright.

CARAT

Carat refers to a diamond's weight. One carat is equal to one-fifth of a gram. Just because your diamond is heavy, however, doesn't make it great quality. Check and pass the complete four "C's" test before you hand over that credit card.

Care and Storage for Your Sparklers

- Put jewelry on last when you're getting ready, because perfume and hairspray can be corrosive to the metal.

- Wipe jewelry with one of those cloths you get in a sunglasses box after wearing it; sweat and germs can also cause bling to look dull.

- Windex or butter (not soap and water) is the best remedy to remove a ring that's stuck on your finger.

- Store precious jewelry in separate compartments in a jewelry box, or in little velvet baggies, to prevent scratching.

- A sprinkle of detergent and warm water, scrubbed with an old toothbrush, will clean gold and silver jewelry the best. If you're cleaning silver this way, rinse the detergent away after a minute; some oxidized surfaces can change color otherwise.

- Soak gold in an eggcup full of gin to bring its shine back.

- For brass and anything plated, clean with mild soap and warm water.

- For stones and crystals, use cold water and even less soap. Baby soap is a great, gentle option.

- Display and organize your jewels by shopping in the office and kitchen departments of stores. Cutlery organizers are fantastic for placing in drawers and holding long necklaces and bracelets. Butter dishes are gorgeous ways to store rings, and a cocktail or butler tray is a nice way to display your favorite pieces. Add a scented candle and antique perfume bottle to the tray for a truly girly, boudoir feel.

- Use an office corkboard to hang necklaces and earrings. The more you see in the morning, the more variety you'll wear.

JEWELRY TRENDS

TRENDS COME AND GO IN THE WORLD OF JEWELRY and, just like with clothes, my advice is to spend your money on the timeless staples you will love for the next twenty years and choose the cheaper option when it comes to a hot, but fleeting, new trend.

PEARLS

Thanks to the polished look of Taylor Swift and the Madonna throwbacks from Lady Gaga, pearls are no longer old-fashioned. Wear them with a red lip, and if you're going to splurge on proper pearls, rub one against your tooth. If it feels slightly gritty, it's not a fake, it's real.

MIXED METALS

I see fashionistas here in L.A. mixing up their metals, too. No rules apply when it comes to bronze, silver, yellow gold, and rose gold—wear them all at once! Just make sure they're evenly proportioned around your body.

BODY AND BELLY CHAINS

I think it's super sexy to see a thin chain going down a woman's torso under her T-shirt: Rosie Huntingdon-Whiteley is a big fan. Make sure the chain is delicate, and that the whole thing hangs loose and comfortably.

STACK IT

Bold, chunky costume jewelry is fun to play with, too. Try stacking clunky wooden bangles and cuffs up your arm.

CHOKERS

The '90s obsession with chokers rolls back into town now and then, and for once I'm going to say a big fat NO. Chokers sit high up and tight around the neck, and cut you off just where you should look statuesque and streamlined. Chokers make me think of Britney Spears, whose music I love, but whose style I do not. Think about how chokers make her neck look thicker and shorter. Instead, use jewelry to attract attention to your décolletage, with a delicate pendant that falls a couple of inches below your clavicle. Too low and it gets lost in your cleavage, but slap-bang on the sternum and hey, you look like a lady!

ODD EARRINGS

One look I'm loving that you may be able to rock from what's already in your dresser, is mismatched earrings. I prefer the look with studs rather than dangly earrings, but contrasting pairs have a playful vibe. Ear cuffs are cute, too. Check out Forever 21, Aldo, JustFab.com, and CatBirdNYC.com for lower price points.

Where to Buy Your Bling

FOR BARGAIN DEALS, resale sites, such as BibandTuck.com, have some incredible steals. Auctions are a fun way to invest as well. Pieces are always on display at the auction house a few days prior, with information on the history of each piece.

Antique fairs and vintage shops are great spots for one-off pieces, but remember you can't always guarantee the true history and worth of a gem. So here it's better to shop for costume jewelry, or with a limited budget in mind.

The big jewelers with the famous names are an expensive option, but will have experts on hand to educate you about your piece. It's also a little-known fact that jewelry is one area of fashion where you can haggle a better deal, especially in the bigger stores. So don't be afraid to politely ask for a discount.

Be mindful of where your jewelry comes from. We've all heard about blood diamonds and mining conditions for workers and their families can be horrific in some areas of the world. You want to be proud of wearing your jewelry, so make sure it comes from a fair-trade, eco-friendly brand. Chopard, Gemfields, and Tiffany & Co. are fine jewelers that all partake in charitable, eco-friendly endeavors. For lower-priced brands, check out the Little Market, an online store set up by Lauren Conrad to bring together ethically sourced jewelry and fashion.

HOW TO CULTIVATE YOUR LOVE OF HANDBAGS

There's something innately personal about a girl and her handbag—the stylish buddy that comes with you everywhere and lies patiently across your wrist or shoulder all day, every day. Handbags are way more than just a means to carry your belongings; they're a signature part of your look.

There are gazillions of shapes and styles of handbags out there. I'll go through the most popular versions to make shopping less of a minefield, but to be honest, shopping for a bag should be more about falling in love. When I first started working in the fashion industry, the phenomenon of the "it" bag had just begun. If you didn't carry a Mulberry Bayswater or Balenciaga Lariat by day and a Fendi Baguette by night, who were you?! The status of your bag was everything, and, like fashion robots, everybody I knew joined the waiting list to blow many months' salary on exactly the same bag. Sad really. Well, thank goodness things have changed.

Yep, there will always be popular designer bags each season that people hanker after, but thanks to the plethora of fashion bloggers making the industry less elitist and the explosion of global street style, finding your own favorite bag from—well anywhere you like—is far cooler. So forget what the label says, forget what your friends have, and make it a passion project to shop for your dream handbag.

Choosing the One

I REMEMBER WHEN I got my first paying job. I was a features assistant at *InStyle*, and I always had it in my mind that the thing you spend your very first paycheck on should be something you remember. Okay, so in my impoverished bank balance's mind, this was the first *few* paychecks! But I saved up and trotted down to London's Bond Street one lunch hour. I bought a little purse from Louis Vuitton. It wasn't even a proper handbag; it was an inner compartment from a huge Louis Vuitton trunk, but it looked like a clutch and for some reason they sold it to me separately. The cheapest thing in the store, and I was in love! To me, this little piece of monogrammed leather was a chunk of fashion, a zipper-worth of glamour, and it represented a pat on the back for the year-and-a-bit I'd worked my butt off as an intern, without being paid a cent.

So when you decide to buy *that* bag; to invest in something that may or may not melt your credit card, ponder these thoughts first:

- Does this bag give you butterflies, or at least make you want to stroke it? (Not even kidding. I'm very affectionate with my favorite accessories. Sometimes I say hi to my shoes.)

- Is this bag versatile and will it complement my style? Can I think of three completely different looks that I could carry this with?

- Is it so gorgeous that I want to keep it forever and pass it onto my daughter?

- Is it stylishly timeless?

- Is this bag well made? Is it as beautifully crafted on the inside as the outside?

- Will this bag lose its shape? Slouchy is cool, but structured bags hold their shape and pristine feel much longer.

- Will this bag hurt my back or shoulder to carry?

- Can I fit everything I need in here? (This is something I will actually try out in the shop, being careful nothing leaks.)

Once you've answered most of these questions with a big, fat YES, it's time to bag it. Pun intended.

A Glossary of Handbags

ATHLETIC OR DUFFEL BAG

These are long and sausage-shaped, traditionally for carrying sports equipment, but great for a weekend away, too.

BACKPACK

I have a brown leather one from Asos. Not only do they look cute; they're very practical when you're running around town all day.

BOWLING BAG

Roomy with a wider bottom and tapered top, these bags are structured, often with bright piping. They were originally designed for carrying bowling balls (who would've guessed it from the name?!), and they have a retro, 1950s feel.

BUCKET BAG

Deep and with a wide mouth, these bags usually have long straps. Great for throwing in all the items you could possibly need for the day, although it can be tricky finding them again.

CLUTCH

Oh, how I love a clutch. The "no handles" bag is my favorite thing to carry out in the evenings. They come as solid little boxes, embellished *minaudière* bags, flat envelopes (the easiest style to throw under your arm), and clutches that fold in half.

HOBO BAG

A medium to large crescent shape that hangs from your shoulder and has a main compartment closure (unlike a tote, which is usually open at the top).

MESSENGER BAG

A flat, square bag with a long strap that is usually worn cross-body.

SATCHEL

A medium-size bag with a long strap and a flap to close it. Traditionally a bag for students to carry schoolbooks, it looks good worn across the body.

SHOULDER BAG

A small bag on the end of a long, thin strap that is often a chain, worn on your shoulder. The most famous example of this is Chanel's original quilted 2.55 bag.

TOTE OR SHOPPING BAG

A large bag with parallel edges from top to bottom, usually featuring long straps, this can literally fit your grocery shopping into it. Well, a bottle of champagne and a pint of strawberries . . . what else does one need from the supermarket?

HOW TO WEAR YOUR SCARVES

I have enough scarves to open a little boutique. Scarves are the ultimate collector's item in a closet; a staple of any wardrobe; a timeless accessory to make even the most basic outfit pop; a warm snuggly friend on any long journey. I'll never suggest throwing them out. I am a gigantic fan of the printed scarf. They just don't date, so your money will never be wasted on a fleeting trend.

I have a blue patterned silk Hermès scarf from my mom, which was made in the 1960s and looks just as relevant today. I've got leopard and stripy scarves from the 1990s, ikat prints from five years back, and laser-print watercolors I bought this season. I wear them all in rotation, and for my fellow neat freaks out there, they look like a cute candy store all folded meticulously on a shelf, or hung on little hooks.

Choosing and Styling Your Scarf

SCARVES COME IN DIFFERING SHAPES, fabrics, and weights, so it's important to check these before you buy.

LARGE RECTANGULAR SCARF

My absolute favorite is an oversize rectangle in a lightweight, lofty linen or cotton. These hold their shape when you wrap them around your neck. I have a few of these from Theodora & Callum, who make stunning prints inspired by Mexico and India. This shape of scarf looks best with a crisp white shirt, bright flats, and jeans. The scarf is voluminous and definitely the star of the show. Drape it loosely around your neck twice, so that the ends meet at your sternum. Tie them gently together and hide the knot under the rest of the material.

LARGE SQUARE SCARF

A large square scarf is best in twill or cotton. Pair it with a thin knit sweater in a neutral tone, a T-shirt and shorts, or faded denim dungarees. Fold it in half diagonally, lay it flat across your chest, then twist the ends once before knotting it at the nape of your neck. Keep it loose and textured, so it doesn't resemble a napkin!

LONG THIN SCARF

I like these in cashmere or gossamer. The less bulky, the better. An easy, chic way to wear this kind of scarf is not to complicate it. Drape it around your neck, over a tunic or white blazer for an androgynous, sexy look (very Charlotte Rampling). Long scarves are also perfect as headscarves. Fold yours vertically, wrap it around your hair, and knot it at the back. This looks super cute with a bold, bright sundress, or anything loose and floaty.

SMALL SQUARE SCARF

The quintessential French woman's accessory of choice, there are a plethora of ways you'll see these draped around a lady's neck in Paris or Cannes. This shape looks best in silk, worn with bright colors that pick up on tones in the scarf's print. For work, fold the fabric diagonally with the triangle facing down your back. Tie the two ends at your collarbone. Alternatively, place the triangle at the front, covering your mouth, then tie the ends over the top at the front, splaying out the material. Then gently pull it below your mouth, so it rests at the base of your chin.

Create a look Princess Diana loved, by again folding your square scarf in a diagonal half. Place it halfway over your shoulder, so that the majority of the fabric lays across your chest and tummy, and tie the ends to the side of your waist. This is a great way to show off the beautiful print, and looks unbelievably polished worn over a trench coat.

Finally, switch things up by making a bandana. Little silk scarves make for great do-rags. Try tying the knot at the top of your head.

HOW TO STYLE YOUR HAT

For the last three hundred years until the late 1960s, hats were an essential part of any fashionable woman's outfit. My granny used to even wear one, along with cotton gloves, to the grocery store. Milliners were just as popular as shoe and dress stores, and women snapped up the new styles every season. But, as dress codes became less formal, hats were gradually omitted from modern dressing, and the art of millinery all but went extinct.

Which makes me sad, because I'm a major flag-flyer for hats. Whenever I take a girl shopping, or perform a makeover on a TV show, hats are the last item she ever thinks about trying. We have this assumption that hats are exclusively reserved for the outdoors or previous eras, like you should only wear them if you're playing baseball or joining a Victorian tea party. Or, of course, if you're a celebrity. Kate Moss in a ripped tee, jeans, and faded suede boots? Cool. Kate Moss in that outfit plus a black felt fedora with a wide rim and leather trim? *Epic. Noticeable. Mysterious.* Adding a hat to your ensemble is the ultimate way to amp your look up a notch, to give it a fashionable edge, and to make heads turn.

Matching the right hat to both your look and your head shape is key. FYI—I'll be mentioning the words "crown" and "brim" a lot. The "crown" is the portion of the hat that covers and envelopes your head, and the "brim" is the horizontal part of the hat that shoots away from the head, usually right below a ribbon or seam. So without further ado, here's my style dictionary of hats.

Summer Hats

SUNHAT

Apart from the practical advantage of protecting your delicate skin from the sun, a sunhat with a wide, flat brim reminds me of style icons like Jackie O. and Brigitte Bardot. Perfect paired with a bright maxi dress and dark shades.

PANAMA

My summer staple. A true panama will keep its shape even when squished, so it's the perfect companion for travel. Versatile stylewise, you can wear a panama with everything from overalls to a lace summer dress.

VISOR

I had to throw this one in here because I'm a huge fan. Visors used to be a bit nerdy, worn by golfers and tennis players. Well, they still are, I guess—but there's a hot new breed of them made from straw and leather, that look amazing with ripped Bermuda shorts and a tank. Go grab one for your next trip to the beach.

BOATER

Always made out of straw, these remind me of summer days drinking Pimm's and watching the rowing regatta at Henley, a super-posh festival on the River Thames. Boaters have very shallow crowns, so leave your hair down as most of your head and face will be exposed. Modernize yours with round sunglasses and denim cutoffs, Alexa Chung–style.

PILLBOX

More like a headpiece, pillbox hats are decorative and, in the U.K. especially, worn for formal events, such as weddings and horse races. Depending on how bright they are, pillbox hats are good for any season. Make like Kate, the Duchess of York, and pin yours toward the front and side of your head. Add a little netted veil in the same color for a femme fatale vibe.

Winter Hats

FEDORA

The wider the brim on a fedora, the better. I like mine made from felt, with a deep crown (so I usually buy a size up), and in a warm tone, such as olive green, navy blue, or maroon.

PORK PIE

Pork Pie hats are a brilliant fashion statement. They're named after their resemblance to a pie dish: flat along the top, a very shallow crown, and a short, horizontal brim. In the 1930s and '40s, jazz and blues band singers began wearing them across America, and that's the image that comes to mind when I think of pork pie hats. The hat is formal in shape but looks best when contrasted with a relaxed or girly outfit. Why not switch things up and wear yours with a long, printed skirt and denim jacket, sleeves rolled up?

BOWLER

Bowlers have a very deep crown and a short, up-turned brim. Made famous by Charlie Chaplin, the surrealist Magritte painting named *The Son of Man*, and New York City bankers in the midcentury, bowler hats have a very masculine history—which is why I think they look super awesome on girls. Wear with ripped skinny jeans or leather leggings.

TRILBY

A short brim, with the front turned down and the back turned up, the trilby was given its name after an awesome novel by George du Maurier I studied at university. That's probably the nicest thing I've got to say about them though. They never seem cool or modern to me—for some reason I way prefer a wider-brimmed fedora.

BEANIE

I can't live without my chunky-knit cashmere beanie. I take it on the plane to sleep, I wear it around New York in the winter, and I live in it when the weather turns chilly. Opt for a baggy beanie, and wear with a leather biker jacket and flat boots.

BERET

About as French as you can get! These are adorable and give a chic androgynous vibe worn with high-waisted pants with a crease down the front, Annie Hall style.

CLOCHE

Cloche hats have a deep, rounded crown and a short, sloping brim, and sit low on the forehead. With a cloche hat, you can channel your inner Daisy Buchanan from *The Great Gatsby*. The epitome of 1920s flapper dressing, this style was all over the runways in New York in fall 2014.

HOW TO BUY AND
SELL VINTAGE CLOTHES

Vintage clothing is a way of wearing history. Vintage items can be far more than just secondhand; to some they're an art, a collector's passion, with sentimental value and a story to tell. Officially, something isn't vintage unless it dates from 1920–1980. Earlier than that and it's antique; later than that, and it's secondhand or thrift. When shopping for vintage, I have to warn you there are a number of "vintage don'ts" to consider:

- Don't buy anything with sweat marks, rips elsewhere than the seams, mildew, or mothballs. Unfortunately, a cleaner cannot fix any of these problems. If a garment has moth holes, but you've fallen head over heels in love with it, take it to the dry cleaners and then have the holes fixed by a tailor or seamstress. Usually your dry cleaner will recommend a tailor they trust, and even have it sent there and returned for you. Don't store it in your closet before this is done; keep it airtight in plastic, otherwise the larvae could infest your whole wardrobe.

- Personally, I steer clear of vintage shoes because they tend to fall apart. I once shelled out $130 on a pair of leopard-print Biba platforms in the window of a cool store in London. I was an intern at *Elle* at the time, so that was a ton of money! I proudly donned them and showed them off to the office that afternoon, only for the strap on one side to break, and the sole on the other to literally fall off. Sometimes it's better to have something inspired by Studio 54 rather than something that was actually *there* and is now too worn out to ever dance again.

- Most important, if you are going to invest in designer vintage, it is important to be able to spot a fake. Again harking back to my intern days, I once spent almost all the money I had on a pair of "Gucci" sunglasses and a "Burberry" trench, only to find out later from a fashion editor that Gucci had never made a design like mine, and then when the label fell off my very scratchy trench coat, I knew that was a pile of poop, too. If you're excited at finding an alleged designer garment at a rock-bottom price, chances are it's probably too good to be true. Check for dodgy stitching (even though clothing before the 1960s was hand sewn, the stitching will be precise and neat). Rogue traders tend to use slap-dash, haphazard sewing. Check the quality, the craftsmanship, and if you see any "Made in China" labels—run for the hills! Fabrics such as nylon and polyester were only introduced in the 1950s, so if it's labeled as older than that but there's stretch to it, you've got a fake.

- This isn't pleasant, but true vintage clothing tends to have a smell to it. An easy way to remove odors from vintage or thrift clothing is to spritz them with a mixture of vodka and water.

- The safest items to shop for in the vintage world are bags, jewelry, belts, and dresses. Wedding dresses can be wonderful, unique purchases, too, because they tend to encounter much less wear and tear. Wedding dresses have (hopefully) only been worn once, jewelry can last for centuries, and it's obvious from one glance at a handbag what kind of condition it's in, so you know what you're getting—unless the bag is designer, in which case there should be a certificate of authenticity and hopefully a dust bag that comes with it.

Where to Shop for Vintage

THERE ARE SO MANY SOURCES to find your vintage clothing. It could be a fun weekend to wander around a flea market, a charity store, or a dedicated vintage fair. The higher quality the goods, the more the seller will be able to inform you about each piece, but the less you'll be able to haggle. Charity shops in wealthy areas of town are a great place to find the designer wares dropped off by neighboring millionaires. Auction houses are a wonderful way to bag vintage items. For some reason, auctions have a reputation for being snooty, elitist arenas, but actually, regular members of the public can and should frequent them regularly. Department stores and big chain stores have started dedicating corners to vintage clothing, but this would be my last port of call. Not only are the items highly curated (which takes the fun out of the hunt, in my opinion), but they're way overpriced and often altered and embellished by the store. If the buttons on my vintage coat are going to be changed, I want to be the one to pick the new ones!

The Internet is a valuable source for vintage clothing, too. You can access pieces from all over the world without getting up from the couch. But beware that clothing before the 1960s does not have sizing, so it's best to liaise with the dealer and ask for specific measurements. Photos can be deceiving, too, so choose a website with many angles and, if possible, with clothing displayed on a model, such as BillieGoatVintage.com. I also love browsing RustyZipper.com and MamaStoneVintage.com. For secondhand designer clothing, I donate and buy from Vaunte.com—it's fantastic!

Vintage Cyber-shopping

THERE'S A ROARING TRADE in buying and selling clothes online. It's the perfect way to cut out the middle man and get your hands on a quick buck, if you're selling—or some serious bargains, if you're buying. At first, I was wary that cybershopping for used pieces could get me into trouble. How can you buy something without trying it on or even knowing the brand or person selling it? But over the years I've picked up tips on how to navigate the gauntlet of vintage cybershopping. Here's how.

BUYING

- **INCLUDE SPELLING MISTAKES IN YOUR SEARCHES:** For example, items entitled Channel instead of Chanel or Mui Mui instead of Miu Miu. One man's mistake is another man's hidden treasure. Or in this case, one woman's amazing bargain quilted leather bag!

- **KEEP A POKER FACE:** Well, a virtual one anyway—by not giving your game away and bidding too early, you avoid the price skyrocketing. Set an alarm for a minute before the end of the auction, so you can swoop in last-minute, or if you're a real pro, use Bidnapper.com, a "sniper" website which bids for you a split second before time's up, leaving your competitors in the dust.

- **USE PAYPAL:** Sounds like a pain at first having to fill out all the information, but PayPal is the easiest, safest way to purchase. Your money is also protected; you get it back if there's anything shady going on.

- **DO YOUR HOMEWORK:** Read the small print; check the item description, seller history, similar pieces by the same designer or era and what they're selling for; check for high postage costs, and don't be afraid to e-mail the seller any questions you may have.

- **LEARN TO SPOT FAKES:** The trade in fake designer goods is roaring, so it's often a good idea to ask for close-up pictures and a card of authenticity (most designer handbags have these inside). Uneven stitching, misspelled logos, and unbranded rivets are suspect. If it's a modern item, pull a close-up image of the original from the designer's official website and compare.

- **DON'T BE AFRAID OF INTERNATIONAL DELIVERIES:** If you fall in love with an item that doesn't deliver to your country, AmericanGoodies.co.uk will act as an intermediary service. Just be sure to check the shipping costs beforehand. It could end up more than the original price of the item!

SELLING

- **CHECK OUT THE COMPETITION:** Don't out-price yourself by charging more than others for the same item. Timing is everything. Close an auction on a Sunday or Monday night, when most people are likely to be at home.

- **HONESTY IS THE BEST POLICY:** If your item has flaws, admit it. Taking photos of any damage and posting them will help you avoid complaints later. Keep your description brief, but detailed about size, age, and condition.

- **SEND UPDATES:** Make sure you send a sale confirmation e-mail to your highest bidder, a payment received e-mail, and a dispatch confirmation. It will pay dividends for your reputation when they leave you stellar feedback.

- STEAM CLOTHES, POLISH SHOES, AND DRY-CLEAN STAINS: Trust me, spending the cents will earn you dollars later.

- SNAP THE RIGHT PIC: The photo will sell your piece, no doubt. So take the time to get a mannequin, great lighting, and decent focus.

MY FAVORITE VINTAGE STORES AROUND THE WORLD

IN **LOS ANGELES**, I head to Ampersand Boutique, the Rose Bowl gigantic flea market, Decades, and Sielian's for ball gowns.

In **NEW YORK**, What Goes Around Comes Around and Mr. Throwback are the best.

DALLAS is a major hotspot for vintage glamour. Head to Dolly Python Vintage.

MIAMI's gem in the vintage crown is Las Tias.

In **LAS VEGAS**, Gypsy Den is totally rock-and-roll.

In **LONDON**, I always stop by Alfies Antique Market, and Grays, right under Bond Street (it's a total secret, no tourists ever find it), great for jewelry and bags.

The mother ship of all vintage shopping, however, is in the one place you'd expect it: **PARIS**. Porte de Clignancourt is an established market where the serious collectors go. Here you'll find authentic designer wares, and even haute couture. If you're ever in Paris, get up early, grab your coffee and croissant, and go. Even if you don't snap anything up, just to window-shop and soak up the atmosphere is an experience you'll never forget. I remember feeling totally in awe of my surroundings there. I was immersed in the history of fashion, surrounded by people who loved it, and reminded why I'm so passionate about the industry.

A Final Thought on Vintage

PUTTING YOUR VINTAGE PIECES into an outfit brings out the inner stylist in you. It's important to keep the rest of your outfit modern, so that the look doesn't become a period costume. With that in mind, think about shopping for vintage much closer to home: try Mom and Granny's closets! I have the best fun helping "reorganize" my mom and granny's closets, with the ulterior motive of scoring some new pieces—like a black patent handbag and a costume jewelry brooch (thanks, Gran), or a pair of high-waisted leather pants and a sequin batwing top from the 1980s (best discoveries ever, Mom). Playing around with how you wear them and seeing your family member's face when they see their old garment reborn is brilliant fun.

HOW TO SHOP SMART, SPEND LESS, AND SAVE MORE

Hit the kids' departments. Tax-free and much cheaper, buying children's clothing and shoes in the largest size they make is a major money saver. I once bought a blue blazer with gold buttons from the Ralph Lauren Boys shop (where kids sizes actually go up to age twenty), for a third of the adult price range.

Sell your old clothes at a consignment store and ask for shop credit in return. Guilt-free shopping! I sell a lot of my old pieces on Pose.com, where there's an incredible array of trendy bargains.

Be strict with new purchases. Hang them at the front of your rail with the tags still attached and the receipts taped to the hangers. Only remove the tag once you're heading out the door wearing it. If you haven't put it on two weeks after buying it, return it.

Online, use the price filter in the sidebar. Restricting yourself to items between fifty to one hundred dollars stops you from being tempted by things you can't afford.

If a retailer has a live chat option, ask which coupons are available. You'll often score 5 percent off and free shipping.

Be smart about coupons. Download apps, such as CheckPoints and Shopkick. They help you rack up rewards for gift cards and discounts when you scan merchandise barcodes. Friend your favorite stores and brands on Facebook or follow them on Twitter and Instagram for exclusive sales and promo codes. Type in your zip code at SaleLocator.com for a list of nearby sales, and visit FreeShipping.org to see which retailers offer complimentary shipping. Sign up for store credit cards—but only if you shop there a lot and if you're certain you can pay off your bills. The discounts associated with these are tempting, but be careful not to get sucked in at the checkout every single place you shop.

How to Shop the Sales

SALES ARE HIT OR MISS. Try not to have your heart set on a specific item because chances are, you might miss out or it might not be as discounted as it should be. It's better to enjoy and have a potluck attitude. Capsule wardrobe classics are a good bet, such as a blazer, a crisp white shirt, or a leather pencil skirt. Quality, luxury fabrics—such as cashmere—are worth spending more on during a sale, and avoid anything too trendy: there's a reason why the pink neon netting vest is on that sales rack!

Shoes and handbags are by far the most popular sales sections. Hit the accessories section first before crowds mess up the heels grouped by size and it turns into a chaotic jumble sale.

Shop for whatever is *not* in the store's target market. By that I mean, head to the men's section for an extra-small sweater, head to the swimwear section if it's winter, and look at the little corner of handbags in a shoe store. A product that isn't to the taste of a chain's demographic, won't sell. The longer it sits there, the more discounted it will become.

Get up early. Beat the crowds by hitting the sales as soon as they start, or better still, shop them online. Most department stores start their online sales at midnight, and once the store itself opens at 8 a.m., a lot of the good stuff is gone. Big department stores have so much stock to re-tag, they often secretly begin their sales a day or two before advertised. There might not be giant sale signs up, but chances are the reductions will already be in their system, so you'll bag a lower price.

Wear comfy flats and an outfit that slips on and off easily, for trying things on. You need to be faster than the competition! Wear a little self-tan and makeup, and flattering underwear, so that under the harsh changing room lights, you give the potential purchase its best chance of looking hot. If you're trying on eveningwear, ask for a pair of heels in your size to borrow, or bring a pair in your handbag from home.

Don't be afraid to ask for further discounts. If you wait for prices to go down later, the item is going to be gone. You can usually haggle an extra 10 percent off over a missing button or unraveling seam, both of which are easily fixed—often by a seamstress that works within the department store itself!

Beware of old merchandise that gets brought back out for a sale. Stores are cheeky; I've seen items up to four years old being dragged out onto the racks again, just so they can get rid of it. Never buy something just because it's on the clearance rack. You need to *love* it.

Remember that most discount sales are final in-store. Online, however, you have more rights. Distance-selling regulations give you seven days to change your mind and get a full refund, including delivery, even during sale periods.

Research the trends by skimming your favorite fashion bloggers and Instagrams that morning. See what inspires you. If a certain color or fabric is going to be big this season *and* next, then it's definitely worth the investment. You'll be ahead of the game picking up a fuchsia skirt now, if that happens to be the big color for next winter.

Don't be limited by any season either. I was recently shopping with a friend who shied away from an unbelievable discounted leather jacket, just because it was summer. If you're in love with it, you'll still adore it come the fall, when the temperature starts to drop, and vice versa if you spot that perfect spring dress when it's still snowing outside.

Many Internet sites have constant sale sections that you can return items to if they don't fit or suit you. Stick to reputable sites, which display the padlock sign—meaning they guarantee secure payment. For designer, hit Net-a-Porter.com and ShopBop.com. For diffusion lines, go to My-Wardrobe.com and TheOutnet.com. For high street, Asos.com, Missguided.co.uk, and NastyGal.com rock. Piperlime.com is a personal favorite with free shipping and returns.

Designer sample sales are no longer just for the fashion press. These are sales of runway pieces and press samples that are no longer needed, and the discounts are eye-wateringly awesome. Prepare for a scramble though! In the past I've bagged a silk Prada pencil skirt, a Miu Miu dress, and numerous pairs of Jimmy Choos, for an absolute steal. I will never forget the time my editor friend from *InStyle* magazine and I hit a big sample sale in London. She was so pregnant she used the bump to jostle other shoppers out of the way, as she grabbed hanger after hanger. She was too pregnant to bend over and try on shoes, but she bought six pairs anyway. Did I mention it was her due date? Suddenly, after shrieking over a gorgeous Armani skirt, she went into labor. We rushed off to the hospital, but not until after she'd paid for her goodies. True story! Now that's commitment to fashion! Check sites, such as Racked.com, Gilt.com, and Haute-Look.com, for insider info on the sample sales.

THE SALES BY MONTH

JANUARY: Winter clothes and accessories will be crazy-discounted after the holidays.

FEBRUARY: Because of Valentine's Day, you'll find specials on jewelry and lingerie.

MARCH: Final, rock-bottom sales on winter fashion.

APRIL AND MAY: Summer preview sales and discounts on athletic gear.

JUNE AND JULY: Great deals on anything you'd take on vacation, like swimwear, caftans, sandals, and sunglasses. If you can wait until July, prices drop super low. Every department store wants to get rid of their summer stock by August.

AUGUST: Back-to-school and back-to-work promotions apply this month.

SEPTEMBER: Labor Day sales! And promotions on early fall pieces. Any summer leftovers will be on the clearance rack.

OCTOBER AND NOVEMBER: Some department stores offer preview sales on winter coats and boots, but hold out for Black Friday, the day after Thanksgiving. This is a chance to get ridiculous discounts. Crowds swarm and even camp outside major retailers though, so I'd advise shopping online late the night before, when many sales start.

DECEMBER: It's holiday shopping! Depending how well or badly a brand has done that year, sales often begin midmonth. Keep an eye on announcements; if you wait until the 26th, as tradition dictates, you may miss the boat.

HOW TO FIND
THE PERFECT UNDIES

In my years working in the fashion industry, and in my years of, well, just being a woman, it has occurred to me there are two types of women: those who don't care about underwear whatsoever and throw the nearest pair of holey, graying panties on every morning without really looking; and those whose underwear is an integral part of their outfit, that contributes to their mindset. For the latter, underwear is about making them feel sexy even if their outer layer consists of a baggy T-shirt and denim overalls. Okay, granted, often the reality of a busy, stressful morning distracts even the most fashion-conscious of girls from giving two hoots about her smalls, but, if you invest a little time into what suits your body and your look, you might be amazed at the results.

Too frequently, the women I make over forget the importance of underwear. The right bra and bottoms have the power to flatten your tummy, cinch your waist, uplift and boost your boobs or, conversely, make them smaller. When I tell you that your figure and clothes will look completely different with the right kind of underwear, I'm not exaggerating. That's why every stylist I've ever met comes armed with a suitcase full of shapewear to every fashion shoot. You simply can't put a great outfit together without careful thought of the undergarments, too. And, aside from changing your silhouette, the feeling of power and seduction you'll get by donning a set of lingerie you feel sexy and comfortable in is awesome. And the look on your other half's face? Priceless.

In our minds, I think we categorize sexy lingerie as something that's not for us. It's expensive, it's slutty, or only for Victoria's Secret models. It's uncomfortable and unrealistic to wear day-to-day, and, at best, it's reserved for Valentine's Day. So can I please break that myth for you guys? Over the last couple of years, the variety of sizes, shapes, and fabrics on offer in the underwear department has expanded like crazy. Finally, manufacturers and retailers are realizing that women come in all shapes and sizes, all have the right to wear sexy underwear, and women want a happy medium—a bra that is both pretty and comfortable, undies that are sexy but wearable for a fifteen-hour day on your feet.

Shapewear (you know, the big Bridget Jones undies) is now being designed beautifully, with lace and bow detailing, and a retro feel. An elegant lace bra no longer costs the earth, and plus-size bras no longer look like a 1920s swimming cap. There's a new breed of lingerie on the market and it's for every woman, every day. Now all you have to do is find the types that suit you best.

Yes, Sexy Lingerie Is for Everyone

BACK IN VICTORIAN TIMES, underwear symbolized repression. The corset was worn day and night, limiting a woman's breath, rearranging her internal organs (seriously—sometimes with fatal consequences), and limiting her physical movements in a big way. Yes, it gave her a great hourglass figure, but it was certainly not a way to embrace her curves and femininity. Underneath the corset came layer upon layer of cotton, with the sole purpose of covering up her body: a chemise, drawers, knickerbockers, petticoat, crinoline, bustle, corset cover . . . how a woman didn't look like a walking Laundromat I don't know.

The point is, today we live in a world where most of us are free to embrace and celebrate our female form. At least, that's what I hope all of you reading this already do, or will learn to one day do. When I worked at Vogue.com, I conducted an interview with a very stylish, wonderful woman, who taught me a fascinating lesson. Lou Doillon is a fashion icon and the daughter of an even bigger style icon and actress, Jane Birkin. I had been in awe of her style for years, and finally got to chat to her during a shoot in London. She went off track during the interview and started talking about lingerie and her obsession with its power. She told me that underneath her baggy jeans, she wears a suspender garter belt every day with a matching bra. Nobody knows they're there except her, but they make her feel like a seductive, powerful woman. "That is how great lingerie should make you feel," she said.

I pondered that idea for a while, and totally bought into it. Whatever shape and size you are, whatever your budget, you deserve to invest in one gorgeous set of lingerie. Not for the benefit of whoever gets to see you in it, but first and foremost, for you. Don't save it for special occasions. Wear it any time you want to feel good about yourself.

Lingerie shopping is fun. Most high-end boutiques—like Agent Provocateur, La Perla, and Kiki de Montparnasse—make it an experience, providing champagne and allowing your gal pal, GBF, or boyfriend to come into the changing area with you . . . the perfect Saturday afternoon, after a cocktail at lunch!

Finding the Perfect Bra

MEASURE UP

Get fitted professionally for a bra. A whopping 75 percent of women are wearing the wrong size. Even if you've been fitted before, go to a reputable underwear or department store again. We fluctuate year to year, and it's worth wearing the right size. It will change the shape, height, and comfort level of your bust for the better.

If you want to measure yourself, it's not too difficult. To measure the band, wrap a tape measure around your ribs, just under your breasts. Then take a second measurement by wrapping the tape snugly around your back, just under your arms and across the top of your chest. If the numbers differ, take an average of the two. This is your chest size, i.e. the number part of your bra size. To measure your cup size, start the tape measure at your sternum, and lay it over the widest part of your bust, carrying on until it hits your rib cage just below. Four inches is an A cup, five inches is a B cup, six inches a C cup, and so on. If you're somewhere in the middle of a measurement, size up.

Bra sizes vary from brand to brand and store to store, so it's worth bothering to try your bras in-store. Plus, as I'm about to explain, different styles of bra make your chest look completely different, so it's worth testing everything out in the dressing room first.

ARE YOU SURE YOUR BRA ACTUALLY FITS?

A bra should support, but also make you feel a little bit (or a whole lot) sensual. It's the first layer next to the skin in an intimate area, so what you put there, and how it feels, is important.

You should be able to fit your thumb underneath the fabric where your ribs meet, between the underwire cups. The band shouldn't dig into your ribs, but it should be tight enough that you feel supported by it. If the band is fitted correctly, it should lift your boobs, like they're sitting on a shelf, and your straps should not weigh down on your shoulders.

Underwire should gently hug underneath and around the sides of the breasts, but not dig in. If it digs in, try a cup size up.

The top of the cup should lie flat. A double boob, where your cup runneth over, is not a good look and will create a funny shape through clothing, so go up a cup size. If the top of the cup gapes, this doesn't necessarily mean you need a smaller size. More likely, you haven't put the bra on properly. I have to admit, not being blessed with a huge chest, it wasn't until I researched this part of my book that I came across the "pour and shake," or the "scoop and swoop" method of putting on your bra! Stay with me, I promise this ends up making sense.

Most breasts, unless enhanced with an implant, are tear-shaped, holding the bulk of their weight in the lower half. Often, they get squashed and flattened into the lower half of the bra. So next time you put on your bra, put your arms through the straps first, then bend forward, holding the sides of the band, and let gravity do its work. Then stand up and fasten the clasp. Now your bust will sit properly in the cups, being lifted instead of just covered. This actually gives a completely different shape, and stops you from being fooled into thinking you were a size too small for any gaping cups.

WHERE TO BUY YOUR BRA

Personally, I like to keep it simple, but full of lace—kind of French-inspired. I love bright colors, but I prefer plain lace over anything frivolous, such as satin, frills, bows, or patterns. And I don't like the feel of underwire or padding. I love to shop at Cosabella, Asos, Hanky Panky, American Apparel, Mimi Holliday, and once in a while, I'll splash out at La Perla.

Other brands I love: for super-sexy pieces, Victoria's Secret, Agent Provocateur, and Kiki de Montparnasse are *va va voom*. For girly, gorgeous negligees and bras, Elle Macpherson, Stella McCartney, and Eres and are great options. Wolford, Nordstrom, Calvin Klein, and Marks & Spencer make chic, plain basics, and for shapewear try Spanx, Yummie, and Target.

For a variety of larger cup and back sizes, check out Figleaves, Bare Necessities, and HerRoom. Rigby & Peller is one of the oldest lingerie companies in the world, the official bra-fitters of Queen Elizabeth (wow!), and their sizes go all the way from a 28A to a 52N. Yup, I said 52N!

TYPES OF BRAS

WIRELESS BRA: With no underwire, these are not supportive for a larger chest but sufficient for smaller and medium ones. A wireless or wire-free bra is comfortable and great for traveling.

T-SHIRT BRA: Seamless and smooth, these give the perfect shape under clothing. T-shirt bras come molded, but not usually padded.

BALCONETTE BRA: Cups are underwired, usually padded, and cut low and straight. They expose the upper half of your chest and create sexy, I-stepped-out-of-*Pride-and-Prejudice* cleavage.

PLUNGE BRA: Great to wear with V-necks and low-cut tops, the shape of the cup slants diagonally to sculpt, enhance, and create cleavage.

PUSH-UP BRA: Similar to a plunge bra but enhanced with padding or gel inserts, these are great for creating curves.

MINIMIZER BRA: Designed to reduce you by one or two full sizes, these tend to have thicker straps to distribute weight evenly. They are designed to make boobs look smaller, not flatter.

CONVERTIBLE BRA: It's handy to own one of these. The straps are removable, but also clip into different positions, such as crossover, one-shoulder, and halter neck.

STRAPLESS BRA: These can be tricky, because they lack shoulder support. They need to fit extra snugly to avoid a sagging chest or worse still, popping out of the top. Try one a cup size smaller than your normal bra size, and make sure the cups separate your breasts, to avoid one giant uni-boob!

SPORTS BRA: These are extremely supportive and made exclusively for exercise. I wouldn't wear one long after you're done with the gym, because they're designed to hold everything tight and still, so you might feel constricted after a while.

In terms of fabric, nylon is best for bras; they're breathable and stretchy, yet also supportive. Silk and lace are lovely, too, but be picky about what you wear on top: silk can easily give a case of smuggling peanuts (you know, when it's a bit nippy on a cold night?!), and a beautiful lace can actually look lumpy and weird under a thin shirt.

Before we move on from bras, remember to check your breasts regularly for lumps and bumps, and have any abnormalities checked out by a doctor right away. Sadly, one in nine women will be affected by breast cancer, so try to be as watchful as possible.

Choosing Your Panties, or, as We English Call Them, Knickers!

MINIMIZE A VPL (visible panty line) with seamless knickers. And choose a pair that doesn't cut into your butt or hips. Choose a lightweight, non-frilly or non-frivolous fabric in a thong shape that cuts above the cheek, not into it.

If you don't like the idea of a thong or G-string, a French cut is a half brief at the back, and far more flattering if you're self-conscious about your bottom.

Boy shorts—the loose, silk variety—are floaty, sophisticated, and easy to wear under long skirts or in bed.

If you're wearing low-cut jeans, purchase hipster undies. These are cute, and avoid any kind of whale-tail-on-display situation when you bend over.

Sculpt Your Body with Shapewear

OKAY, TIME TO REMOVE any cringe-worthy *Bridget Jones* associations from your head. Shapewear is actually sexy these days; not something to be embarrassed about or surreptitiously whipped off in the bathroom before your man-friend gets to see. Every girlfriend of mine owns at least one pair of tummy-flattening support pants, no matter what size she is. High-waist and long-leg briefs are, in fact, life-changers. They, along with girdles, bodysuits, and corsets, manage to lift, smooth, flatten, and cinch everything to a more flattering position. I'm talking killer results—just wait until you put your favorite dress on and see how differently it clings to your curves.

HOW TO CARE FOR YOUR GARMENTS

L ooking after your clothes is paramount, and there are tricks and tips—some centuries-old—that will fix any disaster.

Treating Stains

BLOOD: Soak the item in salt and cold water. For dry, older blood stains, leave it to dry, brush, and then try the salt and water combo, adding a few drops of ammonia to the solution.

WAX: If you spill wax on your clothes, let it dry before chipping off as much as possible with a butter knife. Then, after taking the garment off, lay a paper towel over the area and rub a warm iron over it. The wax melts and sticks to the towel instead. Repeat with fresh paper towels until all the wax has disappeared.

GRASS: To remove grass stains, soak a cloth in rubbing alcohol and apply to the underside of the stain, before laundering as usual.

GUM: To get rid of chewing gum, place the item in a plastic bag and chuck it in the freezer for an hour. The gum will freeze rock-solid, and can be gently chipped off.

INK: Ink can be moistened with salt and lemon, before being held over steam. Felt tip pen can be treated with rubbing alcohol.

GENERAL STAINS: Blot, don't rub, when you spill your supper on your clothes. Wiping or rubbing will actually further ingrain the stain into the weave. When applying any stain remover, dab it from the back of the fabric, not the front, so that the mark doesn't spread any deeper. If there's any sheen or shine to the material of your clothing, first try a baby wipe to remove the stain.

Laundry

I HATE IT WHEN TOWELS OR T-SHIRTS get scratchy and stiff. Revive that box-fresh softness by using a little less detergent and adding a cup of white wine vinegar to the wash. White wine vinegar is a natural fabric softener, and has the added bonus of removing yucky odors. I swear by softener sheets in the dryer, too.

If your whites are graying, add a capful of bleach and wash on a hot setting. For yellow armpit stains, soak the garment pre-wash in a solution of ¼ cup baking soda, ¼ cup hydrogen peroxide, and ¼ cup warm water. Leave it to soak for thirty minutes before giving the targeted area a good scrub with an old toothbrush. Prevent these stains by checking if your deodorant contains aluminum. If so, switch to an antiperspirant without that ingredient.

Add a ½ cup of distilled white vinegar to the final rinse cycle while doing laundry to maintain the wash of your favorite pair of dark jeans.

Put an old perfume bottle or room-freshening sachet into the bottom of your laundry basket to freshen up the smell.

Always fold heavy wool or knit items; hanging them will lose their shape.

I like to hand-wash my delicate lingerie, lace, and knit items with a gentle, nontoxic detergent, such as the Honest Company, or one made for cleaning cotton baby diapers!

Dealing with Moths

MOTHS ARE A TOTAL PAIN IN THE BUTT. Hard to detect until they've eaten a hole or two in your favorite sweater, moths need very specific treatment to eradicate, not just a quick spritz of disinfectant. First, check if you have moths by looking for little holes in clothes, and (I am retching at the grossness of this) look for larvae. Larvae are the size of a grain of rice and tend to target the folds and creases of your sweaters or dresses. Moths like warm, dark, crowded closets, and will eat their way through wool and cashmere.

Wrap your infested clothing in a plastic or brown paper bag and store in the freezer for a couple of days. The low temperature will kill the eggs. Then, have the same garment dry-cleaned.

Remove any old carpet lining the floor to your closet. This is a popular breeding ground for moths.

Another cure for moths is to make little cotton sacks filled with cloves and sandalwood chippings, and a few drops of peppermint oil. Or you can buy these sachets to save time! Lavender sachets also do the trick. Hang them in your closet; not only will it smell delicious but moths can't stand any of those scents, and they leave. The same goes for orange peel and bay leaves.

For a serious infestation that none of the above is fixing, it's time to get the experts in. Call pest control for a quote.

Delicate Materials

LEATHER

Leather needs to be looked after. If it dries out, it will crack and lose its shine. Scotchgard your leather, or at least polish it, as soon as you get it home from the store.

To remove pen marks, spray a little hairspray (use a good quality brand though), and wipe away the stain.

To remove other marks and give it a burst of shine, use at-home leather cleaning wipes, or better still, a dab of coconut oil. Be sure to use a clean, cotton cloth. I have to say, a pair of old panties works a treat!

Windex restores the glossy sheen on patent leather without doing any damage.

SUEDE

Remove suede stains by placing garments over a boiling kettle (raising them about fifteen inches above the spout), and then gently brush marks away with an old toothbrush. A pencil eraser also works wonders on suede stains: rub in circular motions.

To give suede a new lease of life (wear and tear can make it dull and flat), sprinkle talcum powder over it to soak up any excess oil, and then brush with short, sharp strokes to raise the nap and remove any dust. The best types of brushes for this are those with bristles made of brass or horsehair. Finish off the process by vacuuming over the suede.

CASHMERE

The word cashmere comes from *Kashmiri*, the Tibetan name for the special type of goat, whose soft hair is woven into our favorite sweaters. It actually takes four of these goats just to knit one top. Cashmere is without doubt the most luxurious, soft, and cozy material to wrap yourself up in, but it tends to come at a price. I still firmly believe that every woman deserves just one cashmere item in her closet, even if it's a pair of socks for those winter movie nights spent curled up by the fire. Wearing cashmere is dreamy.

Cashmere can be hand washed or taken to the dry cleaners, but never, ever shove it in the machine. My mom did this to my first ever cashmere cardigan, and it came out ready to fit a doll! I was so upset, but hey, these things happen. I would refer to the brand's instructions and see what they recommend for washing. If you decide to hand wash, don't make the water piping hot, and use a cashmere shampoo, which can be found online. I know all this sounds like a pain, but if you're going to save up and spend on this special item, then you might as well look after it properly, too.

To dry, place your cashmere onto a light-colored towel and roll it gently into a tube. Don't squeeze or ring it, but let the excess water seep into the towel. After a few minutes, unroll it and place flat on a different, dry towel.

To reduce pilling (those annoying little balls that creep up on the fabric), look for a mix of nylon, cotton, angora, or silk in your cashmere. You only need a tiny percentage, perhaps 2 percent, but this will really lengthen the life and look of your softest sweater. Frequent washing actually keeps the bobbles at bay. Contrary to popular belief, it's the dirt and oil from your skin that causes them, not the friction from too much washing.

MOHAIR, ANGORA, MERINO, LAMB'S WOOL

To stop these sweaters (you know, those super-fluffy ones) from shedding, fold the garment and place it into a zip-top bag and freeze it for at least three hours. It's best to do this the minute you buy it, and your top will have a longer life.

Special Garments and Accessories

DRESSES

Dresses need to be hung up, and if long, try to hang them on a high hook or rail, where the hem will not touch the floor. For heavy, embellished dresses, hang them on strong, broad hangers, and add foam padding to each side of the hanger. This spreads the weight of any heavy beads, buttons, or gems, helping the dress keep its shape.

For very heavy dresses and evening gowns, place bubble wrap or an old blanket on the floor underneath where it hangs. Should it fall, this will prevent any damage.

TIGHTS

Spray tights with sticky (read: cheap) hairspray to avoid holes and runs.

If you do get a small run or ladder, dab transparent nail polish at either end to stop it spreading. But if the ladder is remotely visible, throw them out. Especially in a work environment, it sends out the wrong message and a new pair is incredibly cheap.

HATS

Straighten bent hats—such as fedoras and panamas—by steaming them. Stuff the hat with scrunched-up newspaper and leave overnight, to help get its shape back.

HANDBAGS

Store handbags in dust bags or covers to prevent moisture from tarnishing any metalwork on buckles and handles.

If you get an oil stain on your favorite handbag, coat the mark with baby powder and let it stand overnight. By morning, the stain should be gone. If a bit still remains, repeat the process until the stain is completely gone. For tiny grease stains, rub a little lighter fluid on the area, or, as I was once told by the queen of handbag designers, Anya Hindmarch, rub a little oil from your own forehead into the mark. Anya said she'd seen workmen from her factory work out a scratch this way, and it works!

If your favorite bag gets soaked in the rain, patience is a virtue here. Don't be tempted to rest it by the heater or, worse, point the hair dryer at it. Instead, stuff it with tissue paper to keep its shape, and leave it in a dark, dry closet until it is bone-dry.

For vintage bags, take a trip to your nearest rare or classic book dealer. These guys have all the best local recommendations for replenishing old leather.

For light-colored leather and any exotic animal-skin bags, always go to a professional cleaner, and ask around for a good recommendation first. It's not worth the risk of taking matters into your own hands and making things worse.

SHOES

Get rid of sticky or slippery shoe soles with sandpaper, and the outsite of banana skin makes for a brilliant substitute shoe polish.

Be careful how you store patent shoes. It drinks color from darker pieces next to it, leaving a permanent oil-slick stain. Be sure to give patent shoes space, or keep them in a shoebox. If you do get a stain, try rubbing Windex onto the area, or a cotton ball dipped into rubbing alcohol. Be extremely careful and specific with the area, however, as these products can remove shine from the shoes.

Part Three:

Beauty

BEAUTY DOESN'T HAVE
TO BE PAIN

Vivienne Westwood once told me a story during an interview that I've never been able to forget. She said that vanity has always led women to extremes, and that during Elizabethan times women wore those tall, elaborate wigs, which became so sweaty and dirty that lice and tiny insects infiltrated the weave. To remove the lice, ladies placed miniscule wooden boxes, filled with a drop of honey, into their hair. The lice gravitated toward the sugar, and every few days the boxes would be replaced. Cue me retching, and realizing that life has gotten a lot easier when it comes to looking after our hair and skin. Err—or has it?

Beauty treatments are almost as terrifying and prolific nowadays. Living in L.A. it's hard not to notice the Botox, fillers, face-lifts, acrylic nails, hair extensions, and even eyebrow transplants (yes, you read that right), that go on. If it makes you feel better, then I say go for it. But I often worry about the toxic chemicals and trauma from elective surgery we put our bodies through. One thing I do draw on from Vivienne Westwood's story is the smart use of natural materials around us. My advice for today's beauty regimes? Take advantage of them. Every once in a while, though, your skin and hair will thank you for a non-processed, non-chemical treatment.

SECRETS TO GLOWING, CLEAR SKIN

When I lived in London, I would look at images of Hollywood stars on the red carpet and just imagine they spent all day tanning in the L.A. sun, because their skin sparkled magically, ethereally, like something out of a fairy tale. Now that I live here I know that actually they don't.

There are exfoliators, peels, scrubs, oils, primers, spray tans, and illuminators to create the magic. Jessica Alba, whose skin is like gleaming caramel that I just want to lick, is my ultimate luminous skin queen. But there's also a huge trend now for pale, porcelain skin. Starlets Carey Mulligan, Emma Roberts, and Emma Stone have brought bright, light skin complexions into the spotlight. Then there's my fashion darling, Lupita Nyong'o, whose dark skin is clear and glows, and looks so stunning next to the zingy bright prints she wears on the red carpet. So no matter your complexion, here are some universal tips and tricks to transform and nourish your skin. Make your skin look younger and fresher, with my smart lifestyle habits.

Sleep, Exercise, Eat Well

YOU SNOOZE, YOU . . . WIN!

Deep sleep produces hormones that stimulate the production of collagen and elastin (the key ingredients that keep skin youthful, but that we produce less of naturally as soon as we hit our twenties). Aim to get between seven and nine hours of sleep a night. I need a minimum of eight hours a night, otherwise I notice a complete difference in my skin: it's lackluster and dry, and makeup just doesn't hold to it in the same way. Lack of sleep overall causes dark circles, eye bags, and in the long term, crow's feet and frown lines, so skip that late-night movie and get to bed!

NAMASTE

Exercise boosts the oxygen and nutrient supply to skin and helps remove toxins, meaning you'll glow. But make sure you throw some yoga, Pilates, or power walking into your workout mix. Too much extreme cardio puts stress on the body, which in turn can unbalance hormones and cause dehydration. The same idea goes for stress in everyday life. The more irritated you get with situations, the more facial muscles start to stiffen, leading to lines; all the more reason to relax and chill out.

AVOID SUGAR

Every nutritionist, personal trainer, and doctor I've ever spoken to says that sugar is a bigger evil than all the naughties in our diets, including booze, caffeine, and simple carbs. Certainly in terms of aging the skin, having a sweet tooth can backfire. Here's the science bit: sugar creates these things called "advanced glycation end compounds" in our bodies, which damage collagen and neutralize antioxidants. In a nutshell, sugar messes with the clear, dewiness of your skin and eventually makes it look grayish and thin. I'm not saying never have frozen yogurt ever again (I wouldn't swap anything for that) but be aware that sugar hides away in things like white bread, sauces, and dressings. So switch white bread for whole-grain, white rice for quinoa, and pasta for sweet potatoes, and if you have time, make your own dressings from scratch. You'll see a big difference.

BUT EVERYONE HAS GUILTY PLEASURES

I'm a big fan of treats, and no healthy lifestyle is fulfilling without them. Giving up the foods and beverages that make you happy, quite frankly sucks, and will make you crave them even more. So instead, make a few adjustments.

If, like me, you can't go without your milky, sweet breakfast tea in the mornings, then switch to almond milk and sweeten it with agave nectar or stevia, both natural alternatives to sugar.

Have a sweet tooth? Switch your candy for dark, organic chocolate, at least 70 percent cocoa. This has way less sugar and is a potent antioxidant, too.

Giving up alcohol completely is definitely not on my radar, either, so reach for the more natural, less processed or sugary options. Switch your white wine for an organic red. Switch your margarita for a silver tequila on the rocks, with at least four wedges of fresh lime (I can vouch for this one, it is my *drink*!), and switch your usual sweet cocktail for a vodka, soda, and dash of cranberry juice. *Hangovers, be gone.*

Want your favorite fried chicken? Skip the batter in favor of a splash of coconut oil in the skillet. This is the best oil to cook with; it's super healthy. I make my turkey burgers with this. Check out that recipe and others in the Lifestyle section.

If there are other favorite treats I haven't mentioned here, have a look at Bodyism's book and website for ideas and alternatives. It's written by James Duigan, a no-nonsense trainer who still understands that we are human and need our goodies! In general, if there are more than six ingredients on the back of a packet, don't do it. The best rule of thumb I learned from him is to stick with foods that still look like their original state, when they were picked from the tree or the field.

Beat the Face Bloat

IN TRADITIONAL CHINESE MEDICINE, the skin under the eye indicates how healthy your liver and kidneys are. One of the biggest factors it shows is how diet, exercise, and rest can affect the aging process of your skin. Excess alcohol and coffee are acidic, which can lead to blemishes and zits. Secondly, those drinks are dehydrating, which results in a puffy face because cells are desperately holding on to any moisture left.

To get rid of bloat, cool the skin down. Try sleeping with an extra pillow to elevate your head and prevent fluid from pooling around your eyes. Lay cold cucumber slices over your eyes (yes, it's an old trick, but an effective one). Keep an eye gel in the fridge, and spritz on a cooling mist.

I filmed a TV show in Malaysia in 2014. It's an incredible culture, with beautiful scenery, but boy was it humid. I battled blistering heat and 90 percent humidity every day. Everything swells up in that weather. It was hard to keep my face from looking like a football! So I sprayed Mario Badescu's Facial Spray with Aloe, Herbs, and Rosewater two or three times a day. It's incredibly refreshing!

Finally, the *pièce de résistance* of beating the bloat: a face massage. When my makeup artist, Rachel Wood, started giving me these at the beginning of every session before filming *Plain Jane*, I saw a huge difference. My cheekbones and jawline became more pronounced; my cheeks were rosier and the dark circles under my eyes were dramatically reduced. The lymph drainage movement not only removes excess fluid, but it brings antibodies and oxygen to the skin, which has anti-aging benefits.

Here are some step-by-step tips to give yourself a face massage:

Using a serum or thin day cream, glide your hands from the center of your forehead outward, applying firm pressure. Spread your fingertips into your hairline and massage in circular motions, before coming down to your temples and adding extra pressure. Pat your fingertips gently but quickly around the eyes, and then press into the upper eye socket just beneath where your eyebrows start, with your index fingers for about ten seconds. With your thumbs, massage all the way along and underneath your cheekbones, and again along your jawline. Squeeze your earlobes and continue small squeezes all the way up your ear. Repeat two to three times.

Feed Your Face

ABOUT TWO YEARS AGO, I started eating an avocado every day—on salads, mashed on toast, as a dip—with anything. I do it mainly because I love the taste, and because they're one of the most nutritious fruits in existence (akin to breast milk when it comes to nourishing a baby—so you could pretty much live off them if you had to). But the added bonus of eating so many *avos* came when my makeup artist said they had totally changed my skin. The healthy fats in avocadoes help skin to stay hydrated and plump. You can put as many creams, serums, and masks on the surface, but true hydration and mineral absorption has to come from underneath.

Drink two to three liters of water per day. Add a cup of unsweetened coconut water every few days if you can find it. The level of electrolytes in coconut water is higher than regular water, so you'll rehydrate even faster.

If you're starting a detox, your skin may well break out on the second or third day, as the toxins have to come out somewhere. But rest assured by day five your skin and eyes will be clearer than ever, you just have to let your skin excrete its junk before it looks clean and fresh again.

My Morning Drink

EVERY DAY I START OFF with hot water and lemon. It kick-starts your system, and helps flush out toxins from your liver, which in turn clears your skin.

My Skin-Brightening Smoothie

I MAKE THIS ABOUT FOUR TIMES A WEEK, and it 100 percent makes a difference to the brightness of my skin and my energy levels. Head to your local health store, Feelunique.com, or iHerb.com to find the various ingredients below, and don't worry if you can't obtain them all. As long as at least four of them are whizzing around your blender, the smoothie will have an effect on your complexion. The consistency should be that of a gloopy milk shake, and taste like a vanilla-cinnamon one. Absolutely delicious, I promise. Here's the breakdown:

3 CUBES OF ICE

1 TEASPOON ACAI POWDER: Acai is a Brazilian fruit and a potent antioxidant that boosts energy and digestion.

1 TEASPOON GOJI BERRY: Grown in the Himalayas, goji berries have been used in Chinese medicine for centuries as a powerful antioxidant that improves circulation. They contain vitamins C, B1, B2, B6, and E, all of which contribute to better-looking skin.

1 TEASPOON CHIA SEEDS: Hailing from South America and having been used consistently in Aztec and Mayan diets, chia seeds are one of the richest plant-based sources of omega-3 fatty acids. Omega-3s help make up the cell membrane that allows nutrients to enter the skin cells. Think of them as the nightclub bouncer, responsible for letting a queue of nutrients inside.

1 TEASPOON GROUND FLAXSEED: Flaxseed provides more omegas, in particular alpha linoleic acid, which keeps the skin and hair hydrated. The human body doesn't naturally create omega-3 fats, so you need to get them from your diet.

1 TEASPOON RAW CACAO POWDER: This is not the same as throwing a bar of chocolate into the blender! Raw cacao is not the same as cocoa. Cacao still tastes good though, and is packed with skin-friendly magnesium, vitamin C, and omega-6 fatty acids that increase blood flow and promote cellular healing.

1 TEASPOON GREENS: You can find powdered greens at most health stores, but the key ingredient I'm talking about is chlorophyll. Chlorophyll is the green pigment in plants and veggies that harnesses the sun's energy in photosynthesis. It fights free radicals, improves oxygen supply, and helps remove toxins, all of which equals much clearer, younger skin.

1 TEASPOON MACA ROOT: Maca is a plant that has been harvested in the Andes Mountains in Peru for 3,000 years. Along with numerous health benefits, it is known to reduce acne and blemishes.

2 WALNUTS: These reduce breakout-causing acidity in the diet.

SPRINKLE OF CINNAMON: Besides smelling like Christmas, cinnamon balances your blood sugar levels and fights off sugar cravings.

½ CUP COCONUT WATER: Antioxidants and cytokinins present in coconut water have an age-defying effect on skin, plus it's full of electrolytes, which makes it a more hydrating drink than water. Make sure you buy the raw, unsweetened variety.

½ CUP ALMOND MILK, UNSWEETENED: A great alternative to dairy, which can cause breakouts for a lot of people, almond milk is full of nutrients like vitamin B2 (also known as riboflavin) and E, which hydrate cells and protect the skin from sun damage, respectively.

Skin-Nourishing Juices

I LIKE TO SWITCH UP between smoothies and juices throughout the week. Their tastes are so different; it makes a nice change to have varying flavors on alternate days. The body has trouble absorbing vitamins and supplements in pill forms, so getting your nutrients from the real deal, the *actual* fruit and vegetables, serves you well. Juicing removes the indigestible fiber from fruit and vegetables, so your body absorbs more of the vitamins and minerals from juice than say, just eating the actual veggie whole. However, since the body also needs fiber to keep running like a fine-tuned machine, there are major debates over which is actually healthier: chewing on your vegetable or drinking its juice. My solution? Switch back and forth between the two. Juicing is a surefire way to fit a large amount and variety of fruit and veggies into your diet, more than you'd have time or space to eat in any one sitting.

There is one other option: the absolute best thing I invested in last year was a Vitamix (NutriBullets are a less expensive version). I have to toot the Vitamix's horn here, because unlike other juicers, it doesn't discard the pulp and fiber of your ingredients, and it is powerful enough to liquefy even an avocado stone. (Yup, for real.) All those yucky bits we're accustomed to cutting off and avoiding on veggies—such as stalks, pips, seeds, and stones—are the most nutritious. So throw them in your juicer, too! I now save a fortune on expensive juice bars and pre-made smoothies, and quite enjoy coming up with new concoctions on my own.

P.S. Try to drink your juice within twenty minutes of whizzing it up. As soon as your fresh juice gets exposed to air, its live enzymes begin to degrade, decreasing the nutritional content. If you leave it longer, it will still benefit you, but be sure to keep it in the fridge.

My Rejuvenating Juice

THIS RECIPE GIVES ME IMMEDIATE ENERGY, clears up my skin after a few days, and is best sipped on an empty stomach.

1-INCH GINGER SLICE: Great for digestion and I love the spicy taste.

4 STALKS TOTAL OF CUCUMBER OR CELERY: This acts as a diuretic, draining excess water.

½ OR WHOLE APPLE OR PEAR: A great source of fiber and it sweetens up the drink.

HANDFUL OF KALE, SPINACH, OR ROMAINE LETTUCE: The darker the green veg, the more iron and chlorophyll you're getting.

1 LEMON OR LIME: It gives a zingy flavor and alkalizes the juice.

SPRINKLE OF CAYENNE PEPPER: This is optional, but it gives the juice a kick, and helps with detox, digestion, and circulation.

Beauty Juice

IF I DRINK THIS CONCOCTION four days in a row, on the fifth day I see a huge difference in my skin: my face is clear of blemishes and has a nice glow to it. Even the whites of my eyes get brighter (well, as long as I haven't been at the cocktails, either!). The consistency is on the thicker side, so be sure to serve chilled by adding ice. One glass fills me up for a good few hours.

4 ICE CUBES

HANDFUL OF SPINACH: Loaded with iron and potassium, spinach also contains lutein, which helps eyes to sparkle.

HANDFUL OF WATERCRESS: A powerful antioxidant, with higher levels of iron than spinach, and more calcium than milk.

HANDFUL OF PARSLEY: Parsley is so underrated as a superfood! It has the highest vitamin C levels of any herb and contains beta-carotene, which is converted into vitamin A for repairing and renewing skin cells. Chlorophyll and vitamin K also help reduce puffiness in the face and erase those dark under-eye circles.

½ RIPE AVOCADO: (See Feed Your Face, page 129, for benefits.)

1 PEAR: Pears are high in fiber but have a low glycerin index, which basically means they slow down the release of sugar into our bodies and skin cells. The result? Less damage to collagen and smoother skin.

1 LIME: (See My Rejuvenating Juice, page 134, for benefits.)

Natural Skin Remedies

USING NATURAL PRODUCTS on your body instead of processed potions in a pot is not only kinder on your skin, but also on your wallet. Particularly for those of you with sensitive skin, the man-made ingredients in beauty products (you know, those ones you can't even pronounce) can be difficult for your face to take day in, day out. Next I'm going to show you why paying more attention to the supermarket shelves, rather than the beauty aisles, could save your skin.

HYDRATE WITH MANUKA HONEY

A rich moisturizer and a godsend for dry skin. Apply a thin layer as a face mask once every two weeks (alternate with your actual, packaged face mask), to smooth and soften the skin.

CLEANSE WITH APPLE CIDER VINEGAR

Another wonder product with many health benefits, apple cider vinegar has taken Hollywood by storm. Lady Gaga uses it daily and lots of actresses are into it, too! Besides killing bacteria and balancing the skin's pH level, it absorbs excessive oil, to help prevent outbreaks.

Mix ¼ cup of vinegar with ¾ cup of water. Dip a cotton pad into the solution and apply the mixture directly to your skin, leave it there for ten minutes, then rinse. This solution can be left on for longer if you suffer from acne, psoriasis, or have a sunburn.

My big tip? Be sure to buy raw organic apple cider vinegar, containing the "mother" of the vinegar, which looks like a creamy blob in the bottom of the bottle. This type of vinegar has raw enzymes in it which will work their magic on your skin; whereas the clear variety of apple cider vinegar is processed and won't be useful for anything other than dressing a salad!

EXFOLIATE WITH COCONUT

Sloughing off dead skin cells is the quickest way to boost radiance. Replace your regular cleanser with this concoction two to three times a week. Coconut oil and coconut water are miracle products that can be ingested or applied topically to revive, hydrate, and renew skin.

TO APPLY TOPICALLY:

First, steam your face for seven minutes to open pores.

Mix 1 tablespoon of coconut water or oil together with a handful of cooked lentils, into a paste.

Rub gently on the skin for two minutes before rinsing away. A common cause for skin problems and dehydration is a buildup of toxins, fungi, and bad bacteria. Scrubbing with coconut oil helps to cleanse and neutralize these toxins, fungi, and bacteria on the outer layers of your skin, which not only detoxifies but also helps to build your skin's natural immune system and protective qualities. Some forms of eczema and psoriasis are actually skin infections caused by a fungus, so using coconut oil topically can help with these, too.

PEEL WITH CUCUMBER

If you have very sensitive skin, avoid exfoliators that contain crunchy granules; they can leave your skin redder. Instead, opt for an at-home peel once a week, which works with gentle acids to dissolve dead cells, removing the top layer of skin from your face (it sounds more drastic than it is). Peels leave a silky finish. The application of a homemade dry-skin face peel can help relieve any dry, itchy skin on your face. Natural peels can be made from a variety of fruit, including strawberries and cucumbers. I've chosen cucumbers here because strawberries can stain your skin for a few hours, which is no good if you're planning to go out afterward!

Cucumbers are high in water content, which makes them hydrating and plumping when applied to the skin. They also boast a hyperpigmentation property, which cleans the skin and helps reduce lines and wrinkles.

Here's a recipe I learned from a beauty writer friend, who came over to my house and showed me how to make this. It works!

1/2 CUP OF CUCUMBER PULP

(the easiest way is to mash it in a blender on low speed)

1 EGG WHITE

1 TABLESPOON OF LEMON JUICE

Mix the ingredients together in a bowl. Apply it to the face and leave for ten minutes, then wash away with lukewarm water and pat the skin dry. If your skin was built up with residue, you may find a few peely bits (it feels the same as when your skin peels after vacation). Rub those away with a towel. Your skin may be red and blotchy for about twenty minutes, but after that it will feel clear and smooth and be evenly colored.

SOOTHE WITH YOGURT

The list of things that can cause breakouts and red bumps is annoyingly long—a change in weather, central heating, air-conditioning, stress, diet, new products, menstrual cycle, and more. But here's a cheap, effective product that provides an amazing remedy: natural yogurt applied straight from the refrigerator cools and calms skin. And I'm not the first person to preach its benefits.

In ancient Egypt, Cleopatra was famous for her daily sour milk baths, which kept her skin glowing and youthful. For hundreds of years and still today in India, yogurt is used to clear acne and pimples. Why? Because natural yogurt is full of zinc and lactic acid. This combination is like kryptonite for zits: zinc contains anti-inflammatory properties to reduce red swellings caused by acne or rashes; it has mild anti-astringent properties to help tighten the tissues and generate new cells; it reduces the size of pimples; and it helps regulate oil production in the sebaceous glands to stop future breakouts. Lactic acid exfoliates and moisturizes dry skin, and reduces wrinkles. It also has disinfectant properties, eschewing the bacteria that cause zits. You thought I was finished? Nope, there's more! Natural yogurt contains calcium and B vitamins, which heal and protect the skin from future damage.

Gently spread a thin layer of plain yogurt on your face, with a cold spoon or little paint brush. Wait for about ten to fifteen minutes to let it dry out and absorb. Try not to smile or talk so the mask doesn't crack. Then rinse with cool water. Remember to apply a moisturizer afterward (if you want to stay natural, you can use olive oil), as the yogurt mask can leave your skin feeling tight.

And in case you're away from your kitchen, on the road, or in a hotel, here are a couple more zit-zapping tricks I've picked up along the way: Dissolve aspirin in a cup of water and dab on pimples with a cotton swab to calm irritation and bring down redness. Toothpaste left on a spot overnight will dry it out. If you've picked at it, clean the area and then spray two pumps of perfume onto a cotton swab, before dabbing it onto the spot. The alcohol in the perfume should sting a little, but it will disinfect it.

MY MIRACLE SKIN AT-HOME FACE MASK

The best part about this natural remedy is that you will almost always have the full list of ingredients lying around the kitchen! My mom taught me how to make this mask years ago. The recipe is a one-stop shop to fabulous skin: it exfoliates, hydrates, nourishes, and soothes your skin, all in one fell swoop. Try it with your girlfriends; it makes for some very amusing selfies!

Mix ¼ cup of full-fat yogurt with ¼ a cup of brown sugar. Mix in two table-spoons each of honey and olive oil. For dry skin, throw in ¼ cup of mashed avocado, too (I'm usually too greedy to not eat this part beforehand though). Massage the mixture onto your face and neck, and leave for fifteen minutes. The yogurt calms the skin, the brown sugar scrubs it clean, the honey hydrates, and the olive oil nourishes it.

How to Wash Your Face

THIS MIGHT SEEM ELEMENTARY, but actually, the amount of dirt and residue left on our faces each day after we think we've "washed" it, is a lot. And that's not only yucky; it causes breakouts, too. So try washing your face with my instructions below. Only do all this once a day—I tend to do it at night after a long day of makeup and pollution. In the morning, a gentle wash with warm water in the shower will suffice. Otherwise you risk removing too much of the skin's oils, which are important for hydration. See if your skin feels and looks different after this. I bet it does.

Begin with a double cleanse. This is key to removing every trace of dirt from your skin. First, wet the skin with warm water and massage in your cleanser. Then wash it off to remove superficial makeup, dirt, and sweat. (We sweat about a pint per night in bed. Ew, but true!) Then apply a little more cleanser, about the size of a grape, dampen a wash cloth with warm water, place it over your face, and take a few deep breaths to relax. Then buff your face with circular motions—this will help decongest your T-zone. Splash your face at least four times with fresh water each time. You actually need to rinse more than you think to remove every last trace of your cleanser. If not, there could be product residue on your skin, which will affect the impact of whichever product you put on next.

Then take thirty seconds to wipe your skin with a toner, splash with cold water, or do as Joan Crawford did and dip your face into a bowl of ice. This will close all the pores you've just cleaned. You've also reduced redness, de-puffed, and tightened the skin.

Next up, massage a facial serum (Hydraluron is one of my favorites) into the skin. Leave for a few minutes until it's sunk in, and then go for your day-time moisturizer, tinted moisturizer, or foundation. I like to mix up all three. But whatever you use, and wherever you live (even if it's cloudy every day), make sure those topical products contain SPF. That's key for keeping your skin young, healthy, and protected.

If you're doing this process in the morning, while your moisturizer sinks in and evens out—before you apply any more makeup—brush your teeth to pass the time. My top tip? On particularly sleepy days, use fizzy water for brushing teeth, it's far more refreshing!

How to Treat Cellulite

CONTRARY TO POPULAR BELIEF, cellulite is not actually a fat issue (plenty of skinny people have it!), it's a circulation problem. Here's why: when cells and blood vessels weaken, they can't distribute enough nutrients around the body. Fibers consequently harden and contract around the fat cells just underneath the skin. This causes yucky fat deposits to squeeze up toward the skin's surface and create the bobbly "orange peel" texture we all know and hate. The causes of cellulite have been linked to stress, dehydration, poor or fad diets, inactivity, hormonal imbalance, and, unfortunately, hereditary symptoms. But there is a silver lining! It *is* possible to reduce and remove cellulite. The process is slow—minimum about eight weeks—and you need to commit to an altered way of eating.

First, give up carbonated drinks, and cut right back on your sugar. Both of these things are known to help cause cellulite. Switch up your diet to increase omega-3 foods, which support the cardiovascular system. Dose up on fish (specifically salmon, cod, trout, sardines, snapper, and halibut), but also try walnuts, flaxseeds, soy beans, tofu, and miso. Garlic is also proven to strengthen blood arteries. Vitamins E and C also improve blood flow and repair body tissue, respectively, so up the amount of both these vitamins in your diet, too. Add more almonds, spinach, and shellfish for vitamin E, and peppers, kiwi, broccoli, and citrus fruit for vitamin C. Finally, check out the natural supplement ginkgo biloba. Apart from giving you energy, it is a powerful antioxidant that strengthens veins, and oxidizes those annoying fat cells right below the skin's surface, helping to rid the body of cellulite. Yay!

Start body brushing (you'll need to buy a little dry body brush, available at most pharmacies), at least once a day. Miranda Kerr swears by it. A nail brush with bristles on the softer side will also do. Stand up naked, and using swift, soft strokes along the body, brush up your calves and shins, thighs, hips, butt, and stomach, always directing toward the heart. Then brush the arms, shoulders, and chest. You'll see the skin go pink, which means it's working.

Dry body brushing revs up your circulation, improves lymphatic drainage, and stimulates toxin clearing, which in turn reduces the appearance of cellulite and improves the overall look of your skin, giving it an evenness and a glow. I actually love incorporating this two-minute ritual into my morning. It wakes me up and softens my skin, exfoliating dead cells away and leaving me with a nice glow.

Topical creams and treatments can also help. Look for an anti-cellulite cream with centella asiatica on the label. This key ingredient restores the macromolecules that give the skin its elasticity. Another strange pair of words? Methyl nicotinate. It promotes the decongestion of tissues, reducing the amount of retained liquid and draining toxins.

Whip up your own homemade cellulite treatments, too—this is the cheaper option! Rub coffee granules and olive oil into the affected area, making sure to use real coffee bean granules, not instant coffee, which will immediately dissolve. The rough texture of the coffee combined with the caffeic acid has exfoliating and anti-inflammatory properties that help increase collagen production, bringing back skin's youthful elasticity.

And last but not least, a treatment recommended to me by a fifty-five-year-old Mexican massage therapist who has the skin of a twenty-five-year-old: she told me to mix lemon juice and castor oil, rub it onto the skin and leave for as long as possible before showering. Having done this regularly her whole life, she had not once inch of cellulite.

How to Treat Stretch Marks

ALMOST EVERY CHICK I KNOW has stretch marks, usually at the top of her thighs. They're caused by skin stretching too quickly, either from a sudden weight gain, such as pregnancy, or from a growth spurt. The collagen and elastin splits, and little marks form—starting off pink, then purple, and then turning a silvery white.

Ladies and gents, I have to throw my two cents in here: if your lines truly bother you, then by all means go and seek the treatments I suggest that will follow. However, I will never forget reading an interview with Salma Hayek, who called her stretch marks her tiger stripes. She accepted them and embraced them as a visual reminder of the life's journey her body had been on. High-five your hips, don't berate them, and just be choosy about finding the right lingerie and swimwear to hide any areas you don't fancy showing the world. Amen.

If you do want to tackle them, the newer the marks, the better chance you have of being able to get rid of them. Try Bio-Oil or Clarins L'Huile Tonic, and be sure to rub a generous amount in, twice daily. Use creams that contain retinol to thicken the skin and rebuild collagen, such as StriVectin SD Advanced Intensive Concentrate for Wrinkles & Stretch Marks. Another tip: a good tan (real or fake) will help camouflage lines, too.

If you're willing to cough up some money, newer stretch marks can be eliminated at spas by a pulsed-dye laser. Older stretch marks are more difficult to lose, but speak to a specialist spa about stem cell and PRP Therapy. This treatment uses a micropen to break up the scar tissue, and then PRP (your own blood plasma) is injected directly into the area, which will rebuild your tissue. Sounds gross, but it's not very invasive or painful, and the results are good. However, it's not cheap: usually an area eight by eleven inches costs $1,200 per treatment, and most people need two to three visits. Fraxel laser treatments, microdermabrasion, and peels can also help, but are not guaranteed to produce big results.

CHOOSING YOUR BEAUTY PRODUCTS

What to Avoid . . .

BEAUTY COUNTERS are a minefield. It's easy to get tempted by free samples, pushy sales personnel, and attractive packaging, but taking the time to read your skincare and makeup labels is key. I used to keep getting clogged pores and breakouts on my cheeks, even though I was exfoliating and doing at-home peels as usual. I couldn't figure out the problem until my facialist at Carasoin Spa in Los Angeles asked if I'd changed cleansers. Yes, I had. She told me to beware of the following ingredients, which can clog or dry the skin: talc, mineral oils, and any products containing petroleum (or petrolatum, as it is also known), such as jelly. I don't want to make you panic, but the regulations that beauty products go through before reaching a store shelf are jaw-droppingly minimal. For example, there are absolutely no universal ingredient restrictions, guidelines, or procedures—anywhere in the world—for determining whether or not a product qualifies as being "hypoallergenic," meaning for sensitive skin. So the label is bandied around rather casually, and if you do have sensitive skin, I urge you to still read the label.

Look at it this way: a lotion, face cream, perfume, or nail polish takes twenty-six seconds from application until it enters your bloodstream, so you should really pay as much attention to the list of ingredients on the label as you do your food packaging. Chemicals to avoid, that are still used widely in skincare and cosmetics and can cause irritation or even more serious side effects, include parabens, phthalates, sulfate lauryl sulfate (SLS), formaldehyde, and propylene glycol. Nobody expects you to avoid all of these, all the time, but keep my list on your phone and next time you're shopping take a glance.

There are a few organic beauty product ranges I recommend that are almost entirely natural and are kind to your skin. Try Alba Botanica, Neal's Yard (I use their lavender Beauty Sleep Concentrate), Yes To (I use their cucumber face wipes), Seventh Generation, and Dr. Bronner's (I love their peppermint hand soap).

What to Look For, For . . .

YOUTHFUL SKIN

Looking for anti-aging products? A mix of peptides plus vitamins A, C, and E will keep your skin from wrinkling by speeding up repair and protecting it from harmful pollutants.

ZITS

Looking to avoid breakouts? You need a non-pore-blocking, oil-free moisturizer, such as Neutrogena Visibly Clear Oil-Free Moisturizer. Jouer's Anti-blemish Matte Primer contains salycic acid, which fights acne, but it's also oil-free, paraben-free, and includes calming, natural ingredients, such as aloe, vitamin E, ginseng, and gingko biloba extract.

If you do still get a zit, zap it with Boots No7's Calm and Conceal Blemish Treatment. It's a dual-ended pen with one side to banish the spot, and the other to hide it.

EYES

I always buy an eye gel or serum instead of a thick cream, as you can't always absorb so much in the eye area. Eye treatments containing hyaluronic acid will plump and hydrate the area. Elizabeth Arden Anti-aging and Intensive Repair Eye Serum is a good one, no matter your age.

SENSITIVE SKIN

If it's a chronic condition like rosacea, consult your dermatologist or doctor first. But if the redness or irritation is caused by an allergy or skin sensitivity, it's easier to treat. Look for anti-inflammatory ingredients, such as resveratrol and green tea. Wear an oil-free sunscreen; the sun makes redness worse.

HANDS

Don't forget your hands! My mom always used to say a woman can have as many face-lifts as she likes but you can always tell her age from her hands. And she's right! So treat them with the same TLC you give your face, from the start. Apply a hydrating hand cream with SPF in the day, such as Clinique's Even Better Dark Spot Correcting Hand Cream Broad Spectrum. At night, apply a retinol-based serum. Retinol is a miracle ingredient that tackles everything from discoloration to wrinkles and even acne. If your skin is sensitive to it, look for ferulic acid instead. And get into the habit of swiping any leftover cream or serum that you've just applied to your face, onto the back of your hands.

GOOD OILS

Sometimes my skin gets dry, particularly if I'm sleeping in air-conditioning, and then I'll switch to a face oil at night. Yes, I know, I know, I just ranted on about choosing oil-free products, but face oils made from *natural* oils, are a very different beast to clogging synthetic and mineral oils. Here's what to search for: olive oil (cold-pressed contains the most antioxidants), jojoba oil, and almond oil. In fact, almond oil was used in ancient China, Greece, and India to treat dry skin and improve skin tone. Sounds counterintuitive, but face oils can also be used to regulate the greasiness of oily skin. When you apply face oil, pores are fooled into thinking they have enough oil, and so they stop producing it. Peppermint and grapeseed oil are the best for regulating oil production, although you should avoid putting grapeseed oil directly onto any blemishes. If you suffer from acne-prone skin, try evening primrose or tea tree oil, the latter of which is an antiseptic. A few drops are all you need.

Hair Removal

HAIR TODAY, GONE TOMORROW. Sorry, I couldn't resist! Sick of shaving my legs, I started laser treatment on them about a year ago to remove the hair forever. Here's the skinny on that experience, and other ways to stave off the stubble.

LASER

Pulsed light zaps down the hair shaft into the follicle, where it destroys the hair's root. Within a week or two, that hair falls out, never to be seen again. But hair grows in cycles, so to get completely hairless in any area, it takes around seven sessions, with a touch-up once a year thereafter.

Does it hurt? Where the hair is thicker, yes, it can feel like a rubber band being snapped on you, pretty hard. But other areas, such as arms or underarm, you can barely feel it at all. I chose to have laser on my legs because I have sensitive skin and got sick of rashes after shaving. I wanted smooth legs that would last.

My tip: if you're on the West Coast of America, head to iGlow Med Spa in Beverly Hills, which is the best in the business and where I had my treatment. It was excellent.

ELECTROLYSIS

Okay, ouch, this apparently really hurts, but the results are worth it. Completely permanent hair removal, with no touch-ups required, electrolysis uses a tiny needle that slides down into the hair follicle and destroys the cells that cause growth. The hair will release immediately, game over. This is great for stubborn hair on the bikini area or under the arm, but not for those with a low pain threshold.

My tip: local anesthetic creams and sprays applied beforehand can help numb the pain, so ask your therapist for some.

WAXING

Soy waxes and hard wax are my favorite newer types of wax. Aveda spas make their own and it's way less painful than old-fashioned strip wax. Soy wax doesn't stick to the skin—it just bonds to the hair—so it's a lot kinder and quicker on your body.

My tip: soy waxing removes the entire hair from root to shaft, so it's essential to use an antibacterial lotion afterward to prevent infection. Aloe vera gel, kept in the fridge, is also very calming if your skin is easily irritated after waxing. At-home wax kits used to be more popular. The idea of messy pots of wax melting in the kitchen and attempting to rip strips off your own body: no, thank you. It's far better to visit a professional or if you do want to stay at home, try a depilatory cream, described on page 152.

SHAVING

Contrary to popular belief, shaving does not make the hair grow back coarser—but, unlike other options of hair removal, the effects are very temporary. Razors have come a long way in the last few years, and sometimes I think men's razors can be better than women's. The Gillette Fusion ProGlide Power Razor has extremely thin blades, a microcomb to guide hairs to the blades, a button to make it gently vibrate so it can get even closer to the skin, and a strip that excretes mineral oil to keep your legs or underarms moisturized. The women's Remington Wet/Dry shaver is a great electric offering, and the Schick Hydro Silk has five blades cushioned by silk guards and makes the shave last days longer than other top brands.

My tip: never dry shave, always wet the skin and use a shaving foam or oil (my favorite is the Art of Shaving's Pre-Shave Oil) first. Make sure you replace your razor every three to four weeks, before it gets blunt.

DEPILATORY CREAMS

Hair removal creams work by dissolving the protein compound that makes up hair, below the skin, so there is considerably less stubble than with shaving. Treatments need to be repeated weekly or biweekly, but are cheap, completely painless, and literally only take about twenty minutes from start to finish. Nair is a very effective brand, but for those leaning toward chemical-free, I also like Nad's Natural Hair Removal Gel.

My tip: apply just before a shower and then wash off with your best-smelling soap. The scent, much like fake tan, isn't particularly pleasant, and can linger.

TWEEZING

Plucking pulls hair out at the root, and it will grow back with the next cycle, in a few weeks. Tweezed hair grows back with a tapered end, meaning it is softer and less noticeable when it first comes in. Eventually, however, it will grow back to its normal thickness.

My tip: Tweezerman make the best ever tweezers for brows, and don't over-pluck: thin eyebrows actually make you look older. Full, arched brows are the most flattering way to frame your face, so take your time, and pull back from the mirror for a better perspective as you go, to keep both brows balanced. Never pluck from above or between brows, unless it's a completely rogue hair growing far from the others.

POST-HAIR REMOVAL CARE

Whichever method of hair removal you decide upon, use an ice cube, cortisol gel, or aloe vera cream to sooth and cool the skin after waxing, shaving, or epilating. This will prevent any blemishes or infections. An ice cube is particularly effective because it also closes pores.

Once a week, exfoliate the areas where you remove hair with a body scrub, loofah, or body brush, to eliminate dead skin and boost circulation. Avoid shaving or waxing during your period, as this is when skin is at its most sensitive. And straight after shaving, avoid swimming or sweating, as chlorine and sweat can irritate the skin.

If you develop an ingrown hair, don't pick at it, or you could create an infection. Instead, rub lemon juice onto the affected area, which will exfoliate the skin and you'll be able to tweeze the hair away.

Self-Tan

I'M HOPING YOU ALL CHOOSE A FAKE TAN, hands down, over a real tan. Burning your skin under the sun is not only dangerous, but super aging for your skin. So when you need a glow, please reach for the bottle, not the beach! Personally, I prefer a spray tan, done by a professional. They know what they're doing, so an even, non-streaky-bacon tan is applied, and it should last up to eight days. Fingernails, toenails, and soles of feet get protected, so there are no nasty stains, and most good spray tanners will spray a primer on first, so the tan lasts longer.

If you want to apply tan yourself though, there are plenty of great brands out there. First up, don't underestimate the importance of exfoliation! Make sure you exfoliate in the shower with a body scrub and a loofah, at least two or three times. Scrubbing away just once won't remove all the dead skin. Doing it right means your tan will go on easier, and last longer. And if you can't get rid of old tan, take a bath with a few drops of aromatherapy oil, and drop two dissolvable aspirin into the hot water. This cocktail will help everything come right off!

Stand on an old towel, so that your feet don't end up orange (trust me, I've made this mistake). Use a mitt, which is usually provided with the tan. Gloves or a naked hand can be tricky—you'll get smeary tan lines, not to mention an orange hand. Start at your feet and work up.

A gradual self-tan is the safest bet, this way you can layer it up each day until you reach the perfect skin tone. For this, I love Jergens 3 Days to Glow. If you're doing it for the night and are a little bit terrified, a wash-off gel like Soap & Glory's One Night Tanned is great. For a longer lasting, deeper tan, opt for a mousse: the airy consistency makes it easy to apply. I recommend St. Tropez's Self-Tan Bronzing Mousse and L'Oréal Paris Sublime Bronze Tinted Self-Tanning Mousse for a natural, sun-kissed look. And if you hate the scent of any tan (in my experience, most do tend to leave you smelling of cookies or curry for the night, so delay date night for twenty-four hours!), Xen-Tan's new scent-secure Daily Protection blocks any weird smells, leaving a cucumber scent in its place. And it works alongside any brand.

Go gently on your face, wrists, feet, and hands, and don't be afraid to mix a little moisturizer into the tan for these areas. It will help smooth the look out. Another good idea is to use leftover tan on the mitt for these areas. Cover your head with a shower cap, but leave your hairline showing. Have a friend finish off your back to avoid patches.

Wait at least eight hours until you shower. I always apply tan after a shower, before bed. Whatever you do, don't apply body oil or serum in the morning. It will dissolve the tan and take it off in patches—again, another mistake I made! It's best to shower and leave the skin alone for another day before applying moisturizer.

If you make a boo-boo and overdo things, or leave a giant blob somewhere on your body, here's how to fix it. A few years back, getting ready for a birthday party rather hurriedly, I managed to turn my entire face *green*, by applying tan over a perfumed moisturizer. Green. I looked in the mirror, and my face was *green*. Wish I had been armed with the following knowledge back then, because instead I just freaked out and burst into tears when nothing would scrub it off! But don't worry, guys, fake tan formulas have come a long way since then and won't turn your skin green anymore if mixed with the wrong thing. So if you mess up, rub the area with cotton balls steeped in nail polish remover before rinsing. Baby wipes work well to tone down the color on your face and neck, and if you need to get it off your face fast, lean over a bowl of steaming water for ten minutes. Then, mix a few drops of lemon or lime juice with a thick face mask, and apply for ten more minutes. Remove with a hot, wet towel. The alpha hydroxy acid (AHAs) in the fruit will help remove the tan.

My Must-Have Beauty Kit

OVER THE YEARS I've been lucky enough to travel the world for fashion shoots, filming assignments, and fashion weeks. Chatting to hairstylists, makeup artists, and spa therapists about their favorite products, I started to hear the same names and see the same bottles, whether I was in Sydney, New York, Cannes, London, or Hong Kong. Some are by completely old-fashioned brands, most are cheap as chips, a lot are 100 percent natural, and some need to be searched for online or in a beauty specialist shop, not just at your average drugstore. Here's my motley crew of essential, non-fancy, *best ever* products.

LOUISE'S OLD-FAITHFUL MUST-HAVES

CAUDELIE BEAUTY ELIXIR:
A fresh spritz to refresh the face, I see this little bottle in every model's bag at Paris Fashion Week.

LUCAS' PAPAW OINTMENT:
From Australia, this is a sweet-smelling balm for dry patches, burns, and dry lips. The red tubed wonder is a staple with makeup artists.

EGYPTIAN MAGIC:
A pot of nourishing balm that's been produced for over twenty years and can be used anywhere on the body to heal and hydrate extra-dry areas. Warm it up in your hands to soften before using.

ALBOLENE:
Again, a product that's been around for generations and not changed its packaging (which kind of makes me love it more, it's retro!). I once wore makeup that just wouldn't come off, and my makeup artist recommended this product, it removes *everything* from your face.

EUCERIN PLUS INTENSIVE HAND CREME:
It's rich and great for sensitive skin.

SHEAMOISTURE AFRICAN BLACK SOAP:
So, at one particularly raucous girly dinner, full of stylists and magazine editors, I found out about this soap, it's amazing! Full of oats, shea butter, plantain peel, tamarind, plant ash, and aloe, it's incredibly soothing for skin.

CAROL'S DAUGHTER LEMON JOJOBA CUTICLE OIL:
It's full of nourishing, natural oils, such as almond, soybean, and jojoba. I apply this to the cuticles on my hands and feet right after the shower, every day.

TRADER JOE'S LAVENDER SEA SALT BODY SCRUB:
A total bargain, smells delicious and, when I last bought a tub, the guy at the checkout told me Jennifer Aniston loves this product! The oil in the scrub leaves you silky and moisturized. Just make sure you stir it up before using.

VASELINE:
I've seen it used during fashion shoots on everything from eyelids and cheekbones, to lips and legs.

HAIR CARE FROM THE INSIDE OUT

There's an emotional attachment to hair that can only be explained in a Samson and Delilah kind of way. It represents our comfort blanket, our strength, our femininity, our style. Think of your hair as another fashion accessory: it should be played up, styled, and switched around to suit your mood and your outfit. But in order to do that, it's key to look after your hair properly. When I started filming shows that required a hot iron and blow-dryer on my hair every day for months at a time, I realized quickly I had to nurse my hair back to life each week, or else it would frizz up and fall out. Here's how I do it.

Protect Your Scalp

SO MANY PEOPLE neglect their scalp, but in many ways it's more important than the hair shaft itself. If your hair is misbehaving, the problem could be product buildup or dry, flaky skin on your scalp—something clarifying shampoo *won't* sufficiently cleanse. The result? Clogged hair follicles, weakened strands, and possibly slowed hair growth. So try rubbing aloe vera, olive oil, or a vitamin E capsule into the skin to keep it hydrated and to prevent irritation. Olive oil is particularly effective, as it contains a natural antioxidant that helps with scaly skin and dandruff. Another tip for getting rid of dandruff: green tea. Steep a cup of green tea until it's cool, then mix it with a large dollop of conditioner. Apply the mixture to wet, shampooed hair and leave it on for five minutes, before rinsing thoroughly.

Invest in a hairbrush that has natural bristles, or soft plastic bristles (these are a cheaper option and just as good), as they won't scratch the scalp. Go for a hairbrush with a wooden or ceramic barrel, too, as a metallic base can heat up and act like an iron, which can cause breakage to the hair and dryness to the scalp. Clean your hairbrush by combing it (yup, use a comb to get rid of the hairs in your brush), then immerse it in warm water. Add clarifying shampoo or a sprinkling of baking soda to get rid of any grease or residue. Then rinse and dry the brush before you use it again.

Feed Those Locks from the Inside

DON'T FORGET THAT what you eat has a huge effect on how your hair (and your skin, and your nails) looks. Add omega-3 fatty acids to your diet. These are found in avocado, pumpkin seeds, and oily fish like salmon. They're also found in the dream hair food: walnuts. Walnuts are rich in biotin (too little biotin can lead to hair loss) and vitamin E, which helps protect your cells from DNA damage. We often focus on the skin, when it comes to sun damage. In fact, your hair can be damaged by UVA and UVB rays, too, causing dryness, faded color, and split ends. Walnuts help combat this in a big way. They are also a source of copper, a mineral

that helps keep your natural hair color rich and lustrous. And sprinkle blueberries on your cereal or add them to your smoothie. One of the most concentrated sources of vitamin C, blueberries help support the tiny blood vessels that feed your hair follicles. Too little vitamin C in your diet can lead to hair breakage.

Look After Your Color

I HAVE BALAYAGE ABOUT THREE TIMES A YEAR, a gentle stroke of honey blonde on the lower half of my hair, which looks very natural and lifts my complexion. Lorri Goddard, the queen of color in Hollywood, figures out how blonde to go by asking, "How long have you been out in the sun surfing—all summer long, or just for a couple of weeks?!" She's a hilarious genius.

If you take the DIY approach to changing your tone, stick within two shades of your natural color. The numbers on the box will determine your range. If you're determined to have a big change, I'd advise hitting the salon and letting a professional take charge.

Don't be fooled, coloring your hair can definitely damage it. The chemical process swells the hair, making it look fuller, but you very often lose shine, moisture, and softness. Color-processed hair needs extra hydration, so whip up one of the nourishing masks I recommend below. In addition, color can fade or alter in tone, so use a color-sealing gloss or glaze, a color-restoring or magnifying conditioner, and a color-specific shampoo to preserve it. Brunette treatments flatten the hair cuticle, smoothing the shaft to keep it shiny. Blonde-specific shampoos work differently. They remove buildup and clarify the hair, brightening up dull strands. There's no point spending a fortune at the salon on a bright, glossy new head of hair, only for it to fade away in a matter of weeks.

Want a natural alternative? Use chamomile tea to gently bleach your roots or brighten your blonde highlights. Steep three tea bags in a brew and let cool, rinse through your hair, and then shampoo. Or, add a tablespoon of honey to the blob of conditioner in your hand. It'll keep the blonde dye shimmering longer. If your blonde assumes green tones caused by swimming in too much chlorine, apply a dollop of ketchup in the shower to counteract the effect. Sounds gross, but it works!

For a brunette boost, use coffee. The pigment in coffee beans makes brown hair look richer by staining it for a few days. Mix five teaspoons of instant coffee in a mug of hot water, let it cool, and rinse through your hair. Repeat, and leave to dry for fifteen minutes. Then wash everything out with shampoo.

Red is the most difficult hair shade to maintain. Why? Red hair dye has the largest color molecule, which makes it difficult to enter the hair shaft. So while your hue may look vibrant right after your salon appointment (while the dye is still fresh on the cuticle), it can fade fast with every shampoo thereafter. To maintain the zingyness of your red hair, try brewing up a cup of beet and carrot juice and soaking your hair for twenty minutes.

If you're noticing some pesky grays coming through, buy a root concealer or a hair color pen, such as Oscar Blandi's Pronto Colore Root Touch-Up and Highlighting Pen. Alternatively, do your own touch-up by crumbling a matte eye shadow that matches your hair color, mix it with a sprinkle of baby powder, and apply it to your roots with a blusher brush. This is great for a day or two of coverage, a temporary fix. Whatever you do, don't pluck more than a couple of gray hairs at a time from your head. It not only thins your hair, but the action can cause infection and stress on the scalp.

How Much Product?

IT'S EASY TO SQUEEZE the whole tube into your hand, but overdoing it with product can ruin the texture of your hair, and screw up the whole look. Always begin by rubbing product, such as cream, serum, pomade, or wax between your hands. You'll notice all professional stylists do this. If it looks gloopy and starts dripping off your palms, you've used too much. I'm going to use money to illustrate how much of each product should be applied.

- **SERUM:** It only takes a dime-size amount. Avoid the root, as it can make hair look greasy.

- **WAX:** A nickel-size portion. Warm it up properly to melt any lumps. This works well on short, cropped hair (think Audrey Hepburn with her elfin cut); be sure to apply outward from root to tip.

- **CREAM:** Dollop the size of a quarter into your hand and it's enough to define even long hair.

- **GEL:** Perfect for a sleeked-back look (try a perfectly straight, center part, and remember to use a fine-toothed comb. Two quarters' worth of gel is enough.

- **MOUSSE:** My favorite product! I apply when my hair is damp, from root to tip, with my head upside down. It really lifts my hair and gives big volume with a matte texture. Pump a scrunched-up dollar-bill amount. For Texas-big hair, dry the hair after applying mousse, then reapply a slightly smaller dollop, brushing it through from the roots.

Going for the Chop

CUTTING OUR HAIR can be exciting, but also scary. We've all had at least one experience of walking out of the salon feeling unsure whether we like the new "do," and there's nothing that makes the women I make over get more upset and terrified than when I put them in the salon chair. But guess what? It *grows back*. So next time you hit the hair dresser's, ask questions about what might suit your face shape, check out magazines and blogs beforehand, and show your stylist pictures. He or she will be honest about what will and won't work with your hair texture, your jawline, and your color. Experiment, and remember a cut should play up your best features. Don't focus on your flaws; look in the mirror and pick your favorite parts. If you love your eyes, draw attention to them with bangs, or have highlights around your hairline. Love your cheekbones? Feather the hair with layers at that level, showing them off. Great jawline or elegant neck? Opt for a choppy bob.

If you're being bold and trying a whole new style, you can always get there in stages. My best friend had a gorgeous crop done, but she went from shoulder-length hair to a bob first, decided she could handle shorter locks, and took the plunge. Another option, if you're going shorter, is to fake it first. Use a foam doughnut, unclipped so it's one long tube, and roll the hair around and underneath, pinning it to the nape of your neck. Tousle the sides so the doughnut is hidden. This faux bob is a great way to see if you like a shorter look.

If you're growing your hair, it still needs to be trimmed. Split ends lead to unhealthy hair shafts and stunted growth, so a little chop every eight weeks can actually speed up the growth rate. I'd also recommend layering long hair. I've had mine long all my life, but I always ask my hairstylist, Adam Campbell at Rossano Ferretti in Beverly Hills, for some movement and texture in there. This adds volume and a more playful, manageable quality.

If your hair is full of split ends and you cannot get to the salon, curling the hair with rollers shrinks up the straggly length and adds volume, giving it more life and hiding breakage.

Never cut your own bangs. This is a recipe for disaster and tears, and resembling a six-year-old girl. Getting a fringe is worth visiting the salon for, as hair needs to be cut vertically, not horizontally, and the detail in the shape and length is paramount to nailing the right vibe. Most stylists will also trim them for free every few weeks; it takes less than five minutes.

Wash

DON'T WASH YOUR HAIR EVERY DAY; it strips the shaft of its natural oils. Every two to three days is fine. Find a shampoo that lathers less. Sudsy doesn't necessarily mean clean; it can even mean the opposite. Shampoos that bubble too much are often overloaded with moisturizing products and chemicals, such as sulphate, which can leave buildup in your hair, making it look and feel dirty and greasy quicker. Sulphates have also been accused of causing frizz and fading colored hair faster. When you're browsing the beauty aisle, look for a label that says "sulfate-free." You might pay a couple of extra dollars and the shampoo won't bubble and lather in the same way, but your hair will thank you for it.

Make sure the water is warm, but not hot. This can make your scalp sweat. And always finish off a wash with a quick rinse of cold water, to seal the hair shaft.

Condition

A DEEP PROTEIN TREATMENT OR CONDITIONER HELPS reinforce weak hair, but you really only need to apply it every six weeks. Using protein on the hair much more often than that can cause buildup that almost strangles the hair, leaving it dry and brittle. However, the weather, and your styling equipment, can affect how often you use a treatment. If you're using a hair dryer on the hot setting, straighteners, or a curling iron more than four times a week, chances are your hair is stressed out, and too dry. It's time to amp up your conditioning treatments and masks. Never slather conditioner on your entire head; you're likely to end up with a tacky film that leads to buildup. The middle of the shaft down to the ends of strands should be your focus.

When I filmed a show in Malaysia, the 100 percent humidity—plus having my hair styled every morning for eight weeks—really took its toll. I used TRESemmé Platinum Strength Renewing Deep Conditioning Treatment every four days, and coconut oil once every couple of weeks when I had the day off, so that the oil could really sink in before I needed to wash it out. That was a temporary, emergency routine, but it worked!

A fix for dry, damaged ends? After washing, mix leave-in conditioner with hair oil. Comb your ends with a deep conditioner, and then rub a drop or two of hair oil into the strands, such as Dove's Pure Care Dry Oil or Moroccanoil treatment. Both products will complement each other to moisturize and de-frizz the hair, leaving it full of luster and life.

And here's one from my mom, who lived in Rio for many years and took this tip from the Brazilian women: once a week, apply a cocoa butter treatment mask, let it sit for a half hour, then rinse it out with coconut water. The combination leaves hair soft and hydrated.

Shine It Up

HERE ARE MY THREE FAVORITE beauty recipes for super-silky, shiny hair, using what's in the pantry. . . .

1. Combine two egg whites with half a mashed-up avocado. Leave it in your hair for fifteen minutes, then wash and condition. It hydrates and flattens the shaft, leaving your hair super smooth.

2. Run a tablespoon of olive oil through your hair with your fingers, from scalp to tip, once a week. This helps to nourish, condition, and improve elasticity, while also eliminating frizz.

3. Rinse your hair about once a month in apple cider vinegar, the kind with the "mother" in the bottle, and see how glossy your locks turn.

On vacation, I like to soak my hair with coconut oil or almond oil and leave it in for up to twenty-four hours. Both oils are full of vitamin E and fatty acids, which soften and repair strands. Heat up a strawberry-size amount of the oils in the microwave or rub between your hands before combing it through. The effect is incredible, not to mention the delicious scent. Just remember to sleep with a towel on your pillow so you don't ruin the sheets, and that you'll need two to three shampoos to remove the oil completely.

Caring for Black Hair

BLACK HAIR HAS TINY NICKS in the cuticle layer, which means the hair can break easily, and which makes it harder for natural scalp sebum to distribute to the ends. A big myth about black hair is that it is coarse, when in fact coarse refers to the strand size, and not the texture. Black hair is rarely coarse; it tends to be finer than any other group, which is why it needs to be handled with extra care. Asian hair is usually the coarsest, strongest hair type.

Be gentle with wet hair. Your hair is most fragile when it's wet so take your time on wash day.

Go low on heat. Try not to use hot tools more often than twice a week.

Use temporary color, and use brands with conditioning rinses.

If you're going to relax or chemically straighten your hair, don't relax it poker straight. It will weaken your hair, making it easier to break. Eighty percent relaxed is about the maximum recommended. Leave at least eight weeks between relaxing appointments.

Deep condition with any of the ways I've suggested, from masks to conditioning treatments and oils. This helps to keep hair flexible. Look for conditioning products containing aloe vera. It is PH4, the same as your hair, and will close your cuticles to keep it smooth.

Sleep on a silk or satin pillowcase, or in a silk scarf. Curly hair dries out easily, and cotton pillowcases literally suck the moisture from your locks, undoing all the lovely oils and masks you've applied. Silk and satin have the added bonus of being great for your skin. Silk pillowcases cause a lot less friction and stress than cotton, and spread less bacteria. Plus, I think the idea of sleeping in a beautiful printed silk scarf, is about as glamorous as it gets! High-heeled fluffy slippers, too, anyone?

Drying Your Hair

DON'T MAKE THE TOWEL TURBAN. I know, I know . . . putting these on is a rite of passage for being a girly girl, but actually, keeping wet strands wrapped in a towel for a half hour as you do your makeup will cause frizz. The roughness of the cotton forces your hair cuticles open, making them more likely to go haywire. Instead, squeeze out excess water as soon as you're out of the shower and let your hair air-dry for five or ten minutes before blow-drying, or, wrap it in an old T-shirt made out of microfiber, which is smoother and ideal for drying hair.

Never let a hair dryer be too hot or too close, it will burn (and you will smell it, eww), and it'll dry out the hair to the point of dulling it. Keep the dryer moving, constantly. Finish drying with a blast of cold air—or do this beforehand in the shower, with a blast of cold water over your head before you get out—this seals cuticles and adds shine.

When using a round brush to dry your hair in sections, start from the roots and dry all the way to the ends, letting the brush linger at the tips of your strands. Let your hair cool off like this on its own for five seconds, then repeat on another section. Alternating between heat and cool-down time helps set your style, and your blowout will have more body.

For fine hair, point the nozzle skyward and underneath sections to amp up volume. A larger barrel brush will also create more height. To smooth out thick hair, direct the nozzle down on top of sections. To keep curls springy, use the diffuser attachment. Once the hair is 100 percent dry, then it's time to start styling it. Hot tools like curling or flat irons dry out wet hair and scorch the follicle. Hair should always be 100 percent dry before using a heat styling tool.

And if you're not rushing out of the house, the best thing you can do for your hair is to give it a rest. At least once a week, comb it through after your shower and let it air-dry.

Protect and Style

ALWAYS APPLY A HEAT PROTECTION SPRAY before you style. Not only will it protect your hair from your tools and the sun's rays, it will also add shine and gloss. The sun and hair tools can dry out or break your hair, and ruin your color. I can't emphasize enough the importance of spritzing this on, from root to tip. Sunflower oil is a natural sunscreen that protects hair from harmful UV rays. Apply twenty drops to your ends before heading to the beach.

Give your strands a break from curling and flat irons every now and again. Set the hair in old-school curlers to minimize heat damage. These give beautiful, bouncy curls and, while your hair's in those rollers, grab some cute selfies!

Apply products ten minutes before you style. Whether you're curling or straightening, applying product ten minutes in advance helps it fully absorb into your strands so you get all of its benefits and more bang for your buck.

Use dry shampoo whether your hair is clean or dirty. I live by this stuff—TRESemmé works best on me. Instead of waiting until your locks need a dirt-fighting savior, spray short bursts of dry shampoo to your roots (from at least ten inches away, so you avoid the white patches), immediately after you curl or straighten them. Give your scalp a quick massage to rub everything in. Though your hair's already clean, the barrier will stave off the debris and absorb any oil that usually greases strands throughout the day. Dry shampoo will also buy you an extra day after a blow dry. By using it on day two to spruce up the look, you'll maintain the shape and texture until day three.

Keep an afro comb or a teasing comb in your desk drawer. Either of these is a quick way to revive flat hair after a long day's work, giving you bounce as you head off for cocktails.

Smooth flyaways by spraying your hairbrush or an old toothbrush with hairspray, or by softly rubbing laundry dryer sheets from root to tip.

Accessorize

HAIR IS FOR PLAYING WITH, have fun! Experiment with braids, twists, clips, bright hair bands, head pieces (I love wearing my gold chain head piece!), clip-in bangs, and clip-in extensions. Be sure to match up the extension color to your own in natural light—which might mean taking it to the store window. Extensions come in different lengths; just beware of not buying the longest one if it's a lot longer than your own hair. This will look super fake. Finally, extensions can be synthetic or made from human hair. Synthetic extensions cannot be dyed, curled, or straightened. Human hair is sold predominantly in two forms: Remy and non-Remy. Remy is human hair where the cuticle remains intact; it can be styled and colored. Non-Remy is human hair that has been stripped of its cuticle. It can't be heated or colored, but it won't ever tangle, so it does have its advantages. Enjoy trying out new styles—you should switch up your hair as often as you switch up your clothes.

HOW TO APPLY MAKEUP LIKE A PRO

I distinctly remember the day I decided I needed a makeup kit. I was thirteen and just starting high school, and saw the older girls smudging kohl under their eyes. I was intrigued. With a mom and two older sisters in the house, I didn't even need to hit the mall. I emptied my cutest pencil case, decided to be a charming little sister for once, and went begging, bedroom to bedroom. They donated generously! The half-finished purple eye shadows, sparkly pink lip gloss, blue mascara (yeah, I know, but this *was* the early '90s), and almost-empty pot of bronzer, was quite possibly the most

electrifying treasure chest I'd ever seen. I spent the afternoon desecrating my face, not having a clue how to use anything, looking like a cross between Liza Minnelli and a clown. But I had discovered a new, lifelong friend, and I was deliriously happy.

There are many reasons why I way prefer being a girl, compared to say, being a boy. Numero uno? Makeup. Sure, guys can wear guy-liner and man-cealer if they fancy it (and living in West Hollywood, I know some damn-beautiful drag queens), but in my opinion, that's not quite the same. We girls can change the way we look. We get to enhance, illuminate, or conceal areas of our faces with all the pretty products makeup has to offer. We get to play dress-up with our faces! We get to have fun trying products with our moms, sisters, and friends. It's quite possibly the girliest of all girly rites of passage. Makeup can be used to create a character, to express your mood, to enhance the features you love, and to help conceal little blotches you don't. You can achieve every look from a subtle, natural glow to a full-blown red-lip and cat-eye femme fatale.

Makeup has been worn by women for thousands (yep, *thousands*) of years. Cosmetics were used throughout history because of practical concerns, such as protection from the sun, because of snooty class systems, for religious reasons, or more often than not, for plain old vanity!

You won't believe what different nationalities used, either. Way back in 4,000 B.C., Egyptian women applied a mixture of copper and lead ore onto their skin, for definition. The ancient Greeks used crushed mulberries for blush, and the Romans made foundation out of chalk and white lead (which often resulted in fatal poisoning—eek). Centuries later, redheaded Queen Elizabeth I set a trend for alabaster, pale faces (which also showed you were posh because you didn't have to work outside, and therefore get a tan), and her version of foundation consisted of egg white, flour, sulfur, and white lead. Not only was this extremely poisonous, but it would have smelled disgusting! Luckily, cosmetics have come a tremendously long way.

Avoid shopping for makeup at the end of the day, or straight after a vacation. Your skin will either be too tired and oily, or too tanned, and the colors won't be accurate for future outings. Go clean-faced earlier in the day, and arm yourself with a list of questions for the beauty counter assistant. Choose a reputable department store that you trust, as they will be able to offer a variety of brands, to suit your skin best.

Now here's my complete guide to buying and applying your makeup.

Foundation

BASES HAVE COME A LONG, long way since the thick, opaque liquids and chalky powders of your mom's day. I love the fact that makeup now creates luminous, glowing, flawless skin, without looking like you're wearing makeup at all. In fact, complete coverage and powdered, matte faces are outdated, and remind me of corny newsreaders. So when it comes to finding your base, think about mixing up products, for a bespoke color palette.

FINDING THE RIGHT COLOR

No matter your skin type, always choose a foundation or tinted moisturizer with SPF in it. Cleanse your face (or ask the store attendant to) before shopping; foundation needs to be tested on a bare cheek. Never test the color on your arm or hand. Those areas tend to be a very different tone and texture to your face. After application, try to find a window in the store, to see the product in natural light. If it's disappeared into your skin, it's a winner.

There's no need to buy lots of different foundations depending on the season. Instead, think about adding different products to create the perfect cocktail. That could be a drop of highlighter for extra glow in the winter, or a little shimmery bronzer on summer vacation.

Fair skin can easily become pasty and tired, so warm up the porcelain tone just a fraction, for a subtle glow, with a pink or peachy-colored base.

Medium skin already has a warmth to it, so match the color exactly, with a yellow-based product. If you have oily skin, look for oil-free makeup.

Dark skin needs more definition than just one color, or else it can look flat. Give dimension by picking a color that matches the jawline, and lightening it by mixing in a little highlighter for areas under the eyes, above the top lip, and along the cheekbone.

HOW I PREP MY SKIN

Every morning, after I wash and moisturize my face, I mix a little primer containing SPF with tinted moisturizer and a very thin liquid foundation. I love the sun-kissed, clean, glowy look it gives me.

It's important to hydrate your skin before applying makeup, but opt for a light serum, day cream, or gel-based moisturizer, to create a non-greasy first layer and to help makeup last. Make sure your moisturizer has sunken into your skin; give it a few minutes—go make the bed or brush your teeth!

Primer is the second step. A much-ignored yet essential stage of your makeup, primer prevents creasing and fading of makeup, and smoothes imperfections. It's amazing. I can't leave the house without mine. I use Jouer, Maybelline, or Boots No7, all inexpensive brands.

HOW I APPLY FOUNDATION

Mix your liquids onto the back of your hand, then dab color onto your forehead, cheeks, nose, and chin, blending with clean fingers or a cosmetic sponge. Always blend makeup out toward the hairline and just below the jawline.

Keep the application thin. You should still be able to see freckles under your foundation.

Check your face in natural daylight, making sure everything is blended.

Some makeup artists use a brush to apply liquid foundation, but I find it easier to blend with a sponge or my good old hands. A brush is better for applying concealer and powder.

Concealer

CONCEALERS HAVE A THICKER COMPOSITION than foundation, and are available in cream, stick, tube, pot, and liquid form. I think it is an absolutely key product for your makeup bag. On days when I feel like wearing very little on my face, I will forgo the foundation and eye makeup, but I will always dab a little highlighter under my eyes, to brighten up my complexion. A good concealer can make your complexion flawless. It can cover up pimples, hide blemishes, remove under-eye circles, and for me, get rid of those annoying tiny blue spider veins that pop up under my eyes when I'm exhausted.

TRY BEFORE YOU BUY

Don't rush up to the beauty counter, grab the first concealer you see that sounds (by the pretty name) like it will suit you, and rush out with it. Unlike blush, eyeliner, or even lipstick, concealer is a true try-before-you-buy product. Test the color on your neck or cheek. It should be a fraction lighter than your foundation. Take the time to get it spot-on (excuse the horrendous pun). Too light and you risk looking like a raccoon. Too dark and you've got blobs of dirt on your face. You may also need a lighter concealer shade for winter than you need for summer.

Now, this is a fact I only learned last year: I thought I knew a lot about cosmetics, but it turns out I was clueless about covering up my blemishes. Concealers can be pink-based, yellow-based, or orange-based. Fair complexions lend themselves well to pink-based, olive skin looks great with yellow-based, and dark skin looks better in orange-based concealers. I had been using a pink-based concealer for years, and wondered why my complexion looked a little *off*. As soon as I switched to a yellow-based one, suddenly my eyes were bright again, and my bronzer looked like it fit with the rest of my face!

EYE CIRCLES

For a moderately thick concealer to cover under-eye circles, I recommend Benefit's Erase Paste and Bobbi Brown's Corrector, which are peach-tinted, and counteract the blue-purple hue of eye circles (orange-peach is the opposite of blue on the color wheel, and thus the colors balance each other out).

HIGHLIGHTER

If I've been filming for weeks, and my skin is starting to show signs of exhaustion, Rachel will top my concealer off with a few drops of highlighter. These reflect light particles and brighten the skin. I love YSL's famous Touche Éclat, and Laura Mercier Secret Concealer, a creamy, light-reflecting brightener. Enriched with vitamins E and A, it softens the skin around the eyes and virtually "fills" fine lines. But beware! Don't use highlighter on a spot or scar. It will draw attention to the area like a lighthouse beacon! Highlighter is also great at freshening up under the eye. But use sparingly—a couple of drops is enough. Too much can give the effect of white rings under the eyes, and look weird in photos.

HIDING PIMPLES

A yellow-based concealer will neutralize the redness in a spot. CoverGirl's Invisible Cream Concealer and Make Up For Ever's Camouflage Cream are both great for hiding pimples, and they won't cake.

VEINS, SCARS, AND TATTOOS

If you are covering up blue veins or faint scars, look for a yellow-based concealer that matches your skin tone exactly, and test the consistency by dabbing it on the blue veins on the inside of your wrist. If it covers it up, you've found a winner. MAC's Studio Finish SPF 35 will stay put all day, and protect your skin.

To cover tattoos and bigger scars, layer a heavier-duty concealer, such as Dermablend Cover Creme or Kett Crème Fixx concealer.

APPLYING YOUR CONCEALER

Apply concealer after your foundation, otherwise it will just get wiped away from its specific area. Concealer looks most natural when you gradually build up delicate, thin layers. Apply several dots under the eyes, not too close to the lashes, without forgetting to dab along the inside corners of the eyes (this is an area some makeup artists I've worked with have missed, and it ruins the whole look). You can use your little finger to tap (never rub) the concealer, or try a small-headed brush with firm bristles. Blend it all in. Dab a dot or two onto other uneven tone areas of the face, such as the chin or nose. Apply highlighter over the top of your under-eye concealer. Dust a thin, fluffy layer of fine, loose powder over your face to set your concealer. HD or translucent powder is best.

HOW TO COVER UP A SPOT

Use a tiny, stiff brush to dab on a dot of concealer that matches your skin tone. Only apply to the zit, and be as detailed as possible. Let the concealer dry. If the concealer slides off the blemish and won't dry, the blemish may be very oily. Dab a loose or pressed powder onto the affected area, then reapply your concealer, which will now grip a hold of the zit.

If you find you overdid the concealer, moisten a cotton swab with makeup remover and gently apply to the pimple. Then re-cover the pimple with concealer.

ACNE SCARS AND POCKMARKS

Disguise a pockmark or scar by using a small, angled brush to apply concealer a shade lighter than your skin. Fill in the center of the pockmark, being careful not to go over the edges, and then finish off with a dusting of translucent powder. If the scar is raised, use a concealer that matches your skin tone and then set it with powder.

AVOID THE CAKE

Not that kind of cake! If you have dry skin, it may cause your concealer to go cakey on your skin. Case in point: after a long flight or too many cocktails the night before, my makeup sits completely differently on my face—meaning it doesn't sit well at all! I fix this by adding extra moisturizer to my face beforehand and blending my concealer with a drop of foundation in the palm of my hand. This helps break up the thickness of the concealer, which can sit heavily on the face.

Brushes

YOUR TOOL KIT IS JUST AS ESSENTIAL as the products you apply with them. Brush kits can look like a minefield, and there are always two or three that sit in my vanity table pot, never being used because I haven't got a clue what they're for. So, the basic brush kit every girl needs consists of:

2 EYE BRUSHES (e, h)

- A small, flat, soft brush for eyes. Great for blending eye shadow.

- A tiny pencil brush. This is very precise and stiff. It is used for smudging kohl liner and getting into the tiny nooks around the eye.

2 OR 3 CHEEK BRUSHES (a, b, f)

- A contour brush, which you only need if you're going to use a contour kit. This is a medium-size brush, with relatively stiff bristles, often tapered into a point at the middle, or angled to a point at the side.

- A large bronzer brush, super-soft. It spreads bronzer lightly over the face. A duo fiber version of this helps spread the color even more evenly.

- A round blusher brush, this one has shorter bristles and is great for circular motions on the apples of the cheeks.

2 BASE BRUSHES (C, G)

- A small concealer brush, which can have soft or hard bristles, depending on what you prefer (I have sensitive skin so I don't like the scratchier types).

- A large, soft brush with long bristles, perfect for dusting finishing powder evenly over the face.

1 BROW BRUSH (d)

- An angled brow brush is neat and short, allowing you to thicken your brows with absolute precision.

Clean your brushes at a minimum every couple of weeks. Professional makeup artists clean theirs every single day, because bacteria spreads like wildfire in beauty products, and breakouts on the face can often be attributed to dirty brushes. Dish soap or any old shampoo works fine. It takes two minutes and really is worth the time. Lay them out on a towel to dry overnight.

(a)   (b)   (c)   (d)   (e)   (f)   (g) (h)

Blush and Bronzer

WHEN I WAS SMALL, I would watch my mom apply her makeup, sitting up so elegantly at her glass-topped dressing table. She sat on an upholstered stool, sprayed perfume from an atomizer, combed her curly hair, and brushed rouge onto her cheeks with short, fast strokes. It was mesmerizing to behold; there was something magical about it. I couldn't wait for the day I got to be like her, and partake in the same ladylike rituals. Suffice to say, that day took a while. I wasn't allowed to wear any makeup before I was fourteen (and looking back, I'm now grateful she was so strict about keeping me a kid as long as possible), but there was one thing I was allowed when I was a little girl: *blusher* (that's what we primarily call "blush" in England). My mom called it "roses," and on special occasions like Christmas and birthdays, she would paint the teensiest amount onto the apples of my cheeks.

Bronzer is a key part of my makeup routine. In fact, second to my eyebrow pencil, it's my favorite item to use. Bronzers give a sun-kissed glow to the face, and if applied correctly, bring out your cheekbones and jawline, making you look like you just stepped off the beach after a long vacation. But we've all seen fake-tanning disasters, and picking the wrong shade of bronzer can make your whole face look flushed or orange. It's important to take your time picking the right bronzer, and applying it gently so you can build up to the final effect.

FINDING THE RIGHT BLUSH AND BRONZER

Blusher is not like foundation or tinted moisturizer, in that it doesn't have to match your skin tone. Blusher and bronzer is designed to enhance your complexion, and you can choose whether you want English rose pink cheeks, a radiant tan, or a youthful, peachy glow. Pick a color that works with your undertones, a quick trick to find your perfect shade is to pinch one cheek, then test a product on the other, to find your ideal match. Otherwise, a beauty counter assistant will be able to help you out.

Pick a bronzer just one or two shades darker than your natural skin tone. Avoid anything too dark that could look muddy, and avoid anything too orange. If you have fair skin, a rose or peach-based bronzer is for you. For olive skin, a copper-based bronzer looks gorgeous—this is the type of skin that can handle the most orange in a bronzer without looking unnatural. For dark skin, a bronzer with blue undertones and more of a shimmer will highlight and warm your cheeks.

To give you an idea of what I mean by undertones: when I'm tanned, I stick to peachy blushes to complement the darker pigment of my skin. Something too pink would make me look flushed and like I'd just run a marathon. In winter my skin is pale but still has a yellow undertone to it, so I go for darker, golden-hued, or coral shades. Have fun testing these out with a friend; it's what Saturday afternoon mall trips were made for!

BLUSHERS AND BRONZERS COME IN DIFFERENT TEXTURES

Powder blushes and bronzers are either pressed, loose, or sold as a pot of little tiny balls. The balls are my favorite! They are usually all slightly different tones, so they give a very natural glow when you apply. Many powdered blushers and bronzers now include skin-nourishing minerals and SPF protection (BareMinerals is a great compact to try).

Some bronzers already have different colors mixed into the palette, such as Guerlain Terracotta Light Sheer Bronzing Powder and Body Shop Shimmer Waves. Rub a little powder between your fingers and check if it's grainy or chalky.

It should be neither. The ideal powder bronzer is silky smooth, and won't leave your fingers dried out.

Liquid blushes (like Benetint) are like food coloring. They work by staining your skin, so you only need a drop. These are great if you never wear foundation, but want a little rosy flush to your cheeks. Plus, you can use these as a lip stain.

Gel blushes and bronzers are easier to use than cheek stains, because they don't dry as quickly and are easier to blend. Their color is less concentrated, so you can achieve a more subtle, transparent look; however, I do find with these, that they can disturb the layer of foundation underneath, and make it look mottled. So when you try one out, wear makeup underneath to test it.

Cream blushes and bronzers (such as Nars and Bobbi Brown) are simply divine. They're hydrating, easy to apply (blend with your fingers), and they often have a discreet shimmer to them.

HOW TO APPLY BLUSH AND BRONZER

Bronzer and blush won't work when applied to blotchy skin, so begin by evening out your skin tone, following my foundation and base tips.

First up, bronze. To get that glowy, sun-kissed look, apply bronzer lightly, using gentle, sweeping motions. Go easy—build up the color in thin layers, and tap the brush each time you dip it back into the pot to remove any excess color. Remember you can always add more bronzer, but it's very hard to tone down an orange face! Focus on the areas that the sun would naturally hit, such as your forehead, chin, jaw, and the tops of the cheekbone. The easiest way to get this down is to imagine drawing the number "3" pattern on either side of your face starting in the middle of your forehead and working toward your chin. Then draw a Nike "swoosh" shape from just under the apple of your cheek, up to right above your ear. Keep going into the hairline for a centimeter—this looks more natural.

I like to use a big brush, because it distributes the bronzer in a more even, natural way. The teeny-weeny brushes you get free with most compacts are almost useless. So even if you're traveling, make the space in your case to pack the big brush. And P.S. you do need separate brushes for powder, bronzer, and blush. All three have slightly different colors, and you don't want those to mix; it will ruin the contours you're trying to create.

Having applied bronzer, I like to add a little peachy or rosy blush onto the apples of my cheeks, on top of my bronzer. Just a little. It gives me extra radiance. A good peach blush is L'Oréal Paris True Match Super-Blendable Blush in Rosy.

Find the apples of your cheeks by smiling, and apply with little circular motions. Then, drop your smile and check in the mirror that all is blended to perfection, and that the blusher isn't overwhelming, or heading into clown territory. If it is, dusting off loose powder will tone it down.

For extra staying power, use two different textured products over each other. For example, a powder blush over a cream blush will lock in the look. And after applying the color to your cheeks, apply a dab of highlighter or shimmer to the edge of your cheekbones, to make them stand out.

If you happen to break a new blush or packed-powder by dropping it on the floor, crush it up into a fine dust in the compact, add a capful of rubbing alcohol, and leave open overnight. The alcohol evaporates, leaving the makeup whole again.

What Is Contouring and Why Do I Need It in My Life?

TWO WORDS: KIM KARDASHIAN. The princess of makeup put contouring on the map—literally a face map—by posting photos of her face covered in tan, taupe, and brown lines, shaded areas and highlighted ones, that made her face look like a toddler had scribbled all over it. But there was serious method to her madness. These marks actually create the illusion of angles, hollows, and arches. So what can contouring do? It can enhance the shapes of your face. A cheekbone is suddenly larger and higher, a brow is lifted, a nose is sculpted and slimmed, a top lip is made plumper, and a jawline more defined. Of course, drag queens and professional makeup artists have used contouring for decades, but I'm giving KK credit for convincing the rest of us all to have a go.

HOW TO CONTOUR

It takes a little artistry and a lot of precision to master the technique, but I couldn't recommend contouring more emphatically. Invest in a palette, such as Smashbox's Step by Step, where you'll find browns, taupes, beiges, and creams. Use the dark, matte shades on areas you want to recede and absorb light, such as along the sides of your nose, beneath the cheekbone (suck in your cheeks to find the hollows—this is a little lower than you'd apply a regular bronzer), and beneath the jawline. This creates depth and has a slimming effect. Use a small, round brush.

Top tip: when contouring, avoid dark bronzers that contain any shimmer or orange pigment. You're looking for a matte brown or taupe tone. Be sure to blend this in like crazy, using swift, circular motions. Otherwise you can risk looking like you got hit in the face with a mud pie.

Use your medium colors on the apples of the cheeks, on the cheekbones, and on either side of your forehead. This makes those parts stand out. A slightly larger, soft brush is perfect for this. With the lighter, shimmery colors, highlight along the top of cheekbones, onto the cupid's bow of your top lip, along your brow bone and if you wish, dust a little on the top of your chin. You can also pat this onto the bridge of your nose, starting between the eyes and brushing the color about halfway down your nose. This step brings your complexion to life, giving radiance and a lifted, three-dimensional effect to your face.

An optional extra? A dash of rosy blush on the apples of your cheeks.

Finally, it's time to set the contours. With a large powder brush, dust a very thin layer of finishing powder over your face. Sephora's Hourglass Ambient Lighting Powder is a good one.

A more subtle way of contouring is to avoid using any finishing powder whatsoever on cheeks (just mattify the T-zone, because it can get shiny fast), and instead of using a contouring palette, create the glowy highlighted effect by dabbing serum on top of your bronzer and blush, along the cheekbones, nose, and forehead. I see this on models at Fashion Week all the time, and I've begun to notice the same trick being used on the red carpet. It's a subtle, fresh look tried by dewy-skinned celebrities who wear little makeup, such as Zoe Saldana, Sienna Miller, and Jessica Chastain.

Lips

WHY LIPSTICK IS HISTORICALLY AND POLITICALLY SIGNIFICANT

Lipstick has always been a weapon in a woman's style arsenal. The right shade of lipstick can symbolize confidence, sex, glamour, youth. It can change the shape of your lips, and it can change the look of your face, and I'm not kidding when I say lipstick can be powerful.

When I said hello on the first page of this book, I mentioned that in Great Britain lipstick was never rationed during the Second World War. Winston Churchill himself declared that it was too significant for the country's morale. So while women used margarine wrappers for moisturizer and ink stamp pads for blush, the sales of lipstick actually soared. But it didn't start there.

Such was lipstick's power that centuries prior, in the year 1650, British parliament actually tried to ban lippy altogether, calling it "the vice of painting." The bill didn't pass, thank goodness!

Fast-forward to the middle of the twentieth century, and Queen Elizabeth II commissioned her own lipstick shade to match her robes at her 1952 coronation ceremony. She named the soft red-blue the "Balmoral Lipstick," after her Scottish countryside castle.

In that same decade, style icon and movie star Elizabeth Taylor, allegedly forbid any other women on her film sets to wear bright red lipstick.

The packaging of lipstick is more significant than you think, too. I remember watching an entire mesmerizing documentary on the millions of dollars spent by cosmetics companies on obtaining just the right *click* sound when you snap shut your lipstick lid. It makes us feel good to hear the right click, apparently. In fact, cosmetics companies rate a lipstick's subliminal effect so highly, that there are entire "flick and click" departments devoted to research on how many twists it should take to raise your lippy, what the packaging should look like, what shape and size your lipstick should be, and what noise it makes to click shut.

But out of everyone, Dolly Parton perhaps put it best, saying, "The only way I'd be caught without makeup is if my radio fell in the bathtub while I was taking a bath and electrocuted me and I was in between makeup at home. I hope my husband would slap a little lipstick on me before he took me to the morgue."

TEXTURE

Choosing the texture of your lipstick is just as important as the color. If the label reads, "matte," "opaque," or "highly pigmented," the color will be dense and without shine, which I love experimenting with. I rarely wear bright lips, but when I do, I go for a matte red with orange undertones (MAC's Morange and Nars Velvet Matte Lip Pencil in Dragon Girl are my favorites), and then keep my skin as dewy and shimmery as possible. The contrast of textures on my face really switches up my usual look.

If the label says "sheer" or "satin," then the color will be thin and gleaming, allowing your own lip tone to blend with it. Corals and peaches work for this texture, and are perfect for a bronzed, summery, laid-back look. Plus, they have the added bonus of making your teeth look whiter.

If you choose a pigmented gloss, expect a high shine, wet-look finish. These can sometimes be sticky and gloopy, so squeeze a drop from the tester onto your finger, and see how it feels first. A red, glossy lipstick signals full-on glamour, so channel your inner Marilyn, curl your hair, and wear heels. *Va va voom!*

If you read "frosted," "iridescent," or "pearl" on your lipstick, then go get a perm—you've accidentally stepped back into the '80s. Just kidding! These are back in fashion in a big way, but if you wore them the first time around, I'd give them a wide berth. For younger peeps, these will have a metallic, shimmery feel to them, and often come in sorbet pinks, peaches, and purples. They look awesome with an edgy, urban outfit.

COLOR

When it comes to lip color, every hue in the rainbow has a way of being styled and worn, with every fashion trend imaginable. That's good news if you're shopping, because whatever your tastes, there is bound to be one that suits you. Here are my favorites. . . .

ORANGE, OR TANGERINE-INFUSED REDS: As I mentioned above, these look better matte, and I prefer them worn with minimal eye makeup and dewy skin. It's an edgy, editorial look to skip the mascara. Try it and see how different your face looks! If that's too bold for your taste, try a sheer version with a peach or coral hue for a less-striking statement.

BERRIES: These rich pinks and almost-reds look wonderful with a dab of a darker hue added to the middle of the lip. To get the look, use a brighter shade on the entire lip and double up your application just in the middle. I like berry shades in the day worn with casual clothes: boyfriend jeans or skinny cargo pants create a chic contrast with your makeup. Shop for Revlon ColorBurst Lip Butter in Raspberry Pie, Sephora Collection Hot Hues Neon Lip Balm in Funky Fuchsia, or L'Oréal Paris Color Riche Balm in Heavenly Berry.

SORBETS AND PASTELS: These are young, fun, and edgy. Think Pepto-Bismal–inspired pink and dense, light purple. These are very opaque and pack a punch. These are best worn with messy hair, a mix of prints and ripped denim, and high tops. Think supermodel Cara Delevingne or Katy Perry. I like Wet n Wild Mega Last Lip Color in Dollhouse Pink, Elizabeth Arden Exceptional Lipstick in Pink Vibrations, and YSL Rouge Pur Couture Vernis à Lèvres in Violet Edition.

GRAPE, WINE, AND OXBLOOD: The femme fatale of the lipstick family, these dark hues are showstopping and vampy. A dark, burgundy lip is sexy, and with the right bold eye makeup, a dark purple can be stunning. This takes guts though, and looks best with a simple black, white, or gray ensemble. I have to be honest, the darker you go with your lipstick, the more aging it can be, so only go for this if you're sure it suits you. Try adding extra color to the center of your lip, for a geisha twist, also seen on the runways. Look for Clinique Different Lipstick in Plum Brandy, or CoverGirl Lip-Perfection Lipcolor in Euphoria.

NUDE: Okay, let's get one thing straight: nude shouldn't mean the actual color of your skin, because wiping that across your lips will make you look like a corpse. Nope—nude lipsticks should brighten and enhance the face, making it youthful in an elegant way. So keep it one or two shades warmer than your skin tone, and infused with hints of peach or caramel. Now add some shine, with a slick of gloss over the top. I recommend Smashbox Lip Lacquer in Creamy Soft Peach (this is already shiny, so you don't need to add gloss), or Maybelline Color Sensational Lipcolor in Warm Latte.

SHOPPING FOR LIPSTICK

Finding the perfect lipstick is equivalent to finding a killer pair of jeans. You may need to try on a few until you find the perfect fit. I also believe in owning a lipstick hat-trick: three contrasting shades to switch your face up according to your mood, your outfit, and where you're going. So snap up three different shades: a subtle, nude tone that's versatile to work with jeans and a tee or a sexy smoky eye; a trendy pink or berry shade to brighten up your look in the day; and a bright, timeless red for life's glamorous moments. You can also play with blending them yourself, for new, custom colors.

On the day you shop, wear a plain black or white top so you're not remotely distracted or distorted from the lipstick color. Wear some foundation or tinted moisturizer to even out your skin tone. If your skin is looking blotchy or has notice-able blemishes it will only be enhanced in the mirror, especially if the lipstick you choose is bright. You want to notice the lipstick, not a pimple on your nose! Apply some mascara beforehand, too; it will help balance the look of a strong lipstick.

Mark the back of your hand with stains you like, to see what they look like on skin. Then, try your final choices on your lips, but always clean the tip of the tester with a hygiene wipe first.

Carry a compact with mirror when shopping, so you can go outside into day-light and see how the shade looks.

Kiss your hand—does it all come off? If most of it stays put, you're onto a winner.

LIP LINER

Lip liners get a bad rap, because some chicks (Lil' Kim and Pamela Anderson, I'm talking to you), use way darker shades than their natural lip color, and it looks plain weird. But, last year I was sent a lip liner that matched my lip color to a tee. Used correctly, lip liner is genius. The pencil should have a soft and creamy texture, and keep it sharpened so it's never scratchy to apply. E.l.f. Studio and Lancôme make wonderful lip liners. This beauty product serves as a great foundation for your lip-stick to grab a hold of, so your lipstick lasts longer. But the best part of using lip liner is the plump, full shape it gives your lips. I pencil the underside of my bottom lip, and along the very top line of my top lip, to create a plump shape. Beware not to go any farther out than that, as it will end up looking clownish.

HOW TO APPLY LIPSTICK

Exfoliate your lips first. I only recently discovered the brilliance of a lip scrub. I'd read about them in magazines but never bothered to buy one, until my lips got

extremely dry and chapped while working on a TV show filmed in the boiling hot heat of Asia. My makeup artist gave me Satin Lips Lip Mask by Mary Kay, which I wipe on in the shower and rinse off two minutes later. It makes a huge difference, leaving me with soft, smooth lips. You can also exfoliate lips using a dry toothbrush, or with a gentle face exfoliator. Starting off with a clean slate allows the color to go on smoothly.

Apply a little lip balm. Your lips should be moistened but not glossy, otherwise the color can run. Line your lips with a pencil color akin to your lipstick (or your natural lip color), then fill it all in, all over the lips.

If you're going to be out a long time, and really want your lip color to stay put, apply a thin layer of foundation or primer onto the lip first. Add a little concealer and powder on the skin around the edges of your lip can help color from bleeding.

Makeup artists usually apply lipstick with a thin brush. However, that's often for hygiene purposes because they may have a bunch of different clients. If you're the only one using your lippy, apply it straight from the stick, or for a more casual stain, use your finger. For dark or bright colors, a lip brush is better, to obtain perfect edges.

Define a cupid's bow for a retro look, or paint straight across the top of the lip for a fuller, more modern vibe. Often people have an uneven cupid's bow, with one side pointy and the other side round. Choose whichever side you like better, and draw the same, symmetrical shape on both sides.

Next, blot or pucker your lips between a piece of blotting paper to remove any excess oil or moisture, before applying another layer of color. You can use tissue for this part, but blotting paper is far more efficient at absorbing oil.

And here's a trick Marilyn Monroe used to use: to stop any lipstick from coming off on your teeth, suck your finger (yes, really), and then dab a little Vaseline on your teeth, which creates a sheen.

If you get stuck without your makeup bag and only a lipstick in your pocket, the color can also be used on cheeks. Drew Barrymore likes to do this. Just be sure to blend it all in carefully, as the pigment is much thicker than regular blush.

RED LIPS

Red lipstick deserves a section unto itself. From Marilyn Monroe to Gwen Stefani, Dita Von Teese, and Taylor Swift, women who wear red lipstick have a boldness and elegance to them that will always call to mind Hollywood sirens of the silver screen. Rachel Wood, my makeup artist and very good friend, is a red lipstick aficionado. She has written her guide to finding the perfect shade of scarlet lips, especially for *Front Roe*.

RACHEL SAYS:

If you have **PALE**, **IVORY SKIN**, you can pull off a variety of reds. Blondes with pale skin suit retro crimsons from the 1950s. Channel your inner Grace Kelly.

REDHEADS look wonderful in vermillion, a terracotta-based, brick red.

For **MEDIUM SKIN TONES**, berry and blood reds fare well. Persimmon-toned reds can look great, too, but be cautious that brighter shades can give a kitsch, pop art look, rather than a classic finish.

If you're **OLIVE-SKINNED**, plum or cherry reds tend to work best. Avoid blue-based red tones, as these can look garish on olive skin. Opt for warm tones versus cold undertones when choosing your lipstick.

Maroon and claret-wine reds look amazing on **DARKER SKIN TONES**. A red gloss will make an awesome statement—think Grace Jones in her heyday. Brown-toned reds will create a more subtle finish. My personal favorite on black skin is a matte orangey-red. Lupita Nyong'o pulls this look off to perfection.

RACHEL'S FAVORITE RED LIPSTICKS:

- **CHERRY LUSH BY TOM FORD:** An opaque creamy texture that works on pretty much all skin tones and hair colors.

- **REVLON COLORSTAY ULTIMATE LIQUID LIPSTICK IN TOP TOMATO:** This is blood red in color and high in shine, very chic on blondes.

- **MAC RUBY WOO:** A matte lipstick in a fuchsia red, a great "notice me" color for pale skin, especially when worn with a bright, rosy blush.

- **RIMMEL LASTING FINISH LIPSTICK IN ALARM:** A warm, wintery red which looks beautiful on olive skin.

- **CHANEL ROUGE ALLURE INTENSE LONG-WEAR LIP COLOR, NO. 98 COROMANDEL:** A timeless red, stunning when worn with matching red nails and a crisp white shirt. It doesn't get more French than that!

Eyes

EYELINER

There are three different types of eyeliner: liquid, pencil, and gel or cream. It took me a while to find my favorite. My mom used a waxy kohl liner for years, and the softness gave a gorgeous smudged, laid-back effect. But as I got older and started hosting on TV, I began wanting a more precise definition on my eyes. On days that I do a photo shoot or a live red carpet, I wear a black or brown liquid liner, with a thick cat-eye flick. It reminds me of Sophia Loren, and I instantly feel more glamorous once it's applied. Liquid liner is like a fine ink pen. You need a steady hand and plenty of practice to apply it. I like Urban Decay and Lancôme liquid liners.

Pencil eyeliners give a smokier feel and can be blended with your fingers, a brush, or a cotton swab. It's easier to smudge and move if you don't like where you've put it. On my days off, I wear brown pencil along the tops of my eyes and smudge it with my fingers. I actually prefer not to sharpen mine constantly, as the softer and rounder the tip is, the smoother it goes onto the skin. Check out NYX Chubby Pencils and Bourjois Mini Pencils.

Gel or cream eyeliners are what professional makeup artists tend to use on long shoots because they just don't budge. On long days filming, I always wear a cream eyeliner, which is applied with a brush, from a pot. Make Up For Ever Waterproof Cream is fantastic for humid weather, or a long day's work with no breaks to fix your makeup!

HOW TO APPLY THE PERFECT CAT EYE

The trickiest part of getting it right is to get both "flicks" going in matching upward angles. Oftentimes, when trying to attempt a cat eye, one flick ends up pointing straight out horizontally, and the other flicks up. So for the wing, tilt your head back and aim the flick to run in line with the end of your brow. It should simply be an extension from your natural lash line. Start from where you want the flick to end, and work toward the eye. Never stretch the skin outward; you'll distort your line. Instead, paint with small, fine strokes that join together, and if you're going for a thick, 1960s vibe, draw an outline of your flick, and then fill in the triangle. Continue to paint the lash line all the way into the gaps of bare skin at your lash roots. Skin on show here is a bugbear of mine; it ruins the look. Once the overall silhouette is as you want it, go over for a second coat, and keep pulling your face away from the mirror mid-application, to check your progress.

Don't forget the final step: two coats of mascara. I like to use waterproof mascara on my lower lashes, otherwise it runs. But for my top lashes, I use volumizing mascara, such as Maybelline's Great Lash, which I have used since that day I begged, borrowed, and stole a makeup kit from the female members of my family at age thirteen. It's just a really good mascara. Be sure to take your time applying: let each coat dry properly before moving on, to avoid goopy spider's legs.

A QUICKIE ROUTE TO CREATING YOUR FIRST CAT EYE BY RACHEL WOOD

A CHEATER'S WAY TO APPLY PERFECT, SYMMETRICAL FLICKS is to take a piece of scotch tape, or a credit card, and place the card on the skin from the outside edge of the eye upward toward the outer tip of the eyebrow. Then paint on the flick as short, long, thick, or thin as you desire, and gently pull the tape or card away. Start thin; you can always make it thicker by adding more.

If you make a boo-boo, don't panic, just dip a cotton swab into makeup remover and fix. A perfect cat eye does take a bit of practice, and my biggest tip? Don't try your first one when you're heading out that night. Give yourself a quiet Sunday afternoon to mess it up and try again.

I love a dramatic eye paired with a bronzed, dewy cheek and a nude, shiny lip. But if you're heading out to a glamorous event, go for it full-pelt with a scarlet lip. It doesn't get more glamorous than that.

CHOOSING EYE SHADOW

Eye shadow comes in three looks: sheer, matte, and shimmer. And as you might imagine, their names describe exactly how they appear on your lids. I'm still learning more and more about eye shadow, and how mixing up colors and texture on the same eyelid can create shadows, hollows, brightness, and character. If you've ever seen a drag queen at work on his eyes, then you'll know it is truly artwork. Not that I'm trying to turn you all into drag queens, but you get what I'm saying: master the art of applying makeup, and you'll have a lot of fun playing dress-up.

HOW TO APPLY EYE SHADOW

To avoid those yucky creases and keep shadow in place, start with a primer or a drop of liquid foundation rubbed onto the lid. MAC Prep and Prime eye pots are awesome. I even like the color of it, and sometimes just wear that as my shadow! But if you want to add a pop of color, shimmer, or shadow to your eye socket, next apply your base eye shadow color with a small, round brush or the tip of your finger. Make sure it's blended, especially if you're using more than one shade. The tones should effortlessly intermix in a soft line.

Many brands sell multicolor compacts, including a tutorial on where to apply each color. Sephora, Bobbi Brown, and Boots No7 are my favorites.

To amp up the look for evening, carefully pat on shimmer powder around the inner corners and if you like, underneath the lower lashes. This counteracts shadows that may form around the bridge of your nose, or under your eyes, bringing a translucent glow and lifts your whole face, so that your eyes sparkle. Gold and silver shimmer powders are best. Choose between the two depending on the color of your shadow and liner. I'm usually wearing brown liners and shadows, so I stick to gold shimmer. Lancôme's Ombré Magnetique Ultra

Lavande Eye Shadow in Disco Silver looks incredible with a black smoky eye, and gets you ready to rock that dance floor on a Friday night!

Finally, dust a thin layer of translucent powder over the top of your eye shadow, to set colors in place.

GLITTER

I love wearing glitter on my eyes! It's glamorous, edgy, and different. But it's also a messy nightmare to apply—a nightmare that is well worth it, I might add—but get ready for sparkles all over your dressing table and floor. Here's how to handle glitter.

Make up your eyes before the rest of your face. You will 100 percent drop glitter onto your cheeks and nose, so don't bother doing your foundation until later. Cleanse the rest of your face as normal, but don't apply any moisturizer or primer, as glitter will stick to that, too. Under each eye, dab a generous amount of translucent loose powder. I'm talking a lot, like Casper the Friendly Ghost levels, to catch all the glitter. This is an easy clean-up technique.

Line your eyelids with a cream shadow, Vaseline, or even lip balm.

Dip a small brush into the glitter pot, tap it gently, and then slowly pat and press the glitter onto the eyelid, without any sudden movements.

I like to focus glitter on the center of the eyelid and leave the outside corners alone. I also like to dab some under my eye, to balance out the color.

Before mascara or any other makeup is applied, use a coarse makeup brush to remove any glitter pieces from the eyelashes and face.

I'm a big fan of copper and bronze tones on the eye, but I also go nuts for really bold hues, such as electric blue and red. If you're wearing glitter, my advice is to make a statement. Go big or go home. And, of course, don't stop fluttering those eyes all night; you are the sparkliest belle of the ball!

EYE TRICKS EVERY GIRL SHOULD KNOW

CURL YOUR LASHES

I usually remember about three times a week, but curling your lashes makes a huge difference to your eye makeup. Your eyes look bigger, your lashes longer, and by lifting the lashes up, more light is cast onto your eyeball, making them brighter. Warm your curler under the hair dryer or the hot tap for a few seconds (beware not to scorch it though!) as this curls the lash much more effectively. Give the lashes two squeezes: at the base and in the middle.

MAKE YOUR EYES LOOK AS HUGE AS BARBIE'S

Use a flesh-colored pencil to line the inside of the lower lash line. This trick was used in the '60s but with white liner (and a less natural effect), but it basically makes your eyes look enormous.

TRY A BRIGHT MASCARA

Don't spend a fortune on one, but experiment with a purple or navy blue mascara. The tone reflects light more than black or brown versions, which has the effect of brightening the whites of your eyes and giving them a twinkle. A TV host told me this a few years back in London, and I didn't believe her until I tried it. It really works for photos, the perfect New Year's Eve beauty trick! Try Rimmel Extra Super Lash Mascara in Electric Blue.

VAMP UP YOUR DAYTIME LOOK IN A FLASH

To go from the office to cocktails, smudge a soft, brown eyeliner right into the upper lash line. Keep your eye open as you look into the mirror and aim it right into your lashes. Then apply black (liquid if possible) liner along the inner lower rims, to make your eye pop. The effect is smoldering, but still subtle and warm, because it's not a huge, dramatic line. For some reason, even if your hair's a mess, and your skin exhausted, this trick peps your face up after a long day at work. The mix of black and brown is hot, trust me—I used to whip this look on when I worked at Vogue.com in London, right before hitting the town for a date!

LEARN HOW TO APPLY FALSE LASHES

Ladies, I cannot stress this one enough. A lot of women shy away from falsies, but whether you use a full strip or individual lashes, the effect is huge. And it's not so hard to do; practice makes perfect. Don't spend a fortune on lashes. I use a mid-length black strip lash from brands like Ardell and Eylure. Buy a little tube of white glue that dries transparent. Don't use the baby tube free with the box of lashes (this usually sucks), and don't ever go for black glue—it dries dark, and if you even remotely screw up, your eye will look like you've been sucker-punched.

Start by curling your lashes. Take one strip lash out of the box first, and gently bend it, to create a crescent shape. Place it along your eyelid, for size. Finely trim the edge of the strip to fit the length of your eye. Cut off one lash at a time and check the size by placing it on your eyelid, pre-glue. Professional makeup artists always do this; if the strip is too long, it will overhang and look fake.

Dab a few drops of glue in a line on the box (never directly onto the lash, this gets messy). Then glide the strip along the glue blob, so it's covered in white, but not covered so much that it could drip. Blow on it for ten seconds. Now, lean your head back as you look in the mirror, and gently place the false lash right along your real lash line. It should lay as low as possible, directly on top of your real lash line. Gently finagle it into place using your pinkie finger or the blunt end of your tweezers. Small, soft movements are best until the glue is dry. Then you can apply your mascara and eyeliner.

Don't forget, you can reuse your lashes once or even twice, by taking them off gently at the end of the day, cleaning them with a cotton swab and eye makeup remover, combing them through with an eyebrow brush, and then placing them back in the box, to keep their shape. This saves a fortune.

Eyebrows

BROOKE SHIELDS IS MY HERO! I love her thick, dark brows. I grew up swooning over photos of her and British supermodel Yasmin Le Bon, both dark brunettes known for their stunning, statement eyebrows. Everybody has their own idea about a favorite, defining feature, but for me and my face, my brows are my *most* important feature. They frame and lift our eyes and cheekbones; they draw someone's gaze toward your eyes; they give symmetry, definition, and power. Think about silver screen sirens like Elizabeth Taylor or Audrey Hepburn without their statement eyebrows; you simply wouldn't recognize them.

I find it fascinating how much importance cultures all over the globe have attached to eyebrows throughout history. Did you know that in ancient Egypt, heavy brows were painted on with kohl as an homage to the gods, and to ward off evil spirits? It may be a major beauty foul today, but the unibrow was once the epitome of power and status, across many cultures. A mosaic from the Byzantine Empire depicts the empress Theodora, with kohl-rimmed eyes and a heavy-set unibrow. She became such a style icon that women of that period actually sported false brows made of dyed goat's hair and attached with tree resin, to enhance their looks. I mean, if that is not the definition of suffering for beauty, then I don't know what is.

During the Qajar dynasty in Iran, thousands of years later, connected brows were still considered beautiful. Then just last century, Mexican painter and total icon Frida Kahlo exaggerated her own unibrow in self-portraits—have a search on Google of her images, they are stunning.

About a hundred years ago, commercially created cosmetics hit the market. In America, thin, arched, painted eyebrows were all the rage at the time. In 1919, T. L. Williams created his Lash-Brow-Ine, inspired by his sister Mabel's habit of applying Vaseline mixed with coal dust to emphasize her brows. The product was later christened Maybelline.

Your brows are yours to play with and shape. As Rachel reminds me, eyebrows are sisters, not twins! Nobody has an exact pair, but you can match them more closely by enhancing areas with makeup. Fabulous eyebrows are not always perfect or symmetrical, a little variation can be a cool quirk. But I have to admit, whenever Rachel says that to me, I tell her emphatically that I must have identical twins! Obsessed much? Me?

SHAPE

Brows should begin directly in line with the inner corners of the eyes. I like them square, but it can look chic if they feather toward the center, à la Cara Delevigne.

The arch should peak just past the outer edge of your iris.

The outer tip of the brow should never drop lower than the level of the beginning of the brow.

To balance wider set eyes, start brows a little closer together. For closer set eyes, slightly farther apart.

PLUCK

Don't pluck them into oblivion. Thin brows are aging, and if you over-pluck for too long, they may not grow back as thick as before, ever. As we get older, brows tend to thin and lose their color, but the good news is, you can bring them back to life. Here's how.

Pluck in front of a regular mirror, not a magnified one, for better proportion. Start by plucking strays well below the arch, and as you get closer to the line you're after, stand back every couple of plucks, and reassess from a distance. This is the safest way to keep both brows the same.

Pull skin taut to ease discomfort and tweeze hair in quick, swift motions in the direction of growth. If your skin gets irritated, wipe with aloe vera, and always disinfect your tweezers between uses. For bushy brows, comb them upward to trim the tips of longer hairs. Again, do this slowly, bit by bit.

THREAD OR WAX

These are great alternatives to plucking, just be sure to get a great spa recommendation, that is both sanitary and careful with your brows, beforehand.

I tend to have my brows threaded just once a year, to get the fundamental shape right, and upkeep them myself with tweezers and nail scissors, from then on.

TATTOO

Here's a little secret: every December, when I'm back in England for Christmas, I head to a beauty therapist in London for an hour of eyebrow tattooing. Don't worry! It's not as scary or dramatic as it sounds. Tracie, the owner of Tracie Giles salon, lightly inks a few tiny thread hairs along my brows, to fill them in and shape them. It makes a huge difference, and the color is matched exactly to your hairs. It lasts almost an entire year.

FILL

Double up on your brow pencil color. Mix two similar shades when penciling in your brows, it will look more natural. Define the shape with the darker color, and then fill in with the lighter one, using feathery strokes. A waxy pencil (I use one by MAC), has a great texture, and powder applied with a slanted brush are my favorites. If you use a regular brow pencil, make sure it's always sharpened. If you have fair hairs, use a waxy pencil first. This gives texture for the powder to grab onto. No matter the color of your complexion, avoid eyebrow pencils with a red tinge, or any color too dark. Both will come off unnatural. Never add bulk underneath the brow, you always want to be raising and extending upward and outward. Dab a little highlighter underneath the arches, such as Benefit's High Brow. It creates instant brightness and lifts the brow more.

SET

Run a clear eyebrow gel, or an eye shadow brush spritzed with hairspray, along your brows to keep them in place. I love the inner edges brushed straight up just like my hero Brooke Shields in the '80s.

MANIS, PEDIS, AND THE ART OF PAINTED NAILS

I'm never without painted nails, and they have to be neat and square-shaped. I'm not one of those grungy cool chicks who rocks her chipped nails, I prefer a freshly polished bright red, chocolate brown, or warm taupe. To keep that "just manicured" shine, I wipe my painted nails every couple of days with a cotton ball dipped in rubbing alcohol.

Store your nail varnish in the refrigerator. The cool, dark atmosphere will reduce solvent evaporation, and stop the mixture from getting cakey. It will also prolong the color much better than leaving your bottles in direct sunlight.

The Natural Look

IF YOU LIKE THE NATURAL LOOK, go for a soft pink or peachy-cream color. Or, skip the polish altogether but keep nails clean by pushing them into a lime wedge to remove hard-to-reach grime. Scrub nails with a toothbrush and then leave a little whitening toothpaste on top for ten minutes. This removes any yellow staining. And don't forget nails need regular trimming, just like hair.

Maintenance and Strength

GENTLY FILE YOUR NAILS once a week and seal the edges with a clear polish, which will strengthen and protect them. Buffing the tops of nails brings out a natural shine, and don't forget, you still need to hydrate cuticles by rubbing lip balm, Vaseline, or cuticle oil into the dry skin.

I take Imedeen supplements every day and have noticed my nails get stronger (and my hair get thicker). The capsules contain a protein derived from a deep sea fish, and antioxidants, such as vitamin C and lycopene, which help the body keep skin, hair, and nails strong and healthy. Other nail-boosting supplements to search for in the health store? Vitamin B7, or biotin, which protects against breakage. Fish oil, because it contains omega-3 fatty acids (these are the gods' nectar when it comes to keeping a woman looking and feeling youthful), and GLA (gamma-linolenic acid), which is a healthy fat found in evening primrose oil. Sound too complicated? Just make a note of these names and show the health store salesperson. That's what I do when in doubt!

Manicure Tips

- **GET SUPER-SOFT HANDS:** I like to exfoliate my hands with a scrub and then soak them in olive oil, baby oil, or almond oil every couple of weeks before putting on cotton gloves to sleep in. This keeps them unbelievably supple and soft. I notice a huge difference. The oil helps to prevent redness, chapping, and rough cuticles.

- **FRENCH MANICURE:** Use a thin slice of carefully placed tape to guide your painting for the French tip. Once you've smoothly painted on the white tip, remove the tape and paint over the top in soft, ballet-slipper pink.

- **MIX IT UP:** Going bright but can't find the exact shade you want? Mix up polishes to create your own bespoke range of colors. But instead of painting one shade over another on your nail, mix a few drops of each polish into a plastic cup, with one drop of remover to help them combine. Paint quickly, before the mixture begins to harden.

- **NAIL ART:** Don't be afraid to experiment. There are plenty of design ideas on nail art blogs. PolishandPearls.com gives step-by-step tutorials for beginners. I really like her ladylike ideas. FleuryRoseNails.com is the unbelievable, daring work of a professional manicurist who has worked at Fashion Week and with movie stars. It's great for elaborate, jaw-dropping styles. And MissLadyfinger.com is just a genius. She translates trends and prints from the runway onto fingernails.

- **NAIL STICKERS:** If you want to use nail stickers for your manicure, warm them between your hands for twenty seconds to heat them up. The stickers will be more flexible and easier to apply.

- **DOUBLE UP ON YOUR BASECOATS:** Apply a nourishing one first, such as Butter London's Horse Power Nail Fertilizer, followed by a ridge-filling one, such as Nail Tek Foundation III, to make your nail bed smooth.

- **GEL MANICURES:** I'm also obsessed with gel manicures when I'm filming. The color won't chip for three weeks, which is perfect when I'm on the road and cannot get to a salon. I've just discovered Sensationail, an easy-to-use at-home gel kit, which lasts three weeks, no chipping! Give it a try (and always invest in a system that uses a safe LED light to dry, not a harmful UV light).

READY, PEDI, GO!

HOW TO DO THE PERFECT AT-HOME PEDICURE:

1. Clip, trim, and file your nails before soaking them. This keeps the nail strong and gets the shape ready for some polish.

2. Soak your tootsies in warm water. Add a handful of Epsom salts, which will disinfect any grazes and also bring down any swelling. I use this trick on set at the studio all the time. I take a portable foot-spa and de-bloat my feet from high heels during my lunch break!

3. Exfoliate your feet and ankles with a scrub—I like the Body Shop Peppermint Smoothing Pumice Foot Scrub or OPI's Tropical Citrus Scrub. Rinse and dry. A mask is a great idea, too, to soften your soles. Try Lush Volcano Foot Mask.

4. Buff your heels with a foot file. Doing this straight after a shower or foot soak means the rough, dead skin will be at its softest, and come away easily.

5. Clean up and push back cuticles with a cuticle pusher and pen. Start with the Body Shop's Almond Nail & Cuticle Oil, which smells delicious. Wipe away dead skin and dust with a cotton ball soaked in polish remover. This makes it easier to get a smooth, professional finish with your color.

6. Paint the nails, using toe separators, a base coat, two layers of color, and a topcoat. You may get a little polish on your skin, but once nails are dry, dip a paintbrush or cotton swab into the remover and dab neatly around the edges, for that clean, professional look.

7. Maintain your just-been-painted varnish shine by wiping rubbing alcohol across the surface every few days (that's a great trick a nail technician taught me). And before bed, lather toes and heels with thick, nourishing cream, such as Jergens cocoa butter, slip on some cotton socks, and get a long night's beauty sleep.

8. Finally, keep your feet fresh through the summer with regular spritzes of Earth Therapeutics Tea Tree Oil Foot Spray, or with a wipe of Fab Feet Eucalyptus Foot Cleansing Wipes. Both will deodorize, refresh, and enhance circulation.

FINDING YOUR SIGNATURE SCENT

Y ou've probably heard it said that smell is the strongest form of memory. So it makes sense, if you think about it, that choosing the right perfume is as, if not more, important than the clothes you put on your back or the makeup on your face. "A woman who doesn't wear perfume has no future," said Coco Chanel. Well, I wouldn't go quite that far, but I would point out that it's often the first thing people notice when you walk into a room. It can evoke strong emotions, thoughts, memories—and in many ways define your persona. So think long and hard about smells you absolutely adore, and want to be associated with.

What Is Perfume?

ALL PERFUMES DERIVE from different families of scents. Each perfume always consists of three notes: a top note which evaporates and you smell first, a middle note that develops a bit later, and finally the base note, which is the true, raw scent. The interesting science bit, is that when you spray yourself with perfume, you produce a smell that is completely and utterly unique to you. Your body chemistry, temperature, pH balance, and natural odors interact with the fragile notes of your perfume, to create an individual scent that no other human on earth will have. It's a sort of like an orchestra playing on your skin, which creates a totally bespoke tune, just for you.

We Are Family

SO WHAT ARE THE MAIN FAMILIES of perfumes, and what feelings do their smells evoke? There are six main groups: Oriental, Fougère, Chypre, Floral, Citrus, and Ozonic.

ORIENTAL

As the name suggests, these fragrances' ingredients evoke a feeling of the Orient. There are three sub-groups within the Oriental family, namely smoky leathers, musk, and incense.

Leather scents are dry and striking, often based on raw materials, such as wood, moss, tobacco, and birch tar. The most testosterone-fueled of all scents, picture sitting in an old leather armchair by a crackling fire, perhaps a whiff of cigar smoke trickling by, in an ancient wood-paneled library in some stunning old English country manor . . . you get the idea.

Then there's musk, which is a little more outdoorsy and earthy than leather. Wet moss, dewy grass, sandalwood, amber—it's far more pungent than floral, but evokes a rich sense of nature, freedom, and the outdoors nevertheless.

The final member of the Oriental family is incense. Very potent—too potent for my liking, in fact. These are strong, earthy, and spice-filled smells. Cloves, nutmeg, tarragon, dried fruits—these odors are warm and tend to permeate a room.

Oriental smells are often associated with masculine perfumes. They are strong, sophisticated, free-spirited, mature, and confident.

FOUGÈRE

Herbs, greenery, and woody aromas make up this family. Fresh and perfect for summer, fougère (pronounced "foo-jair") actually means "fern" in French.

Fitting then, that the mix of basil, grass, lavender, mosses, and citrus fruits associated with fougère, evokes images of the beautiful rolling hills of the French countryside.

CHYPRE

Rich and sensual, chypre (pronounced "sheepr") scents are better suited for winter days. Think of cardamom, jasmine, violet, cedarwood, black hemlock, and picture a refreshing but cold, windy walk along cliff-tops, all wrapped up in a big woolly scarf and with bright red cheeks: that's chypre. The scents are definitive, classic, and elegant.

FLORAL

The most popular group of scents, floral can vary widely. They can be focused on one, single flower; a mix of complementing blooms, or a hybrid between petals and say a stronger component, such as musk. Florals can be pretty, soft, and feminine, but some also have a little more bite and attitude. My favorite floral scent, which makes for a wonderfully intoxicating candle, is tuberose.

CITRUS

The raw materials are extracted from the peels of fruit, such as orange, lemon, lime, and grapefruit. Sweet citric scents are ideal for spring. They remind me of exotic vacations. They're very awakening, clean, refreshing, and youthful.

OZONIC

Dream of the ocean, a salty breeze, sand between your toes. Ozonic fragrances are perhaps the rarest to find, but get the right one and you will constantly feel like you're floating in fresh air. For the free-spirited, nomadic, less girly girls— these scents are a far cry from sweet citruses and balmy florals, but addictive all the same.

How to Shop for Perfume

ASK THE SHOP ASSISTANT'S ADVICE. Yes, she's the chick we usually speedily loop around to avoid being sprayed in the face by some new sample, but actually, she's trained to know about different scents. Take the time to explain your favorite smells—it could be your homemade apple cinnamon cider, the way your garden smells when it rains, a certain candle—all these things will give her clues as to which perfume suits you best.

It's worth spending time finding your signature scent, don't rush it. Like a good man or a great pair of shoes, it could be with you for many years to come.

Avoid testing more than three perfumes in one day, or your nose will become confused and muddle them up. Buy a latte on your way, or bring a little bag of coffee beans on your pocket. When your nose starts to get overloaded and confused between scents, taking a good long sniff of the coffee will, in fact, neutralize your nostrils.

Spray a scent lightly onto a testing card and if you like it, ask the assistant to write the name of the perfume onto the card. A fragrance develops with time. It takes between ten minutes and several hours for the base note to develop, so hit the perfume counter first and then head off for the rest of your shopping. After an hour or so, head back and spray your favorite two directly onto your skin this time—one on each wrist. Now the ingredients can mingle with your natural pheromones and body odor, to create an absolutely unique scent that is yours, and yours only. Wait as long as you can (coming back the next day is ideal), and then make your purchase. Waiting before you pay also lets you avoid buying a perfume you're allergic to. If there's no reaction on your skin after an hour, you're in the clear.

Don't buy a perfume simply because you like the commercial, the bottle, the designer, or the celebrity endorsing it. Remember that perfume is an investment into your personality. You're the one who will have to walk around smelling it all day long. It should really appeal to you, it should be distinctive, and it should enhance your aura, not overpower it. Personally, I like to wear a scent by a lesser-known boutique British brand called Jo Malone. It's the smell of my favorite candle, Wild Fig and Cassis, and unusual enough that people ask what it is, but haven't smelled it a million times before.

Pure perfume or cologne can indeed be expensive. But used sparingly, they give best value for money when compared to watered-down, cheaper versions, such as eau de toilette, body sprays, and deodorants, because they have immense staying power.

Steer clear of buying perfume when your body is in a transitory phase, such as pregnancy or during *that* time of the month. All those crazy hormones rushing around everywhere will really affect your sensory perceptions, and certain smells that you like at the time might repulse you later, or vice versa.

If you've got the time to spare before making your decision, take a few testers home. Besides giving you longer to choose the right perfume, these are the perfect size to keep in your handbag for a quick pick-me-up throughout the day. When you finally buy your big bottle, make sure you also purchase an empty baby bottle and a funnel, for the same handy handbag purpose.

Personalized Scent

ONE OF THE MOST SPECIAL THINGS I've ever done was to create a bespoke perfume. Many companies offer this service. I did it on holiday in Hawaii so the memory association is an unbelievably happy, mellow one. After smelling around forty different flavors, the perfumer mixed together notes that firstly I liked, but, secondly, that complement each other. I now save this little bottle for special occasions and to always remind me of a wonderful beach vacation. Check out Ajne.com for your own.

Applying Scent

PERFUME WORKS BEST WHEN APPLIED to damp skin, so after a bath or shower, is ideal. Spritz it onto the inside of your wrists and elbows, behind your knees, and on your clavicle. These are your pulse points, where the fragrance will sustain longer and be emitted most effectively to all the cute boys walking by.

Don't rub your wrists together after spritzing, however, because you'll crush all the fragrance's delicate notes, reducing the effect of the top layer. Same thing will happen if you spray it behind your ears, as the sebaceous glands also alter scent.

I like to put a couple of sprays onto my sheets before bed at night, and into my hair, too, as the scent seems to linger longer and whenever you put your locks up or down during the day, you get a nice whiff!

One round of application will do, don't overkill (it's important for people to smell you when you walk into a room, but you don't want to make them choke!), and don't spray near your nose, or you'll inhale the chemicals and probably end up in a coughing fit. Resist the temptation to soak your best dress or shirt in perfume, too. You risk ruining the fabric, especially if it's silk.

If you fancy feeling like a silver screen goddess, buy an old-fashioned atomizer pump on eBay, and spray your perfume into the air before walking through it. Totally Grace Kelly.

Perfume Maintenance Tips

NEVER HOUSE YOUR PERFUME on your windowsill. The light and heat can break down the oils and alcohol in the bottle, causing the scent to change or even disappear. It's best to store perfume out of the heat (so not right next to the shower or bath, either), and unless it's in a very dark glass bottle, away from bright light. Store it in the refrigerator if you can, just like nail polish—and it should last up to three years from the date it was bottled.

Your local climate is important to keep in mind. Warm, humid conditions will intensify a fragrance, and cause it to evaporate more quickly. So choose lighter, floral, or citrus scents in the summer and apply them more often. Cold weather makes a scent last longer, and is better suited to stronger, spicy, and wood-based smells.

There is absolutely no reason why you can't switch up your scent according to the season—just like you would your wardrobe. Same goes for different occasions. A formal meeting might call for a subtle, sophisticated scent, while a cocktail party or a night out on the town might be well-suited to something more noticeable.

SCENT OF A WOMAN—TIPS TO USE FOR HIM

One of the best ways to make someone you fancy remember you is through scent. Before a date, find out his favorite type of scent if you can, and spray a little on.

Make sure your new perfume isn't a popular, obvious choice, because you run the risk of it matching his ex-girlfriend's, which would be a nightmare.

A genius tip is to pretend you're cold, borrow his sweater or jacket, wear it to the bathroom and spray on a little of your perfume. Just once is enough, or the smell will be too strong and the trick will become obvious to him! But the lingering scent will remind him of you.

And finally, you can now buy unisex perfumes, which mimic the smell of pheromones (the subtly scented chemicals released when we're sexually attracted to someone), and these perfumes are proven to increase your chances of appealing to that special someone you've got your eye on!

Part Four:
Lifestyle

I'M OBSESSED WITH DECORATING

To transform your house into a home is a rewarding and creative pastime. To do it on a budget by visiting flea markets and discount warehouses and see the looks on your friends' and family's faces when they see it for the first time is even more satisfying.

I'm so obsessed with decorating, I rearrange the books and trinkets on my coffee table just for fun, and get the biggest kick out of it. I love the visual awesomeness of a few tweaks here and there, a new splash of color. They're total bargains that have the power to transform a room. I posted the pics to Instagram, and while some people didn't understand why changing a few simple things on my coffee table could make me so happy, others totally appreciated it and shared their tips with me! It gives me such a thrill to bounce ideas off the readers of my blog—who are equally as inspired by interior design—and to see what they recommend making over in their own homes! Geeking out over interior design is something that makes me really happy. Orchestrating a stunning and chic sanctuary makes walking through the door every evening a joy. Home is where the heart is, so let me show you how to create an ambience that welcomes, protects, nourishes, and inspires.

SHOPPING FOR YOUR HOME

Wondering where to begin with a revamp of your place? First, do your research. Earlier in the book, I suggested you do this before shopping for clothes. Having a clear vision before picking the right housewares is even more important. You're going to look at them, and live with them, every day. Pull together images and inspiration from all around you. Create a Pinterest board to serve as a place to keep all of the inspiration for your space. Flip through magazines, home decor blogs, Instagram, and visit high-end furniture stores. I often head to the Pacific Design Center in L.A., which has stunning interior design showrooms, albeit at extortionate prices. Once I've got a mental picture of what I want, I begin the hunt to find matching items, at a much lower price. There's a real thrill knowing you've managed to find an identical or similar item to that on your wish list and saved hundreds of bucks at the same time.

Before you buy anything, first check reviews of the product or seller (if it's eBay or Amazon) online. I've learned the hard way that reviews are crucial. Be sure to check multiple sites for products, so you can compare prices, too.

Be patient for the right purchase. And me writing that is almost a joke, because I'm the least patient person in the world! Once I get it into my head that I want to make, buy, or achieve something, I have to do it *now, now, now*. However, patience is a virtue I'm constantly reminding myself to focus on (when it comes to both furniture and life!), and it's a valuable lesson. The worst feeling is buying something that, once you get it home and put it on display, you don't love. Then I get frustrated trying to make it work elsewhere in the house and end up taking it back to the store. Take your time finding that perfect statement piece that makes you smile every time you walk by it.

HOW TO MAKE YOUR BEDROOM
A SANCTUARY

Welcome to your tranquil sanctuary; your romantic boudoir; your private dressing room. Think about this: your bedroom is probably the one room in the world where you spend more time than anywhere else. It should represent a blissful, serene nirvana; a place where shutting the door means shutting out the noisy world outside, and taking some peaceful rest.

The importance of lighting, decor, and ambience in your bedroom is not to be underestimated. It has a huge bearing on your state of mind and ability to relax after a long day's work.

In the summer of 2014, I moved into a townhouse in a leafy part of Los Angeles. Finally, after years of dreaming about it, I splashed out on my favorite bed: an upholstered sleigh bed from Restoration Hardware. Putting my bedroom together became a passion project. I was inspired by the elegant, antique designs you see in Charleston, with a splash of retro Palm Beach design, and a whole lot of calm, California coast. Everything finally came together—the mix of rich texture, bright and muted colors, and beachy ornaments. If I didn't ever have to leave my room, I wouldn't! Just remember this when you decide to revamp your bedroom: exhaling as you walk through the door and catching some zzz's is one of your very most important actions of the day. So the place you choose to do it deserves attention.

Lighting

I'VE LIVED IN FOUR HOUSES since I moved to L.A.; three in London before I moved; three during college, and a gap year in Australia right after leaving home. That's a grand total of twelve bedrooms. And I can confidently say, through trial and error, that restful, comforting lighting is best achieved with low-wattage bedside lamps. They're way better than overhead lights. Search for lightbulbs below one hundred watts, and lampshades in soft neutral tones, or dark colors.

Window coverings are very much a matter of personal sleeping habits. Some people need pitch black to sleep, while others need the natural light seeping through in the morning to wake up. I'm in the latter camp. I like a squint of light in the room once dawn begins. It makes it a lot easier to get up and out of bed. But during the weekends, it's nice to be able to draw the shades so that you don't feel pressured to get out of bed. So I like thick curtains or plantation shutters, which close all the way shut, in the bedroom.

Plantation shutters are usually painted white or cream, and are a nice way to add texture without taking attention away from focal points. Thick, sumptuous drapes on the other hand, control the light, privacy, sound, and warmth of a room. Their color and texture can unify the atmosphere, providing an elegant framework to look at, but also to shut away the rest of the world with, as you catch up on rest. I love burlap or linen curtains, for a rustic feel, but be sure to line either of those fabrics, as they tend to let the light seep through. Hang curtain rods as close to the ceiling as possible to elongate windows and add height to walls. Pelmets, or a valance, as long as they're not frilly or fussy, are a pretty finishing touch to hide ugly hardware or rails.

Here's an idea: line curtains in a contrasting color or fabric, to give an attractive view from the outside of your house.

Technology

AVOID HAVING ANYTHING EMITTING an electrical signal in your bedroom, other than lights and music. Computers, TVs, mobile phones, and especially a modem, are proven to mess with your sleeping patterns. Turn your phone off at night (not just onto silent) and try to keep it away from the bed. I'm the worst at waking up and checking mine, especially if it's flashing. So not only do I turn mine off but I put it on the other side of the room, where I cannot reach it. Put clocks out of sight, too. It can be tempting (in a horrible kind of way) to check the clock when you wake throughout the night and calculate how much (or how little) sleep you've got left. But that can really rile up anxiety levels, and get your brain ticking, when it should be in "off" mode. The moment I removed the clock from my bedside table, I started sleeping a lot deeper.

LET'S TALK ABOUT THE TV

I look forward to watching TV in a hotel bed; it's become a treat because I don't have one in my bedroom at home. It has been proven that TV before bed disrupts sleep cycles and makes you go to bed later. In addition, what you hear and see last each day matters. The evening should provide a valuable opportunity to chat and laugh with friends, to read a great book, to meditate, to evaluate the day, or—as is one of my favorite pastimes—to enjoy a hot bath. And if all that didn't convince you, couples with a TV in their bedroom have half the amount of sex as those who don't. Crash! I can just hear the sound of TV's being chucked out of bedroom windows right now!

Declutter

THE EQUATION IS SIMPLE: the less fuss, junk, and mess in the bedroom, the better you will sleep. My mind always feels clearer when there's less to look at or worry about in a room. That goes for a cluttered bedside table, so buy one with drawers to hide away your ChapStick and magazines. If your clothes end up strewn all over the floor by the end of the day, buy a basket or trunk to throw them into until you have time to wash or hang them back up. Mount shelves to neatly stack away books or DVDs. Reduce the knickknacks and ornaments dotted around the room. I know you really love the snow globe collection you've had since you were nine, but less is more.

Decoration

MORE THAN ANY OTHER ROOM in the house, a bedroom's color, fabric, and ornament choices should soothe and shield us from the outside world. It's also a place to display personal, sentimental items. For example, on my wall I framed a large, vintage, silk Hermes scarf that my mom gave me (ahem, I know that she'll read this and say, don't you mean "stole"), and now every time I walk into the room it reminds me of her. I had the scarf pressed and framed professionally, as framing fabric can be tricky, but it was still cheaper and far more sentimentally valuable than any artwork I could have bought.

In the hallway that leads to my bedroom, I framed three pages from a beautiful Slim Aarons book. If you do the same, cut the pages carefully, with a Stanley knife and a metal ruler, and buy a sturdy white border for inside the frame, to disguise any less-than-perfect edges. Once they're mounted they look like an expensive print, and in my defense to anyone who says I'm ruining a nice book, I say isn't it far better to have the pages on display and admired, rather than hidden away in the depths of a coffee-table pile? The same can be done with wallpaper (many shops even give samples away for free), and even beautiful gift-wrapping paper. I love a good cheat to chic!

When I moved into my current home, I focused on incorporating accents and accessories that could be translated into feelings of relaxation. I'm a bad sleeper, very restless, so for me, these items serve more than just a pretty purpose. I have a few beach-related things, such as a starfish, which lives on top of some antique leather-bound Charles Dickens books. Dickens is my favorite author. My granny gave me the books, and the starfish makes me feel calm. Triple-whammy home decor right there! I always think themed items should come in threes or fours, so I also have a little coral on the same console table, two terracotta coral sketches hung above the bed, and apothecary jars filled with seashells in the *en suite* bathroom. A running theme between two connected rooms gives a sense of cohesion to your design, too.

Hues are an important aspect to take into consideration when going for a serene look. Perhaps strong colors are your thing, but try selecting a softer or lighter color within the same color chip. For a more relaxed vibe, terracotta trumps red; and sage green or seafoam are more mellow than say a grass green or an electric blue. The color blue has been proven to reduce stress and decrease blood pressure, which are both key factors for a good night's sleep.

When it comes to wood, however, I prefer dark tones compared to lighter or red tones. A warm rosewood or mahogany dresser gives a bedroom depth and comfort.

I'm big on crisp, white sheets. I think they look so much more inviting than bright sheets. If you want to add color to your bed, try a printed cushion or quilt, but again, keep the shades muted.

Your bedside tables do not have to match. As long as they complement each other either in shape, material, or shade, go for it. Keep them within a few inches of the same height, but mismatched tables (and even lamps), can look unique and cool.

What's Onk In My Nightstand

I KEEP A SMALL VASE OF FRESH FLOWERS, usually peonies, next to the book I'm reading (which, at the time of this writing, is *The Fishing Fleet* by Anne de Courcy, a riveting, nonfiction account of the women who headed out to the Raj looking for wealthy, handsome husbands). I also have a little china dish to keep my most frequently worn jewelry in.

Inside my drawer, I keep Badger organic Sleep Balm to rub on my wrists and temples each evening. The heady mix of lavender, bergamot, and rosemary helps clear the mind before sleep. I also keep a notepad and pen in the drawer. When my mind races with ideas, writing them down helps get them out of my head, so I can fall back asleep.

Flowers

WHENEVER I BUY OR AM GIVEN FLOWERS, my first thought is always to display them in the living room for others to enjoy. But there's something fundamentally girly and wonderful about waking up to fresh flowers in your bedroom. Enjoying them all to yourself in your private boudoir makes you feel special and glamorous. These are my favorite bedroom flowers:

FREESIAS: With a strong, heady scent, you'll smell them walking through the door before you see them. Freesias are rather nostalgic for me. They remind me of an English country garden.

HYDRANGEA: Tied with peonies for my all-time favorite flowers, these just make any room look beautiful. They're rustic but bright. I love the purple, green, and cream shades.

DELPHINIUMS: Tall and statuesque, the zingy purple variety look beautiful all bunched together.

PEONIES: Pink and feminine, you only need four or five of these whimsical, voluminous blooms to fill a vase.

HERBS: Used as foliage, try lining the perimeter of your vase with rosemary, thyme, or marjoram. They give the bouquet a quaint charm, and smell delicious.

Don't forget to trim an inch off the bottom of the stalks, in a diagonal direction. This helps the stems absorb more water. Replenish the water for your flowers every two to three days, and to make your flowers last longer throw ¼ cup of clear soda (such as Sprite or 7Up) into the water. The sugar will nourish them. A crunched-up aspirin and two ice cubes is also said to prolong their life, and putting a copper coin or a few drops of vodka into the vase will stop the spread of bacteria (although I can think of better uses for your vodka!). Last but not least, gently spray a small amount of hairspray over petals, to keep them looking fresh. It's worth doing this just to see the look of utter confusion on your housemate or hubby's face. Just tell him flowers need blow-dries, too, and walk away. Priceless.

Scent

I ALWAYS LIGHT A SCENTED CANDLE on my bedside table at the end of a long day. Picking your scent is important. Just like when you're running the bath, the fragrance you choose will set the ambience of the room. My favorites include Diptyque's Baies or Henri Bendel's Tuberose for moody, romantic nights. Just remember to blow out your relaxing candle before you start to snooze! Neom Organics make a fruity Sicilian Lemon and Fresh Basil flavor that wakes me up in the morning. My all-time favorite that I buy in bulk is Beach by CocoCozy. The scent is refreshing and balancing for the daytime; it's 100 percent Californian sunshine in a jar.

A drop or two of essential oil on a lightbulb releases the scent of the oil gradually into the room.

Crack the window, no matter how cold it is outside. The convection currents (yes, I actually remember this specific science lesson I received at age twelve, from Mrs. McCormack), will move your scented-candle-deliciousness around the room faster, when colder air is introduced to the room. Plus, fresh air is crucial when you're lying in the same room all night, preventing it from getting stuffy.

Sound

MAKE BEDROOM PLAYLISTS. I have one for the morning that gets me up, motivated, and out the door ready to take on the world, and a mellow version to relax with at night.

TO JUMP OUT OF BED:

Kiesza, "Hideaway"

Rudimental, "Home"

Sigma, "Nobody to Love"

Beyoncé, "Crazy in Love"

Pharrell Williams, "Hunter"

TO CHILL OUT AND GET SNOOZY:

Daft Punk, "Fragments of Time"

London Grammar, "Hey Now"

AlunaGeorge, "Just a Touch"

Aya, "Looking For the Sun"

Bon Iver, "Beach Baby"

Beds and Bedding

BUY THE BEST BEDDING you can afford. I used to scoop sheets up in a rush, barely opening the packet to feel them first. But since you spend so much of your time in bed, it shouldn't merely be an afterthought. As I said earlier, I love white sheets, but make them interesting by choosing embroidered or scalloped versions, from Osborne & Little, Cole & Son, the White Company, and Serena and Lily. Overstock.com, Gilt.com, and Wayfair.com have high-quality sheets and bedding at wholesale or discount prices.

Change bedding with the season. I used to keep the same comforter on my bed throughout the year, only changing up the duvet cover. Later I came to love the tradition of changing the sheets and switching to a lighter (both in color and texture) blanket once the weather warms up. Sprinkle two drops of lavender oil on your pillow before bed to aid restful sleep.

Many luxury hotels offer "pillow menus." The first time I saw one, I was on a press trip in the Maldives, at a top-notch hotel filled with honeymooners. I thought the pillow menu was a gimmick, a little over-the-top . . . until I tried it. The difference between laying your head onto foam, or feathers, or down, or buckwheat, or an orthopedic pillow, or memory foam, is a very personal choice, and one that I believe truly helps you sleep better. The type of pillow you choose can also help avoid achy necks and shoulders in the morning. I prefer an inexpensive foam pillow. It offers good support and stays fluffed up without me having to bash air into it every morning. Think about it: you spend a huge amount of time with your head resting on this thing, so don't make a snap decision. Take the time to test out different pillows in your local department store.

Always make the bed. This isn't just about having a bed that looks presentable, but it also gets your day started on the right foot. I once heard that if you begin your day by accomplishing something (even if it's as simple as making the bed), it sets the stage for productivity.

Keep a blanket at the foot of the bed. This is one of the quickest ways to make a bed look inviting and it's ideal for impromptu naps.

Every girl has her dream bed. My best friend since childhood lusted after a walnut wood sleigh bed for years, after she slept in one at a hotel in Paris. When she finally got one, I've never seen someone's face light up so much. There's an element of the fairy princess in dreaming of your ultimate bed. If your bedroom has relatively high ceilings, consider a canopy or four-poster bed. They have such a strong architectural shape, whether they're wooden, bamboo, or wrought iron. They make an elegant centerpiece for any bedroom. Personally, I prefer a four-poster with very simple, if any at all, drapery. Keep it clean, open, and with a modern twist. Victorian wrought-iron beds look very stylish, but my obsession with them ended after I bought two at auction for my old flat in London. One rusted and fell apart, and the other was extremely creaky and uncomfortable. No sitting up in bed with a good book there. If you love an old-fashioned style, research online where you can find a similar model, made today.

Your mattress is also worth spending as much time researching as possible. Just think how awesome you'd feel getting up every morning if you'd had the best night's sleep ever. Every day. That's the difference a decent mattress can make. Research suggests it's not necessarily the higher-priced mattresses that are the best. You can't buy a mattress online though. The only person who can tell if "extra firm" means it's really firm enough, is you. So head into the stores and get lying down. Don't just jump up after five seconds, either, stay on the bed a good five minutes, settle in, and concentrate on how your body feels. Memory foam and Tempur-Pedic beds are, in my opinion, heaven-sent. For those with sensitive skin and allergies, there are plenty of organic and hypoallergenic brands to choose from, too, such as LifeKind, Naturepedic, and OrganicPedic (Oprah's fave).

THE BATHROOM—
HOW TO ACHIEVE THE PERFECT
LOOK FOR YOUR LOO

Whether we're talking a tiny powder room for guests, a corridor bathroom you share with your housemates/the entire family, or a spacious *en suite*, the loo is a more important room than you think. It may be the smallest room in the house, but most girls spend a huge amount of time in here (myself included!) and often, it's the only peaceful, quiet alone time you get for the entire day. So make it a pleasing zone to enter, whether that means a loud printed wallpaper, or a tranquil spa.

Scent

I KEEP A ROOM SPRAY (I love Casuarina by my friend India Hicks's Island Living line), a stylish box of matches (taken from a cool restaurant!), and delicious scented candles dotted around the countertops.

When I run a bath, I add a couple of drops of my bath oil to the inside of the cardboard toilet roll: with each turn, fragrance is released.

Keep a window open as much as possible. This helps the room smell fresh and prevents mold, caused by damp.

In winter, place lemon slices in an open bowl, or fresh mint in hot water, to give a fresh, clean smell and to combat dryness and static caused by central heating, which leads to dehydrated hair and skin.

Decorate

A SMALL SPACE IS A GREAT EXCUSE to try a bold look, such as vivid, patterned wallpaper from floor to ceiling (and sometimes even covering the ceiling, too). I've seen some awe-inspiring powder rooms with black-and-gold prints, bright red Oriental artwork, retro green palm tree leaves (inspired by the iconic wallpaper at the Beverly Hills Hotel), and more traditional French toile. Another friend of mine installed antique mirrors around the room, to make it feel larger, and another played with marble, having the same slabs on his wall as on his countertops. If there's a flare for interior design in you, the bathroom is an easy place to flex those decorating muscles! With a smaller space, there's less money to spend on things like wallpaper or granite surfaces, so you can invest.

That being said, I personally prefer my bathroom to be a clean palette, a calm oasis for me to put my makeup on in the morning, or unwind with a hot bath before bed.

Two types of lighting (or the use of dimmers) is ideal—bright lights for doing your makeup in the morning, and dimly lit sconces on either side of the mirror, for the evening. Sconces make for more stylish, intimate lighting than overhead bulbs. Buy colored sconce lampshades to match tones in the paint or wallpaper.

I like the lights low in my loo (if you can't install dimmers, switch your bulbs to a lower wattage). A peach bulb is a nice addition, but be sure there's either enough natural light or additional switches to focus on your face when applying makeup. I will never forget one of my editors at *Vogue* storming out of a very trendy Manhattan hotel because the bathroom was so dark she couldn't apply a scrap of makeup. She ended up blending her concealer in Starbucks!

So, back to my bathroom: the surfaces are a light gray marble. Gorgeous. When I bought the house the walls of the bathroom were white but they needed warming up, so I painted the walls a gray-taupe, and the bathroom suddenly looked ten times more expensive.

Personalize the surfaces with items that mean something to you. I have a large floral, china bowl, given to me by my granny, that sits proudly by the bath. It is Victorian and was used for bathing many moons ago before running hot water existed. I wanted to incorporate a beachy feel, too, so I shopped online for glass confectionery jars and found three in different sizes. Instead of using them in the kitchen as they're intended, I filled them with shells. Apothecary jars also look stylish filled with natural sponge pieces, cotton balls, and bath salts. I also cleaned the leftover wax out of candle jars from Diptyque, once they'd finished burning, and used them to house my cotton swabs and makeup brushes. I also head to kitchen sections of stores to find ceramic dishes, butler trays, and bowls, for use in the bathroom. For example, I recently snapped up a long, skinny cocktail tray, on which I lined up my favorite beauty products. Of course, they're color coordinated, too! The point is, don't be afraid to think outside the box and use household items for a completely different purpose. The unexpected twist can look very glamorous and, of course, unique.

Place hooks on the inside of your bathroom cabinet, to store any jewelry you don't want on display. Be sure to only store costume jewelry this way; fine jewelry should be kept out of the bathroom and away from damp conditions. The same goes for hooks on the back of the door—the more space you can buy yourself by hanging up towels, the better. I hang a gorgeous silk kimono from the one hook in my bathroom that is most visible. Seeing such a beautiful garment as soon as I walk in the door is visual stimulation that always uplifts and inspires me stylewise.

Revamp the look of your bathroom vanity by repainting it and switching out the drawer knobs. Try a high gloss finish for a clean, brand-new feel.

Place a little stool by the bath. This can be more of an aesthetic addition, and looks elegant with fluffy towels piled up, or with a rattan basket full of your prettiest products.

Speaking of rattan baskets, I cannot get enough of them. I've got them coming out of my ears at home! They're cheap and their warm, neutral texture means they go with almost everything. I have one by the loo filled with toilet paper, one on top of my wooden stool filled with perfume bottles, and many more scattered around the house to hold books, rolled-up blankets, and loose photographs.

I also like to decorate with stunning soaps. Discount stores, such as Marshalls, World Market, and HomeGoods, have shelves stacked with brightly packaged soaps. They're so chic, nobody would ever have a clue they cost just a couple of dollars when you display them in a dish by the bath. Make sure the dish also complements the feel of the room. Is it wooden and rustic? Modern and marble? Or hand-painted clay for a Mediterranean feel? Every detail counts.

Fresh flowers in the bathroom are a real luxury. A little vase of a few stems picked fresh from the garden makes a beautiful difference.

Personalize your hand towels with monogrammed embroidery, available at most major department stores. Initially a European tradition, this design idea also took off in the south and East Coast of the U.S. a couple of hundred years ago. The lady of the manor would emboss, engrave, and embroider her personal items, such as handkerchiefs, linens, and jewelry. (I've got *Gone with the Wind* in my head right now, anyone else?) When she went on posh hunting trips, weekends away, or elaborate holidays, this ensured her items would not get mixed up with other guests'. Once she got married, a lady added her married initial to the monogrammed items in her trousseau. This is an elegant touch, but keep your monogrammed hand towel subtle. Stick to two or three overlapping letters in the same shade as the towel, or at least a tone very close to it. Thin, curly calligraphy is a beautiful, traditional font.

Remember bathrooms see a lot of hand washing, so hand towels often suffer wear-and-tear fast. Invest in two or three identical high-quality, quick-drying hand towels.

Decorate a sleek shelf or two with neatly folded towels—a great visual is to choose two patterns and one solid, all in the same color palette. If your whole bathroom is painted white or cream, bright towels can provide an eye-catching pop of color. But if there are focal points elsewhere, play it safe and stick to cream, white, or taupe towels.

Place a handful of pebbles or large crystals between the soap bar and its dish, to prevent soap from going squishy in its own suds.

Keep a good book, pen, and notebook in the bathroom—it's a place where genius ideas are often born!

The Ultimate in Bath Time

THE ROMANS HAD BEAUTY TREATMENTS DOWN. To cleanse and relax, they would soak for hours every day in huge aromatherapy baths, scented with exotic oils brought back from far-flung countries in the Roman Empire.

For me, there's nothing, absolutely nothing, as calming and luxurious as a hot, scented bubble bath. A long, luxurious bath helps you de-stress, let go of the day's problems with one giant, steam-filled exhale, and sleep well afterward. In fact, I never sleep like a baby unless I've had a steaming bath beforehand.

There's no rushing this ritual: whether you're a stressed-out student, a busy mom, or a career girl, this is the one moment of the day that is truly yours, so see it as a rightful indulgence. Firstly, put aside at least twenty minutes (more if possible), dim the lights, and shut the door. Leave your phone outside, on silent. Remove all your jewelry, as body washes and soaps can cause a buildup on silver and gold, often dulling it. Light a candle or two, either unscented or choose a fragrance that will complement, not compete with, your chosen bath oil. Play some soft music, preferably without lyrics, as this is proven to be the least distracting, most relaxing type of music.

Place your fluffiest towel or robe on a warming towel rack or tuck a hot water bottle inside it, ready to cocoon you for drying off.

I like to throw a face mask on at this point, the steam from the bath opens pores, so a mask can really get to work.

Put the aromatherapy oils into the water last, once the bath is fully drawn. Otherwise some of the scent can evaporate too soon.

Get in and concentrate on slow, deep breaths. Enjoy a moment of meditation. Focus on calm scenes that make you happy (for me that is always a beach right before sunset, hearing the waves roll in), and let any worries or anxious thoughts from the day just pass on through. Don't stop to ponder them, just wave them by and let them go.

Have fun picking your oils and salts. For a refreshing wake up in the morning or before going out, eucalyptus, frankincense, lemongrass, or peppermint are great scents to track down (use them separately, not together).

To relax, lavender, geranium, chamomile, or neroli are perfect. Aromatherapy Associates makes a cute little box of travel oils, and the "Deep Relax" is so strong that a masseuse once told me she can only use it on clients once a day because otherwise it puts her in a trance!

If you're going on a date and bathing beforehand, jasmine, rose, sandalwood, or ylang ylang all smell delicious, and have the added bonus of being an aphrodisiac. Watch how your scent makes your loved one swoon.

MIXING YOUR BATH COCKTAIL

Essential oils can be potent. Their scent and properties create a strong smell and mood in the room. Choose carefully, and remember a little goes a long way. Use five to ten drops of the essential oil (a tiny capful) in one tablespoon of carrier oil per bath, unless indicated otherwise on the label. Carrier oils are an important mixer, think of them as the tonic to your gin! They prevent the essential oil from being too powerful, and if you choose carrier oils, such as olive oil, jojoba oil, or sweet almond oil, they have the added benefit of nourishing and moisturizing your body.

Read all of the labels and warnings on your essential oil: some are not suitable for use when pregnant, breastfeeding, or for children. Also, some oils may irritate sensitive skin, so do a little patch test the night before, to be safe.

MILK BATH, CLEOPATRA STYLE

For a non-oily or non-slip bath, make like Cleopatra and add full-fat milk or dairy cream as the base, instead of carrier oil.

LUXURIOUS ROSE PETAL BATH

If you're really pushing the boat out and making an evening if it, consider a Moroccan rose oil bath. The former is a favorite at top spas around the world. Create your own with Ren's Moroccan Otto Bath Oil. Rose petals are harvested at dawn in Africa for this product, which turns the water milky white with its strong, sweet scent. Why not go the whole hog and scatter some real rose petals into the water, too. Go on, spoil yourself!

SOOTHING BATH

And one of my absolute favorite bath bargains: put porridge oats in the end of a stocking leg (cut off at the ankle) or muslin bag, tie the top around the bath tap, and let the warm water—which will turn milky—run through it. This is particularly soothing for sunburned or irritated skin, and makes my skin very supple.

SALTS

These work in a similar way to oils but have the added bonus of reducing retained water in your system. Swirling a cup of scented salt or the king of all bloat-beating salt—Epsom salts—into your bath every couple of weeks can really fit you back into those tight jeans. A personal trainer once told me a hot Epsom salts bath can help you shed up to three pounds of water weight. Perfect if you're getting ready for a night on the town in that cute dress!

Bath salts make for pretty bathroom decoration, not to mention inexpensive gifts. So play around with your own mixtures and scents. Why not throw cedar shavings, scented soap shavings, and dried flowers into the mix? You can even tint the mixture with food coloring. Wrapped in a little muslin sack or Mason jar, tied in a bow with twine or cotton ribbon and a homemade label, these look simply gorgeous.

SLEEPY-TIME BATH

I have trouble sleeping. I'm restless, a worrier, and very often jetlagged. A model friend is constantly on planes and trying to adjust to new time zones and she shared with me her miracle cure. The recipe includes liquid melatonin, a natural hormone that can be absorbed through the skin and regulate sleep cycles in the body. If you'd rather skip the melatonin part, then by all means omit it and this mixture will still lull you into a tranquil slumber.

Mix 1 cup of Epsom salts and ¼ cup of baking soda for the base. Add in one or two drops of liquid melatonin, eight drops of lavender essential oil, and a few more drops of chamomile essential oil. Mix everything together in a bowl before adding to your warm bath water.

LOVE YOUR LIVING ROOM

Drawing room, family room, lounge, parlor, sitting room—whatever you like to call it—the living room is the centerpiece of your home. More than any other room, it's on display. For me, the living room is a place where guests mingle at cocktail parties, where the family gathers to watch movies or play games, where the fire is lit in winter, and the sun streams in through open windows in summer. It's where I relax with a glass of wine after a long day. Striking the perfect balance between elegant and lived-in, between curated yet informal, is key. I want people to appreciate the decor and design in the room, but feel at-home and welcome enough to plop right down on the couch and settle in.

Color Scheme

AN EASY WAY TO SELECT A COLOR SCHEME is to elaborate on one that's already been started in the room by accents, such as bright books, a rug, a cushion, or a piece of artwork.

These are fantastic springboards, and even better if you can kick things off by finding more than one item in the house that fits into the color family. For example, when I last moved, I wanted to add splashes of terracotta and red to my bedroom. The walls, bed, sheets, and lamps are neutral, so it was a blank canvas begging for some warm color. I walked around my old home, stopping to pick up anything that matched the color. A decorative plate from the kitchen, an antique jug from the study, three books that had been scattered on different bookshelves. Suddenly the makeover was coming together, and I hadn't even been shopping yet. I placed them all on the bed, took a photo, and then hit the department stores. I found terracotta cushions at Kohl's (on sale—it was a sign!). In the kitchen section of Macy's I found a terracotta egg holder (yup, I said egg holder), which I knew would make a great jewelry dish. And finally, I stumbled upon a gigantic red lacquered pot in Home Depot, that I knew would be perfect for the pepper plant I was planning to buy. It was a balance between envisioning what I needed, and buying things on impulse.

Or, you can introduce an entirely new color scheme to the house. Be punchy and bold. Try something you wouldn't normally do. A geometric print, a pop of fuchsia, abstract art. There's no reason why your house has to be vanilla and safe. Get those creative juices flowing!

With splashes of color, there are some points to remember. Tonality is key. If the shades are similar but not clashing, you'll create a richness that isn't matchy-matchy. Don't go overboard with your colors; you don't want a candy store. Four bright focal points in the same palette is plenty.

Be aware of how much natural sunlight the room gets. If it isn't very much, steer clear of a darker palette.

Remember to keep your neutrals as the dominant color in the room. Round out your color palette by adding neutrals, such as white, cream, taupe, or gray. These colors give your eyes a place to rest and let the bold colors be the star of the show. The more neutrals you add, the softer your color scheme will become. I repainted my whole house the color Sand Dune, by Dunn-Edwards, and to complement that I painted my bathrooms and bedrooms a few shades darker and warmer, with a hint of gray to it, named Rustic Taupe. I'd highly recommend the brand of paint as great value for money. For an even more luxurious finish, Farrow & Ball are an excellent paint company, and they even mix custom colors to fit your palette exactly.

If you want, add a second bright color into the mix, but check that the two are compatible first. Combine cool and warm colors for balance. In my bedroom, I kept things calm and simple, so it's just warm taupe and terracotta. But in my study, I have a triple color scheme: cream, sage green, and burnt orange. Sounds odd? I promise you it works, you'll have to come over and see it!

A basic formula for a harmonious color palette is 60 percent your dominant color (neutrals), 30 percent your secondary color (your bright focal points), and 10 percent your accent color (if you want to add one).

There's no reason you can't mix different prints, too. Installing two contrasting motifs doesn't have to mean chaos; it can give the room an extra dimension and certainly lifts it in the style stakes. The safest way to do this is to keep one print in neutrals. So a black-and-white geometric pattern, perhaps, against a chevron or tiled floor, contrasted with something more whimsical and bright, such as a floral wallpaper or ikat print chair.

If you stick to just one print, use it two or three times within the room, for consistency. Flavor Paper make some unbelievably creative printed wallpapers. I adore C. Wonder and Allegra Hicks's patterned home decor accessories, and for beautiful tiles, check out Malibu Ceramic Works.

Textures

CONSIDER TEXTURE, TOO. Enjoy the juxtaposition of a shiny, glossy vase next to old leather-bound books, next to a soft throw. Wood or rattan furniture often provides warmth. Variety of texture adds a luxurious feel.

Texture on the wall is fun to play with, too. Elevate a simple monotone with a high-gloss paint. A polished finish is both bold and grandiose. Shine works best in primary or jewel-tone colors (there's nothing more decadent than a ruby-red room), but be aware that gloss highlights imperfections on walls, so have them smoothed out prior. Also, balance the glare out with soft furnishings and plush textures, such as suede pillows and thick rugs. Any additional light-reflecting surfaces, such as marble, leather, or mirror, could become too much. It looks cool in a bar or a hotel, but not in a home.

I absolutely love textured wallpaper for the chic, timeless feel it provides. I've noticed this in upscale spas and boutique hotels, and I'm desperate to try it out at home. Grasscloth wallpaper is the bomb. But anything too gimmicky, or that tries to look like something it's not (brick, tile, wood, or stone wall effect) looks cheap. The simpler, the better. Rapture and Wright make gorgeous wallpapers that feel warm and luxuriously textured, and I like Phillip Jeffries for a huge selection of grasscloth wall coverings.

Remember soft furnishings, such as rugs, curtains, and pillows, lessen the noise in a room. If you just have hardwood floors and wooden blinds, the room will have an echo and feel less intimate.

Antiques

DEFINITELY CONSIDER BUYING secondhand furniture and objects for your living room. It's the perfect place to show them off. I also adore the fact they're a one-off and have a story to them. Don't be afraid to mix eras and designs. I love the look of homes with a mélange of modern and old. Old pieces can be reupholstered or painted into something even more exquisite, and—although many will disagree with me here—don't get hooked on the pedigree of furniture. Who cares if it's by an original designer and worth squillions? If the silhouette and craftsmanship is pleasing to you, then snap it up. Skip the expensive antique shops or trendy "vintage" furniture stores in big cities; these will always be a rip-off.

I once wandered into a quirky interiors shop in Venice Beach. I picked up a rusty, old, charming biscuit tin. It turns out I have a similar one given to me by my dad, which he'd kept pennies in since he was a kid. The tin on sale was $150. $150! Are they kidding? The customer that ends up paying that is, as we'd say in England, a mug. Don't be fooled into thinking something is ever cool enough to overspend on. That same week, I hit Long Beach flea market, an hour outside of L.A. Big surprise: I found a plethora of similar tins, selling for four dollars each. A little extra effort put into your search goes a long way.

I would definitely recommend getting up early and hitting the flea markets, even if it means a long drive. Most of these markets offer an early-bird special entry fee, where you pay a little more to get in before the crowds. Ironically, at that time of day you'll likely see all the owners of said expensive antique shops snapping up bargains, that they'll later sell for ten times the price. Beat 'em at their own game!

Online antique shopping is vast, too. Narrow your search by entering a specific item, era, and texture, such as "mahogany Sheraton sideboard," and you'll cut hours from your search.

Other sources for fantastic antiques include estate sales, thrift stores, overstock warehouses, and furniture auctions. Make it a fun day out. Just be sure to check out the goods thoroughly when you wander around, ask questions about the history and heritage of a piece, and stay focused on what you're after; it's easy to get distracted. Having said all that, the beauty of an antique is the sentimental wonder of it. So as much as I advise being practical, you've got to let your heart do the choosing sometimes, too.

Limit yourself to one or two antique finds per room, and place it somewhere prominent. You don't want the space to feel dated. Plus, the grace and elegance of one killer antique piece, can carry the attention of an entire room.

Storage

THE ONLY NEGATIVE ABOUT MY CURRENT HOUSE is the lack of storage space. It's a cute city townhouse and I'm in love with it, but the one thing I miss is having enough closets. If you're in the same boat, there are many options I've discovered for smart, stylish storage. Wicker baskets serve as great decoration accents all around your home and double up as clutter disguises. They can be used in your foyer, under the coffee table, on the stairs (try the two-tier variety, they're shaped to fit a step), or even in your child's room to conceal toys. Vintage leather suitcases or trunks are a stylish way to hide junk, and tufted ottomans with opening lids also work for extra seating. In my kitchen, I use a gorgeous old picnic basket from Fortnum & Mason (the oldest department store in London and where the queen gets her groceries) to house my coffee, tea, and sugar. Trays and boxes also help neaten up a space. Make them a feature, by opting for bright prints or interesting textures, such as faux snakeskin or Perspex.

Personalize

DISPLAYING PHOTOS OF FAMILIES AND FRIENDS is a lovely way to personalize your space. Instead of standing frames on surfaces, I love to create a gallery on a wall (stairwells and corridors are particularly good areas for this). Yes, you can place piccies in identical frames and hang them in a neat grid, but I'm a fan of giving the wall as much character as your mates and loved ones deserve. Buy a bunch of different frames (keep one element consistent—unite them tonally, or by material), and hang them at different heights and distances apart. For this visual effect to work, begin by hanging the larger frames, and keep everything else clustered pretty close around them.

Perhaps because I'm a bookworm, bookshelves are one of my favorite things in a living room. I love perusing other people's book collections to see the literary journeys they've been on. Books piled high tell a story about their owner; they give a sense of history, culture, depth, and even travel, to a room. Flicking through an interior magazine once, I noticed the brilliant, easy idea of color coordinating books on a bookshelf. Arrange your books according to the color of their spine, and you've created your very own art installation. Another idea? Paint your bookshelves (particularly if they're built into the wall), a bright color. This is an example of where high-shine paint can look fantastic and give the space vibrancy.

I think it's important to integrate any hobbies and achievements into your home, too. More often than not, trophies, prizes, collector's items, and memories get relegated to closets or the attic. But there are modern, stylish ways to put your personal history and passions on display. A study, a corner, or a corridor off the living room can be perfect to house a themed collection. If you're into magic tricks, horse racing, vintage magazine covers, or you just want to remember your wedding by seeing visual reminders of it every day, then consider showcasing items as a group for a captivating impact. Frame old photos, pictures, and posters in mismatched frames. Place other items on long shelves hung either extra low, or extra high on the wall. I'm talking fifteen inches below the ceiling. This creates a border-like feel of decoration. The eye notices these items but they aren't the mainstay of the room. Small glass domes, bell jars, and display boxes are a cool option, too. I recently found some with metal edges and hinges from Pottery Barn.

Space

THERE'S A REASON HOMES without any furniture take longer to sell than those already decked out. We struggle to imagine an empty room laid-out, cozy, and decorated in all its glory. The same applies to rooms in your own home when you want to rearrange the vibe. Some rooms lack personality, or they have difficult slanted ceilings, or columns, beams, and windows in awkward places. Some are just plain odd shapes. Instead of spending thousands on an interior designer, download an app and draw up your own floor plan. These things are game changers. I recommend the helpful apps Home Design 3D and MagicPlan.

Make the focal point a piece of artwork, the fireplace, or a gorgeous tallboy. But please, whatever you do, don't make your TV the focal point of your living room! It's an eyesore; it ruins any sense of charm, style, and peace you've worked so hard to obtain. If you can, mount the TV higher up on a side wall, with an arm attached to the back that means it can be pulled out and angled perfectly to snuggle up and watch a movie, and then neatly stowed away again, in a less obvious place. I just did this with my TV and although you can still see it, it's not the first thing your eye lands on when you walk into the room. In fact, a friend once gave me the ultimate compliment by not noticing it until he was leaving! Other options for hiding the TV include placing it inside a dresser with doors that open up, or incorporating sliding panels of wood or artwork that cover a flat screen. There are slightly more expensive options, such as remote-controlled TVs that disappear into the foot of your bed, or that track along the ceiling into your closet.

If you live in a studio apartment, consider dividing up the space with a temporary wall, a tall, wide bookcase, or a printed silk screen. In open plan living rooms, I like to visually split up the sitting area from the dining or kitchen area, by placing one sofa with its back to the next "room." A console table often works beautifully backed up against the couch. This breaks up and enlarges the space, allowing you to introduce a new color scheme or style to the next section of the home. If sofas line the walls, always pull them forward ten inches or so, away from the wall. It's a common mistake to think it'll make the room larger having sofas packed right up against the wall, but it has the converse effect.

Consider painting or wallpapering one statement wall, to give the room depth and a focal point. Sticking wallpaper up all over a small room can actually help expand it, by extending the corners of the room and giving it the illusion of more space.

Lastly, every living room needs an oversize mirror, to double the size of it, and reflect light.

BEFORE YOU REDECORATE . . .

QUALITY OVER QUANTITY

Don't get carried away by what the neighbors are doing, or what the home-makeover TV show is doing. Showy, over-the-top changes will stand out, but not in a good way. The understated, simple use of high-quality materials and subtle design tweaks will have timeless appeal.

KEEP A SENSE OF PLACE

By that I mean, let the design of the building guide you. If you live in an Art Deco apartment or a Victorian townhouse, then renovating with modern materials could look incongruous. I'm all for the juxtaposition of contrasts and opposites when it comes to smaller details, such as furniture and ornaments, but for building work, stay in keeping with the charm of the building that attracted you to it in the first place.

DON'T FAKE IT

You can't replicate beautiful surfaces like marble and mahogany with cheap imitations, so opt for something completely different instead, or head to the reclamation yard. Invest the most money in surfaces you see and touch every day, like kitchen and bathroom counters.

BRING THE OUTDOORS IN

Especially if you're a city dweller, don't underestimate the aesthetic and emotional significance of having real plants and flowers inside your home. Many behavioral studies show that looking after plants and seeing them grow and bloom increases feelings of wellbeing, intimacy, happiness, and calm in the human psyche. A bamboo palm, rubber tree, or fiddle-leaf fig are three of the easiest houseplants to *not* kill. Plus, they look pretty.

CLEANING WITHOUT HARSH CHEMICALS

et's get one thing straight: cleaning is about as boring as it gets. Unless you're one of those crazies who finds it cathartic and therapeutic . . . and if so, you're welcome any time at my house! But if, like me, you're house-proud, then the cleaning has to be done, because you like your house gleaming and sparkling at all times. I'll cut to the chase: just like beauty products, cleaning products have a bunch of hidden, toxic nasties lurking inside them that can cause anything from skin irritations and burns to respiratory problems. Some have even been linked to more serious diseases, such as cancer. Over the years, I've discovered some natural alternatives that are not only cheaper; they're often more effective. Many of these your grandparents will have used, and I kind of love that we've come full circle, back to the old-fashioned home remedies.

In the Bathroom

REMOVE HARD WATER STAINS on the bath, sink, or toilet bowl by filling the area with warm water, dropping two Alka Seltzer tablets in, and letting them fizz away. Thirty minutes later, brush clean. For really stubborn stains, do the same again but swap the Alka Seltzer for a few cups of vinegar. Leave for a few hours, or even overnight, then flush. To prevent dirt from settling as quickly in the future, squeeze a little baby oil along the surface with a brush; it stops dirt from clinging to the surface.

To make tiles shiny and grime-free, combine two cups of baking soda with a little water, mixing it until you make a paste. Spread it onto your tiles, leave for twenty minutes, and then rinse away. Not only does this magic potion clear away residue, it also disinfects the area.

To remove limescale from a yucky tap or showerhead, soak the head in a bowl of vinegar, preferably warmed in the microwave beforehand. Then scrub with an old toothbrush.

In the Living Room

TAKE THE STRESS OUT of having pretty soft furnishings by Scotchgarding the fabric. This makes them stain-resistant, so you can have a beautiful and kid-friendly living room.

To get stubborn dust off of lampshades and curtains, swipe a lint roller across the fabric. This also works for grabbing crumbs off the table!

In the Kitchen

TO CLEAN THE GREASE OFF GRANITE but keep its shine, mix ¼ cup of rubbing alcohol with four drops of liquid dish soap. Pour this mixture into a spray bottle and fill the rest of the bottle with water, to dilute.

Clean copper and brass items with hot sauce. The various acids in the Tabasco sauce vigorously eat away at copper tarnish. Just rub it on with a soft cloth and then rinse away that dull tarnish.

To soften food splatters in the microwave, fill a cup of water and microwave on high for two minutes. This makes it a million times easier to wipe clean.

If your casserole or soup or whatever's on the stove bubbles over, sprinkle a generous amount of club soda on the spill immediately, and leave it to cool before wiping away.

To shine your stainless steel refrigerator, soak a cloth in club soda (make sure it has sodium bicarbonate in the ingredients list) and wipe vigorously.

In the Bedroom

TO BRIGHTEN UP YOUR WHITE LINENS, add half a cup of lemon juice or a cup of white vinegar to the wash cycle.

Get your duvet dry-cleaned every six months. Most of us don't bother to do this, and until a friend of mine suggested the idea to me, neither did I. But it's the best way to have good-as-new sheets, plus dry-cleaning kills off dust mites and allergens.

Whether to wash or ditch your pillows when they've been around a while, is a hotly contested subject. Most of us do neither, but—and I hate to gross you out—pillows pick up so much dust, dead skin, and mold, they can actually double their weight in three years. That's pretty disgusting. I recommend getting new pillows every couple of years, but if you've spent a fortune on them, they can be thrown in the laundry with your other linens, and tumble dried on hot for extra time.

Clean your curtains once a year. If they touch patio doors, the floor, or a window sill, chances are they've picked up dust mites or mildew from dampness through the years. Check if they're machine-washable and if not, take them to the dry cleaners.

Anywhere

MIX A FEW DROPS OF TEA TREE OIL with four cups of water, and fill a spritzing bottle. This is a really great eco-friendly, gentle disinfectant, germicide, and fungicide to keep around the house, for anytime a surface needs a quick clean. It even works on leather chairs.

To get rid of sticky labels and price tags, soak a cloth in hot water, pour a little vinegar on top, and saturate the glue. Leave it as long as possible, then rub everything off. Always dust with a microfiber cloth. These prevent the spread of germs, pick up dust without leaving streaks, and dry really fast. They speed up your cleaning big time!

If you can't be bothered to mix up your own cleaning products from scratch, I recommend the ranges by Method, the Honest Company, and SunBrite. They're nontoxic and biodegradable.

COOKING UP A STORM IN THE KITCHEN

They say that a kitchen sells a house. Well, it's certainly the first place I make a beeline for when I go back to my parent's home in England. The family congregates around the dark granite bar, sitting on stools or wandering around, rustling in cupboards, catching up on stories at a million miles per hour. The kettle whistles as it boils, ready to make a round of tea. I hear the sound of cookie packets opening, plates clattering, me and my sister's voices gossiping over each other. I can smell dinner in the oven, and see little ones running around playing games, jumping over our feet, and asking for extra cookies. The kitchen is the focal point of family life; a hive of activity, and a place to congregate every morning and evening. Design-wise, the kitchen is a very personal choice, but when it comes to atmosphere, a kitchen should be light and airy, warm and informal.

Me, the Faux Chef

SO HERE'S THE THING: I love to eat and I know a fair amount about nutrition, but I can't cook to save my life. Two years after I moved to L.A., my dad asked me if my oven was gas or electric. I couldn't even tell him. Like Carrie Bradshaw, my oven was used for storage! So with that awful admission in mind, I recently took an afternoon's cookery class at the kitchen store Sur La Table, which I highly recommend. We learned simple but hearty dishes like chicken casserole, spicy pork stew, and shrimp jambalaya—the kind of cooking where you throw everything in a pot and hope for the best. At least I'm learning! I'm still bad . . . but there are a few failsafe favorites I tend to make again and again, some taught to me by (extremely) patient friends, others I've experimented with until they taste good. So here are my essential, healthy cheat's recipes to make you appear like an amazing chef.

This is far from how a typical cookbook would begin, but this isn't a cookbook, so let's kick off with the fun stuff—cocktails!

Festive Mulled Wine

I grew up associating the sweet, spicy smell of mulled wine with Christmas. It's a very traditional drink to serve in England over the winter holidays, and makes the house smell so warm and welcoming. Note with this recipe, the red wine need not be expensive, as the heat and other flavors tend to overpower anything too fine.

SERVES 5

1 bottle of red wine (750 ml)

6 whole cloves

2 cinnamon sticks

Sprinkle of nutmeg

1 orange, zested (for recipe) and sliced
   (for garnish)

Throw everything in a pot and heat on low for twenty minutes. Serve in wine glasses and garnish with a slice of orange.

Pear Prosecco Cocktail

I much prefer prosecco to champagne. I think less bubbles and a sweeter taste is more delicious. So it was with great delight at my friend Kirsty's beach barbecue one summer that I discovered this cocktail made with prosecco. I just had to ask the recipe, and here it is.

MAKES 6

¼ cup brown sugar

¼ cup water

20 whole cardamom pods, crushed

¼ cup pear brandy

1 bottle of prosecco (750 ml)

Thin slices of pear, to garnish

On low heat, mix the sugar and water in a saucepan, until the sugar dissolves. Add the crushed cardamom, bring to simmer over medium heat for 5 minutes. Leave to cool.

Strain the mixture into a pitcher, then stir in the brandy.

To serve, add ½ ounce of the syrup mixture to 6 glasses (I like to use the old-fashioned coupe champagne glasses), then top them off with prosecco and add a slice of pear to garnish.

Louise's Mezcal Kicker

I'm a tequila drinker. I like to sip a good silver tequila on the rocks with ice and plenty of freshly squeezed lime. Tequila is the most crowd-splitting of drinks (who hasn't gotten hammered on tequila and sworn off of it?), but mezcal has made its way onto fancy cocktail lists. It is truly an upper for your mood and energy. So tequila's long-lost, naughty cousin, mezcal, also from the agave plant, is at the top of my list for a delicious drink. The taste is smoky, and mixed with a few herbs and lime, it's refreshing without being too sweet, or too tart. Perfect for a summer's evening with friends.

MAKES 2

4 ounces silver mezcal

Juice of 4 limes

Ice-filled shaker

2 tablespoons agave nectar

1 dried red chilli

Lime wedge, to garnish

2 sprigs of thyme, to garnish

Shake everything (except the thyme and lime wedge) vigorously in a cocktail shaker. Garnish with a lime wedge and the sprig of thyme.

Coconut Cashew Shake

I found this smoothie at a yoga retreat and it tastes just like a milk shake, without the calories. You'll need a high-powered food processor to crush the cashews, or failing that, a mortar and pestle.

SERVES 1

¾ cup raw cashews

Water and meat of 2 coconuts

4 to 6 dates (optional)

1 tablespoon vanilla extract

1 cup ice

Blend the cashews for 30 seconds on high in a blender. Then toss in the remaining ingredients, blend everything together, and voilà!

Cacao Coconut Balls

This is such a yummy dessert, introduced to me by my great friend Anita, who is a fashion stylist always on the go. These are a great snack to take to work or on a flight. The first time I made them, I screwed everything up; just be sure to melt the coconut oil on the stove for a few seconds first, so that everything mixes together easily.

MAKES 12

10 fresh dates, pitted

¼ cup raw cacao powder

¼ cup raw almonds

1 cup coconut flakes

2 tablespoons agave syrup

2 tablespoons coconut oil, melted

Preheat the oven to 350°F.

Mix the dates, cacao powder, and almonds in a food processor for 1 minute to make a sticky, chunky paste. Add the remaining ingredients, plus 2 tablespoons of water, and blend again.

Divide the mixture into twelve balls, each about the size of a golf ball, and place onto a greased baking tray.

Bake in the oven for 10 minutes.

Stephanie's Double Date Dish

My wonderful friend Steph is a fiend of a cook. She has been since university. When the rest of us were proud of rustling up baked beans on toast with a side of ketchup, she was serving roast lamb with all the trimmings for Sunday lunch. No wonder people were practically queuing up outside her front door—a gourmet home-cooked meal was like finding a unicorn at college. Cut to a decade later and she's still teaching me to cook. She recently stayed with me in L.A., and we had the ultimate girly day out: manicures, a beach walk, lunch in Malibu, followed by a stop at the farmer's market. Here we picked out all the ingredients to make the perfect dinner for four. It doesn't take long to prepare but looks and smells very impressive. It's grilled fish with a yummy bean puree, best served with a side of greens, mashed potatoes, and a nice bottle of dry white wine.

SERVES 4

For the bean puree:

½ onion, roughly chopped

2 tablespoons olive oil

1 garlic clove, crushed

2 cans cannelloni beans, drained

1 cup chicken stock

4 tablespoons extra-virgin olive oil

Juice of 1 lemon

For the fish:

4 fillets of fish (cod, salmon, or sea bass work well)

6 tablespoons extra-virgin olive oil

For the dressing:

1 tablespoon fresh parsley leaves, chopped

1 can-cured anchovy fillets (50g), drained

Juice of half a lemon

2 tablespoons extra-virgin olive oil

Brown the onions with the regular olive oil. Then add the garlic, beans, and stock.

Put everything in a food processor, adding the extra-virgin olive oil and lemon juice.

Preheat the oven to 400°F.

Fry the fish for two minutes on either side with the olive oil, before transferring it onto a baking tray and cooking in the oven for 8 minutes.

Meanwhile, make a dressing by finely chopping the parsley and anchovies, then adding the lemon and stirring in the oil. Mix together thoroughly.

Serve the dressing in a small jug, ready to drizzle as you please, and plate the bean puree on top of the fish.

Rachel's Turkey Burgers

My makeup artist and great friend Rachel taught me how to make these. We're on the road filming a lot together, facing long hours, when you stumble through the door ravenous at the end of the day and want something healthy, yummy, and fast. I remember the first time she made these turkey burgers for me in London, I ate about three in one go. And they're delicious served with homemade guacamole and chopped-up mango!

MAKES 8

1 red onion

2 tablespoons olive oil

1 pound of ground turkey

1 tablespoon tomato paste

1 egg

2 tablespoons ground almond meal

Handful of cilantro, finely chopped

Salt and pepper, to season

Juice of 1 lime

Dice the onion, as finely or as thick as you like (I like mine chunky), and then fry in 1 tablespoon of the olive oil until soft and lightly browned.

Mix all the other ingredients, except the lime juice, in a bowl. It's best to use your hands to smoosh it all together.

Split into 8 or so burgers, depending on how big you want them.

Fry the burgers in the other tablespoon of olive oil over a low heat and turn frequently. When they're almost done, squeeze lime juice on both sides.

My Mom's Coronation Chicken

I was raised on this curry chicken recipe. In the U.K., we call it coronation chicken, because the dish was apparently invented in 1953 by Constance Spry, the cook preparing the banquet for the queen's coronation. My mom has her own, healthier version, and whenever I come back to England for a visit, she always makes it for me. I love being a kid again, being told off for scarfing the bowl while it's still in the fridge before lunch!

SERVES 6

1 onion, chopped

1 tablespoon olive oil

1 tablespoon hot curry powder

½ cup chicken stock

1 tablespoon tomato puree

1 tablespoon mango chutney or apricot jam

Juice of half a lemon

10 tablespoons fat-free natural yogurt

1 cooked chicken (about 3 lbs)

Seedless green grapes, sliced, to garnish

Brown the onions in the olive oil.

Stir in the curry powder, stock, tomato puree, chutney or jam, and lemon juice. Stir until boiling and simmer for 5 minutes.

Allow the sauce to cool, then stir in the yogurt, until it's creamy and light brown in color.

Cut up the chicken and mix into the sauce.

Leave to cool further, refrigerate overnight if possible. Garnish with sliced grapes.

Parsley and Cream Cheese Frittata

If I'm going to be on my feet on set all day, I like to eat a big, protein-based breakfast. When we filmed *Plain Jane* across Europe and I stayed in hotels, I often asked the kitchen to make this Mediterranean delight. I've had it so many times when we filmed, it became my *Plain Jane* breakfast staple, a workhorse power brekkie! It's also an impressive, delicious, easy meal to make for brunch with friends, as you can serve the dish hot from the pan or chilled, just like you would a quiche, with a side salad.

SERVES 6

8 eggs

¼ cup fresh parsley leaves, minced or finely chopped

2 tablespoons chives, chopped

1 garlic clove, peeled and minced

3 ounces low-fat cream cheese

Pinch of salt

Pinch of pepper

1 tablespoon avocado oil

Preheat the oven to 450°F.

Break the eggs into a mixing bowl, then add the parsley, chives, garlic, cream cheese, salt, and pepper and whisk together.

Pour the mixture into a skillet lined with a tablespoon of avocado oil, and cook the eggs without stirring until the edges begin to set. (By the way, this skillet will end up in the oven, so either choose one with a metal handle, or go for a little casserole pot instead.)

As the eggs cook, run a spatula around the edge of the skillet and tilt a few times, to help it cook evenly and not burn.

Once the eggs are mostly set around the edges but a little runny in the center, remove from the heat and place the pan in the oven to bake until the eggs are set and slightly puffy, 5 to 7 minutes.

Remove from the oven and slice.

HOW TO BE A
GLAMOROUS HOSTESS

Thank goodness that, over the last few years, the art of entertaining has mellowed out. Throwing a dinner, or a party, has become more about good times, great food, and even better company, rather than the stiff, formal etiquette of bygone eras. Just think of some of your favorite shows for an idea of how stuffy dinner parties once were. To give you an idea, here are some of the ridiculous rules from the pre–First World War era of *Downton Abbey*: ladies would sit down at the table from the right side of the chair, not the left. You would pass the port to the left, dinner napkins had to be between twenty-two inches and twenty-six inches (and woe betide you if you got them mixed up with the luncheon ones, which were eighteen to twenty two inches). A lady would never stir her coffee in circles, let alone blow into it, to cool it. Nope. Back and forth with the spoon, in vertical lines, was the etiquette of the day. And don't even get me started on how to eat soup.

Thankfully, the influx of Americans into the U.K. after the war led to a more relaxed social setting, with louder laughter, fewer rules, and cocktails (an American invention) being served before dinner to loosen everybody up. God bless America.

But even mid-twentieth century, during the '50s and '60s, entertaining was full of facades and traditional roles. In the *Mad Men* school of style, the men enjoyed their scotch while the women slaved away in the kitchen, *Stepford Wives* style. So what's changed? Well, now it's up to *you* how to throw a party. You can go big, or keep it simple, but the essence is always the same: guests want to let their hair down, eat, drink, and have fun. The antiquated rules and pompous etiquette might have gone out the window, but that doesn't mean you shouldn't make an effort. I'm all for letting your creative juices flow when it comes to throwing an event!

A few years ago, when I worked at *InStyle* magazine in London, one of my favorite parts of the job was to help out with the entertaining shoots. Whether it was an article on how to mix retro cocktails for a chic, *Mad Men*—inspired soiree; how to set the scene for the perfect boho garden party; how to cook a farm-to-table Sunday brunch; or how to decorate a room like a Moroccan souk, I absolutely loved helping style these pieces. My love of fashion absolutely translates into creating the perfect setting for a gathering, and sometimes nothing gets me more inspired than entertaining a group of friends.

The key is in the details. The entire setting, from invitations and napkins, to music, decorations, and even scent, is important for creating an ambience. As the hostess, you're inventing a fairytale world away from the office or stresses of everyday life, for your friends to relax into. You want to stimulate all the senses of your guests, from sight to sound, smell, touch, and taste.

So where to start? Think about the kind of party images that inspire you. Is it fun '80s-themed dance parties? Or a super casual BBQ? Perhaps it's an elegant, candlelit dinner party. Personally, my idea of the ultimate, entertaining luxury is captured in almost every Slim Aarons photograph. A famous society photographer in the 1970s, he snapped a plethora of glamorous poolside parties all over the globe, including Marrakesh, Palm Springs, and Italy—shooting women in long, printed caftans lounging on bamboo chairs, sipping martinis from under gigantic, tortoiseshell sunglasses. Check out his images online. Just like with shopping, it's great to have a visual idea of the atmosphere you'd like to create for your party.

While I say yes to splurging on great quality *food*, even if it's simple (nothing beats a yummy cheeseboard with warm French bread and a bottle of red wine, or a wooden board covered with fresh antipasti, in my opinion), don't feel you need to do the same and spend a lot on all the decorations. Don't overcomplicate the theme. Some great summer ideas are "music festival," "at the beach," or "English country picnic." "Fun fair" (think caramel apples and hoopla), "Oktoberfest," and "Narnia" are some fun themes for fall and winter. Or, if you're keeping things simple and just going for a color theme, pick two key bright shades to work with and run with them, leaving everything else neutral.

When you're the hostess, you want to appear pretty relaxed and have time to actually mingle with the guests, instead of rushing around or getting stuck in the kitchen. Put out a relaxed, welcoming energy, one that shows you're happy to have people over, not stressing about it. I even dress in a laid-back way to make guests feel the same: bare feet, a long, floaty dress, and loads of rings and bangles.

The best way to stop yourself stressing about entertaining (well, aside from having your other half pour you a stiff cocktail as you both get ready), is through careful planning and preparation. Make what you can the night before, and say yes to help; delegation is key. What are certain friends good at . . . playing DJ? Mixing cocktails? Making

dessert? Don't be afraid to e-mail in advance asking people to pitch in; contributing only makes them feel more part of the event.

Light candles fifteen minutes before guests arrive. (I like to save the scented ones for the bathroom, and burn unscented ones in the dining room, so they don't interfere with the food.) Get the music on before anyone arrives. This is a *must*. Place fresh flowers in at least two rooms. Your guests are likely to bring you more to fill other rooms, and be sure to place them in vases as soon as you get them. Not only is that polite, but the whole house will be brightened.

Serve some dry nibbles, such as raw cashews and kale chips, which can be put out in advance. And here's another tip: serve hors d'oeuvres in mismatched bowls so it doesn't look like a catering hall. My granny gave me a few hand-painted bowls from Brazil, from when she used to live there back in the '60s, and that sparked my collection of gorgeous little hand-painted bowls. I try to pick a couple up whenever I travel somewhere new and exotic.

Set up a drinks trolley that Don Draper would be proud of—think old-school glam. For this, a side table, console, or even a rolling organizer from other rooms in the house will work. I found a raised butler's tray on stilts and made a display of it, hanging three retro prints above it, and filling it with vintage tumblers and printed napkins I found at a market in the Hamptons.

To make yours, you'll need a plethora of booze, but don't get the predictable brands. I really love finding obscure labels from small or family-owned firms. I proudly display: Tito's Handmade Vodka, Sailor Jerry Spiced Rum, Hendrick's Gin (okay, it's not a small company, but it's the best and the black glass bottle is genius), Tapatio Tequila, and Ypióca Cachaça from Brazil. Buy your tonic and soda water mixers in individual little bottles. These look more like a legit cocktail bar and will keep their fizz. I like to incorporate something green and growing on the cart, too. Currently I'm using a wide glass flower vase filled with fresh, juicy limes. Old-fashioned water dispensers, a baby pestle and mortar for crushing herbs, and kitsch stirrers are eye-catching additions, too. Not only will your makeshift bar look chic, but it encourages guests to help themselves, cutting down the workload for you.

When your dinner party countdown begins, most important, factor in an extra fifteen minutes to have a drink with your hubby or best friend *before* any guests arrive. It will work wonders to help you relax and get you in the mood. Rushing and feeling edgy when you open the front door sets the wrong tone.

Don't feel you need to have everything finished the second guests arrive. Some people disagree with me on this one, but I believe it's a more mellow, friendly atmosphere to have people wander into the kitchen and chat while I finish cooking the main course. I like the banter, the camaraderie; and it's less formal. But do keep an eye on timing. From the time guests arrive to the time they sit for dinner, should be forty-five minutes, an hour max. And although I like my mates to join me in the kitchen, I don't want to be standing there all night. So pick dishes that can be left for a while, if not prepared earlier, and don't require constant babysitting by the stove (yes, I'm talking to *you*, risotto).

P.S. Here's where I—and a lot of my friends from the fashion or beauty industry—go wrong: we want everything to be perfect. Remember that a fun party is not a perfect party. If something goes wrong, laugh your head off about it. The best nights out are always when something outrageous happens, so see the funny side, have a giggle, and most likely another drink!

I remember the first Thanksgiving I moved to America, my job was to bring vegetables to dinner. Experimenting way outside my comfort zone, I Googled a recipe and whipped up some mashed sweet potato, flavored with honey and turmeric. It turned out Big Bird yellow—or nuclear—as my kind friend put it! And after the meal there were twelve plates left around the table, all clean except for a massive splodge of uneaten, nuclear yellow on each one. It was so funny we took a photo of the remains, and I still get ribbed for it five years later. The point is, you don't have to be Martha Stewart. Just have fun, relax, and your guests will, too.

My Ultimate Party-Throwing Tips

PLAN THE PARKING. This is one that few hosts remember to consider, but finding a place to park can be a colossal pain in the neck for your guests. If you have a large crowd coming, consider including a few suggestions for parking arrangements in your invite. For example, if you live near a facility with a parking lot that won't be used during party hours, suggest that your guests park there. If you know in advance that parking restrictions will be in place on your street, mention that as well.

Make a playlist. Or failing that, ask a friend to make one, or play Pandora or Spotify with the perfect theme song to kick off the night. And don't forget to change the mood later. A party should always finish with dancing, so a great, cheesy '90s or '80s stomper will be popular.

Think outside the box when it comes to drinks. Try Prosecco with rose petals instead of champagne, or whip up one of the cocktails in my recipe list. Espresso martinis are a surefire way to get everyone dancing, and make the nonalcoholic drinks interesting, too—anything from an elderflower cordial with sparkling water and fresh mint, to hibiscus or rose cordial–infused soda water served with a sprig of rosemary. And invest in a new ice tray with giant cubes. One that almost fills the whole glass looks very cool.

Don't rush your table plan—and I massively encourage you to make one. I don't throw formal dinner parties, and yet I always set place cards. A good table plan can make or break the party, not to mention set off rounds of raucous laughter, new friends, and hopefully, new romances.

Make the effort with your invitations. This sets the tone, and gets guests excited for your party even before it's begun. I've been sent invitations to New York Fashion Week in all shapes and forms—from old vinyl records (cheap to pick up at any flea market) to fridge magnets and candy. I once wrote out a hundred invitations by hand, on vintage postcards I bought cheaply in bulk online. Get creative making sticky labels on your laptop, and remember almost anything can be used as an invite. Don't forget to ask specifically for an RSVP. People are extremely casual now about bothering to let you know if they're showing up, but if you're going through the trouble of cooking, then it's a must.

Seeing as you may only use your decorations and accessories once or twice ever, I'm a big fan of finding bargains online (Joss and Main, PartyCheap, One Kings Lane, C. Wonder, and Hester & Cook are fabulous), or at discount stores, such as Costco, Target, and HomeGoods. At any of these places you can find everything to create your party vibe—from candles to vases, dishes, bright glasses, scatter cushions, tablecloths—the lot. If you're renting out a particularly beautiful or unique venue, then the location does the work for you (i.e. you can skimp on the decor). The same goes if the location has a wonderful view.

Consider new uses for the kitchen accessories you already own. I use Mason jars as my regular water cups. I have a closet stacked full of them. Try using them to hold flowers from the garden or bright paper straws. And how about filling good old-fashioned julep cups with fresh herbs, such as mint or rosemary sprigs, for guests to make cocktails with? Such quaint Southern charm! Did you know that vintage julep cups are unique to the city or state in which they were manufactured? Collect a bunch from flea markets or thrift stores, and you'll assemble an eclectic mix.

Don't feel overwhelmed to decorate every square foot. Sometimes drawing on the place's indigenous charm can keep things simple and chic. I recently went to a luncheon at the Cannes Film Festival in the south of France. Lining the street were pretty lemon trees, and each table's centerpiece consisted of a few lemons and their leaves. Not even a dish. It looked so gorgeous and cost nothing. If you can't afford too many flowers, fruit and vegetables are a great alternative. Wooden bowls or flower vases filled with limes, apples, pomegranates, or artichokes look very cool.

Lighting transforms a space. Lower the dimmers, or replace a few lamps with lower wattage or red bulbs. You can never have too many candles, and try festoon lighting instead of fairy lights in the back garden (these are bare lightbulbs linked with rope, and they can be rented at reasonable prices). Paper lanterns are gorgeous, too, and if you're a whizz with extension cords, rig a chandelier up to a tree—perhaps not great-granny's heirloom chandelier, but you can find super-cheap versions on eBay. At the end of the evening, never turn on bright lights in an effort to get people to leave faster; this can seem rude or worse, like a tacky nightclub! Instead, lower the music, it's a subtler approach.

Spice things up with a homemade cinema. At a rooftop party I went to once, my friend hung up a white sheet and projected retro surf footage into it. And a bar in London I love has old Cary Grant and Audrey Hepburn movies playing on muted flat-screens around the venue. Choose a film that resonates with the party's theme (think about the vastly different moods you could create with everything from *Casablanca* to *White Christmas*, or *Ferris Bueller's Day Off* to *The Big Chill*). Turn the volume down, so it doesn't detract from the music and conversation.

Deal with drunken guests. Either put them to bed in a spare room or order them a cab home. They'll thank you for it in the morning.

Over-invite by 30 percent. If you're aiming for fifty people, invite sixty-five. That way the room will never feel too empty.

Put your pets away. Cats and dogs get overexcited with crowds and loud music, and although the sight of your two cute Labradors playing tug of war with your coat in the living room is relatively funny on a normal day, it's not so funny if it's Aunt Jessica's new Gucci jacket, and she's not an animal lover. Best to put pets in the garden or another room for the evening.

Keep the neighbors sweet. You have two choices here: invite them or keep the noise down. Oh no, hang on—there's the third absolutely genius option I first heard about when interviewing a newlywed couple who had a large and raucous reception at their suburban home: they left cute packages on their neighbor's doorsteps, containing a polite note, a bag of popcorn, and movie theater tickets for the night of the party. If you're planning a whopping party with over fifty guests, this is a great tactic.

Offer veggie and nonalcoholic options. Since I live in Los Angeles, it's practically status quo for parties to have gluten-free-this and vegan-that on offer, but even outside of the most health-conscious city in the world, do keep in mind it's becoming more common that people may not eat meat, or suffer from wheat or peanut allergies.

You kind of have to entertain, too. Thinking ahead about the different ages of guests means everybody can have more fun. Designate a DVD area for teens, a games area for kids (within view, if possible, of the main table), and a quiet corner where older guests can sit down, away from the noise. If there are going to be more than say, twenty children arriving, it may make sense to hire a children's entertainer for the day.

Deal with a fashion clash like the classy lady you are. I once arrived at an English country wedding in my floor-length, printed Matthew Willamson dress. It had butterflies, it had sequins, it had frilly tiers—the lot. I arrived only to look down the church pew and see the editor of a newspaper I was currently writing for, in exactly the same gown. Eek! My girlfriends and I were sitting in the same row, about ten of us. We whispered a vote, one to the next . . . should I rush back to the hotel and change after the ceremony? They answered yes, and so I did. But I have to say, looking back with hindsight, better to have laughed it off, complimented my editor on her fabulous taste, and taken a photo together for fun. So what, you both chose the same dress, who cares? Have the confidence to pull it off and laugh it off, knowing you look great.

Designate a coat room. Be sure to take guests' coats when they arrive, and put them all in the same place (usually on a bed, in a spare bedroom, is ideal).

When it comes to messy food, either avoid it altogether or put out empty bowls for pistachio shells, shrimp tails, or candy wrappers. A fun gimmick will always draw people's attention: rent a popcorn machine or an ice-cream cart. My friend Tom once paid a taco truck to show up outside his house and serve chicken quesadillas late at night. People absolutely loved lining up, and it became a real talking point. But you don't have to spend a fortune. I once cooked sausages and mashed potatoes (or "bangers and mash," as we call it in England!) and put a baby bottle of ketchup at each place setting. It was a simple touch, but everyone loved it and the table looked bright and fun.

Make sure you have plenty of seating for your guests, even if you're not hosting a sit-down dinner. If guests are going to be eating, make sure there is adequate table space for glasses and plates, so guests don't have to juggle. For every party, there's likely to be at least one spill. Don't stress, just cover it with stain removal powder or failing that, salt, and carry on having fun. If guests see you worrying, it will change the mood of the party—and remember that if worse comes to worst, there are hardly any stains a cleaning company can't shift; it's not the end of the world.

Play old-school games. Hot potato? Musical chairs? These don't get any less fun just because we're grown-ups, you know. But the prizes can be more mature—try a baby bottle of tequila, or a cute pair of bright lace undies.

And if you're a guest, always show up with a gift. It doesn't have to be expensive, just a small token of your appreciation. With gifts, it's best to go one of two ways: make it personal, or keep it simple. If you know your hostess well, bake her favorite cookies, bring her favorite scented candle, a book you think she'd enjoy, or buy a spa voucher (the last is my all-time favorite gift—although this is more appropriate for certain occasions, like if it's her birthday). If I don't know my hostess well enough to buy something funny or that I know she'll use, then my next priority is finding a neutral, simple gift in adorable packaging. A scented candle, bunch of flowers, or good bottle of wine is spot-on. Food, such as homemade preserves and olive oil, or fancy salt and pepper shakers will always go over well, as will bath soaps and bath salts. Really, it's the thought that counts.

And in the age of e-mails and texts, I'm a big fan of the handwritten thank-you letter. People of all generations appreciate a note in the mail, so make the effort. It'll take you five minutes.

How to Throw My Favorite Kind of Party: A Tea Party

HAILING FROM ENGLAND, afternoon tea is in my blood. To me, a piping hot, sweet and milky mug of tea is the most comforting thing in the world to wrap my hands around. I could have had a long, exhausting day on set, but putting the kettle on reminds me of home, of family, and is wholeheartedly uplifting. Henry James had it right when he wrote, "There are few hours in life more agreeable than the hour dedicated to the ceremony known as afternoon tea."

And as my granny says, tea should always be poured from a teapot into a cup, and not straight from the kettle! Making a big occasion of afternoon tea is not only a lovely way to catch up with friends, it's a great excuse to use those cute floral teacups that stay hidden away in the cupboard, to attempt baking, and to be utterly girly.

Usually served with cakes and finger sandwiches, the art of afternoon tea is a tradition that can be dated back precisely to 1840. While the custom of drinking tea actually dates back way further, to China almost five thousand years ago, the hot drink became popularized in England during the 1660s by King Charles II and his wife, the Portuguese Infanta Catherine of Braganza. The concept of a sandwich was made popular in the mid-1770s by the fourth Earl of Sandwich, who ordered his meat between two slices of bread so that he could hold it in one hand and continue playing cards with the other. But it was not until the mid-nineteenth century that all these elements combined and the concept of "afternoon tea" first appeared.

In the year 1840, Anna, the seventh Duchess of Bedford, England, would become hungry around four o'clock in the afternoon. The evening meal in her household was served fashionably late at eight o'clock, so the Duchess asked for a tray of tea, cake, and bread and butter to be brought to her room during the afternoon. This became a habit of hers, and she soon began inviting friends to join her.

The trend caught on socially, and it wasn't long before ladies of high society started changing into decadent, long gowns, white gloves, and elaborate hats for afternoon tea.

I love to get the girls over and throw a tea party, no matter what time of year. I enjoy searching out pretty floral china teacups, saucers, milk jugs, and teapots at the flea market. These are usually sold as a set, but if you only find a few eclectic ones, that's fine. It's super chic serving tea in mismatched china. Buy a tiered cake stand; they are the best way to show off your delicacies.

Have a colorful menu. Make finger sandwiches from interesting breads, such as beetroot bread (which is yummy with cream cheese and cucumber), tomato bread (delicious with mozzarella and fresh basil), or olive focaccia (works well with chicken or ham, and pickle).

Fondants, cupcakes, and macarons are always different pastel colors, and look beautiful together on a cake stand. Dust powdered sugar over the cakes to give them a fairy-tale feel.

The secret to brewing the best cup of tea is to fill the kettle with fresh water that has not been boiled before (reheating water reduces the oxygen content and alters the taste). Once boiled, swill it around the teapot, before adding two teaspoons of loose tea, or one tea bag per cup, plus one extra for the pot. Add the boiling water and leave for no longer than two to three minutes, or the tea will stew and taste yucky. I like mine with a splash of whole milk and brown sugar.

But you don't have to drink tea! Homemade lemonade is a refreshing alternative, or one of my personal favorite ideas: serve fruity cocktails from teacups.

Make your tea party alfresco. A sunny afternoon in the garden is the perfect setting. Put flowers in Mason jars, throw a gingham tablecloth or a bright rug on the grass, and throw some fairy lights up in the trees.

If there are children, plan a few games and don't forget the dress-up costume box, full of feather boas and fun hats.

Give out party bags. Leaving birthday parties as a kid, there were always little party bags to go home with, which made me smile. Channel your inner Peter Pan and do as the kids do: wrap a slice of cake, add a flea market–bought teacup and perhaps some candy or a lip gloss to a small brown paper bag, and tie it with string. I love making old-fashioned nametags by cutting up burlap into rectangles, writing each name in brown felt pen, and tying it to each bag.

HERE ARE MY FAVORITE PLACES IN THE WORLD FOR AFTERNOON TEA

- **SWEET LADY JANE IN LOS ANGELES:** It took me a while living in L.A. to discover this little café on Melrose Avenue, but the cakes are enormous and fluffy. Pretty much every movie star gets their birthday cake made here. I'd single out the chocolate almond crunch as my favorite flavor, closely followed by the triple berry shortcake.

- **LA MAISON ANGELINA IN PARIS:** There is always a line outside but their famous hot chocolate and melt-in-the-mouth macarons are worth the wait.

- **FORTNUM & MASON IN LONDON:** One of the oldest shops in London, and where the royal family has shopped for centuries, the atmosphere here is historic. You simply must have clotted cream and strawberry jam layered onto a hot scone!

- **THE PUMP ROOM IN BATH, ENGLAND:** Loaded with tradition, the Pump Room is not only aesthetically pretty, it is the famous location where Jane Austen's heroines from *Persuasion* and *Northanger Abbey* gossiped, courted romance, and mingled with the upper classes. The first Jane Austen book I read was *Northanger Abbey*, and for the main character, Catherine, afternoon tea became the vital way of meeting up with her man. "With more than usual eagerness did Catherine hasten to the Pump-room the next day, secure within herself of seeing Mr. Tilney there before the morning were over, and ready to meet him with a smile."

- **THE RAFFLES HOTEL IN SINGAPORE:** This is a legendary venue that epitomizes the romance of the Far East. Raffles and its fascinating history has been included in novels by Somerset Maugham, Rudyard Kipling, and Ernest Hemingway. High tea is served in the hotel's historic Tiffin Room, with an enormous array of fragrant loose teas on offer.

- **TEA & SYMPATHY IN NEW YORK:** Situated in the heart of Greenwich Village, this English shop serves an authentic afternoon tea, including homemade jams and pastries.

HOW TO FEEL FABULOUS ABOUT YOURSELF ON A SHOESTRING BUDGET

Feel the Burn

EXERCISE IS ONE OF THE MOST EFFECTIVE MOOD LIFTERS, ever. Raising your heart rate and working up a sweat releases endorphins within five minutes, which creates feelings of euphoria, blocks pain, and reduces stress. Recently, I nearly knocked myself out trying a new aerobics class, and although it was tough, I left with a major spring in my step, itching to go back again. Experiment with different forms of fitness to see which suits you. It might be punching the heck out of the air in kickboxing, letting off steam with friends in a team sport, or taking a peaceful yoga class—but know that cardio is more effective at releasing endorphins than resistance training. If you're short on space and time, take an online class, such as Dirty Yoga (there's nothing filthy about it, it's just really effective!). Or dance—put on your headphones, crank up your favorite tune, and dance around your room, because research says that dancing releases more endorphins than any other sport.

If You Can't Hit the Gym

I AM ALWAYS UP CRAZY EARLY when filming on location, and I struggle to make it to the gym. So, when I can't work out, even ten minutes of stretching and deep breaths makes a difference. And I have the best fitness secret ever: a travel roller. A plastic tube about the size of your upper arm and lighter than a bottle of water, goes to every hotel with me. Twenty minutes in front of the TV rolling out my legs, arms, back, neck . . . this piece of equipment massages, stretches, and realigns the muscles and improves my posture, back pain, and energy levels. It's genius. Any yogis reading this will know the benefits of breathing slowly and deeply.

Inhale for four counts, hold it for six, and breathe out for eight. Repeat five times and remember to drop your shoulders, try to clear your mind, and close your eyes. Try it a few minutes, first thing in the morning, before bed, or even at your desk during a quiet moment. It will make a big difference.

Say Thank You

MY FRIEND CARA used to have an alcohol problem, and is now proudly nine years sober. For nearly a decade, she has made a gratitude list every day, to keep her grounded, mindful, and focused. When I remember to do the same, I swear it gives me a little lift. Try it! You write down what you appreciate. It could be a sunny day, a yummy cappuccino, the person you wake up next to, the great book you're reading—anything.

Beauty Sleep

CLEAN YOUR SHEETS, iron them, and spritz a refreshing linen spray on them. Nothing beats that feeling of climbing into crisp, freshly laundered bed sheets. Add a drop of rose and lavender oil to your pillow before bed. The former reduces puffiness in your face and calms the skin tissue, while the latter enables restful sleep. While you're at it, de-clutter your bedroom (it should be as simple and tranquil as possible), and put fresh flowers in a vase. A lot closer to a five-star hotel than it was before, right?

Say Yes

AGREE TO ONE THING you normally wouldn't. The point is to push yourself out of your comfort zone. Try a new class at the gym, skydive, listen to a poetry reading, begin a new hobby, visit the local art gallery, be a tourist in your own town for the day. Switch things up. If you really hate it that much, you can leave. But showing up and trying is liberating in itself.

Plug In

USE TECHNOLOGY TO UPLIFT YOU by following funny and inspirational people on Twitter, like comedian/writer @MindyKaling, @ActionHappiness, @Pospositive (for uplifting statements), and @FunnyorDie for stuff that will make you LOL. Apparently the nature of the tweets you read really does affect your mood, so keep that feed positive.

Microwave yourself a bowl of popcorn, pour a large glass of wine and watch happy box sets on TV—perhaps something that reminds you of your youth. So for me, that's *Friends*, the original *Beverly Hills, 90210*, *Saved by the Bell*, *Sex and the City*, and oh—any movie with Audrey Hepburn in it. It's popcorn for the brain, and some awesome, mega '90s fashion throwbacks, too—Kelly Kapowski's cropped tops and Levi 501's anyone?

Unplug

UNSUBSCRIBE TO ALL THOSE IRRITATING MASS E-MAILS that make you go "ugh" every morning. I get a weirdly large satisfaction from doing this every day. Turn off your computer, TV, and phone at least thirty minutes before bed. Those lights have been proven to screw up your sleep patterns, and reading an irritating e-mail will fire you up when you should be winding down.

Instead, lose yourself in your own imagination and become a bookworm with some girl power lit. I'm an old-fashioned, printed book kind of gal, but if you love your Kindle, keep it on a low light. These are some of my top choices, spanning the last three hundred years:

PRIDE AND PREJUDICE by Jane Austen

A ROOM OF ONE'S OWN by Virginia Woolf

THE AGE OF INNOCENCE by Edith Wharton

BOSSYPANTS by Tina Fey

IS EVERYONE HANGING OUT WITHOUT ME?
(AND OTHER CONCERNS) by Mindy Kaling

#GIRLBOSS by Sophia Amorusa

DADDY'S GIRLS by Tasmina Perry

People who read on a regular basis are proven to be more likely to take part in charity work, community volunteering, and exercise.

Face Time

PRESS AND GENTLY RUB YOUR TEMPLES, the middle of your chest, and the soft area where your thumb meets your index finger. The latter is particularly good at relieving headaches while pressing the chest eases breathing. Before applying makeup, use facial oil or serum to give yourself a face massage (see tutorials on YouTube). It's so effective at relieving a tense jaw, puffiness, and alleviating under-eye circles. I make sure I have one every day.

Light a Scented Candle

NOT ONLY IS SCENT THE STRONGEST FORM OF MEMORY (so it can take you to your happy place), studies show that certain smells are uplifting. The best ones to induce contentment? Lemon, rose, jasmine, lavender, and licorice. And you should always smell good, too. Whiz through the department store, spritz, and leave with as many samples as they'll hand out.

Makeover Monday

START THE WEEK OFF AFRESH by giving yourself a beauty makeover, dramatic enough to do a double take when you walk by a mirror. Buy a red lipstick. It's not just silver screen goddesses who are allowed sexy scarlet lips, so try on a few before you buy and once you own it, wear it with pride whenever you feel like it (with jeans and a sweater—is to me—much chicer than saving it for a formal occasion). Get bangs cut into your hair, experiment with nail art, get your eyebrows professionally shaped, or book in to a good spa for eyelash extensions. Trust me when I say these things will change your face dramatically for the better: no surgery or makeup required! An instant new, chic, and stylish you.

Nature Trail

DRIVE SOMEWHERE BEAUTIFUL and take a long walk with the dog (for me that means borrowing someone else's dog, but it still works!). I get stressed when I'm locked in a work bubble and forget that life doesn't actually revolve around a desk or filming an eighteen-hour day. So take yourself out of your normal environment, and your problems will most likely seem smaller. Fact: photos of nature on your walls or screensaver—such as mountains, forests, and beaches—cause your mind to feel more tranquil and calm.

Toot Your Own Horn

LIST THREE THINGS YOU'RE GOOD AT, and leave that note on your night stand. It could be that you're good at making meatloaf, good at applying eyeliner, good at kissing, or good at being a caring friend. They all count. Celebrate your successes the same way you would a friend's. Acknowledging and motivating yourself is important. I recently bought myself jewelry for the first time ever, as a reward for getting a job, and I have to say the moment felt pretty awesome!

Meet Me in the Lobby

PUT ON YOUR BIGGEST PAIR OF SHADES, sit in a posh hotel lobby to people-watch, and just soak up the atmosphere. Many places have live music during afternoon tea, which feels like a bygone era. I'm obsessed with Claridge's in London, the Peninsula Beverly Hills, and the Waldorf Astoria in New York. Every city's got a good few!

Find Your Central Perk

BECOME A REGULAR somewhere, be it a café, gym, or bar. Having staff know your name and drink order is really rather comforting.

Hug

CUDDLING RELEASES THE FEEL-GOOD HORMONE oxytocin, which reduces stress and makes you happy.

Cut and Paste

FORGET PINTEREST, BUILD A REAL SCRAPBOOK full of things that make you smile: quotes, old Polaroid photos, messages, magazine tears. It will fast become a mood board for all your inspirations, reminding you of the values and styles you want to live, dress, and think by. I've kept one for several years, and I love flicking through it now and again; updating it on a rainy afternoon.

It's a Marathon, Not a Sprint

IF YOUR LIFE RUNS AT A HUNDRED MILES PER MINUTE, plan an activity with a friend or boyfriend that doesn't involve anything particularly cool, fast-paced, expensive, or cocktail-fueled. Some ideas: take a step back and go for a hike, visit the flea market, or hit the farmer's market with a recipe and then cook up a storm together (and remember—it's okay if you burn everything and end up ordering takeout. It's the activity that counts). Indulge the *Mad Men*—style domestic goddess in you by throwing a tea party (see my guide to throwing an awesome one!). In short: pick up an old tea stand in a thrift store, bake a cake, cut the crusts off sandwiches, brew tea in a proper teapot, make your friends dress up, and enjoy an afternoon of inexpensive, old-fashioned glamour.

Music Alfresco

BUY LAST-MINUTE standing tickets to the opera, to an outdoor cinema, or to a local jazz club. They're very cheap, it still sounds the same, and it's a very romantic idea for a spontaneous date, too.

Grow Green Thumbs

CULTIVATE A VEGETABLE OR HERB GARDEN, even if it's a windowsill box or a few pots on your balcony. Gardening is good for the soul: to nurture something and eventually add your own homegrown fresh basil to a bowl of spaghetti, is epic.

Pretty Women

DRESS UP TO THE MAX with a friend and spend the afternoon trying on clothes at designer boutiques. (Discreetly) take a Polaroid camera and create the best fashion-editorial-Instagram-montage ever. Many high-end stores even serve free champagne while you're in the changing room, too. Woohoo!

Power Hour

SET ASIDE A "POWER HOUR" to complete all the boring admin that comes with being a grown-up: pay bills, clear your inbox, get your taxes in order. Once it's done, you'll feel a weight lifted off your shoulders.

Snack Attack

EAT FISH. Ingesting omega-3 fats (found in fish like salmon and tuna) increases serotonin in the brain, which makes you feel content and calm. Food has an insane effect on how we act and feel. I only really began to realize this as I got older, and read personal trainer James Duigan's book *Clean and Lean*. Processed foods, simple carbs, refined sugar, caffeine—anything with long ingredi-

ents you can't even pronounce—they all give you a quick buzz, and then you drop. This can make it hard to sleep peacefully, make you feel fatigued, give you the jitters, even mess with your mood. For some healthy ideas check out my morning smoothie (page 130) and dessert ideas (page 258).

An Oldie Is a Goldie

CALL YOUR GRANDPARENTS. They somehow just bring calm and the perspective that only an older person knows how to impart. If you don't have a grandmother or grandfather, volunteer at your local home for the elderly. Honestly, the stories elderly people tell are enough to make our modern-day problems seem superficial. According to *The Journal of Consumer Psychology*, the happiest people are the biggest givers to charity.

Soak It Up

MY FAVORITE POET, Sylvia Plath, once declared that "There must be quite a few things a hot bath won't cure, but I don't know many of them," and I tend to agree. Take the time to make this a weekly ritual. Light candles, add scented bath oil, apply a face mask, bring your favorite book—and just soak. It feels so decadent and comforting. Adding a cup of Epsom salts de-bloats your body, too. (No wonder Cindy Crawford admits it's part of her preshoot ritual!) Plus—here's another science bit—physical and social warmth are actually interchangeable, so having a hot bath actually helps get rid of feelings of loneliness. Try it.

Selfie Style

SNAP A TOTALLY GORGEOUS PHOTO of yourself, even if it takes a hundred shots to make the perfect one, then put it into a super-flattering filter. And why not frame it, too?

Find Will Ferrell

GOOGLE THE FUNNIEST MOVIES of all time, rent whichever tickle your fancy, and laugh your head off out loud all afternoon. Laughing reduces blood pressure and releases a huge amount of endorphins, making us feel fabulous. In fact, laughing for an hour every other week can lower blood pressure by five or six points in three months—which is basically the same effect on your health as losing ten pounds! What's more, laughing is proven to decrease levels of stress hormones like beta-endorphin and cortisol. It reactivates digestive, sexual, and immune systems that can be switched off by stress. Pretty amazing, huh? The more easily you giggle, the more you'll be able to apply that response to difficult situations, and trust me, that is often the best way to deal with problems.

THE 10 MOVIES EVERY FASHIONISTA SHOULD WATCH

There is nothing I love doing more on a rainy day than curling up by the fire with a bowl of popcorn and a good movie. Depending on which film I pick, the escapism is relaxing or stimulating, but I love being dragged into a totally new world and story. Personally, I believe old movies have a charm to them that modern ones don't. And when it comes to style sirens and retro settings (Grace Kelly playing with a model boat in a pool in *High Society*, Julia Roberts weeping in her red gown at the opera in *Pretty Woman*)—these are beautiful images that stick in my mind, lift my spirits, and inspire my fashion choices.

- *BREAKFAST AT TIFFANY'S:* Holly Golightly's famous black satin dress was especially designed for Audrey Hepburn by her good friend, Hubert de Givenchy. The dress later sold at auction for $1 million. Natalie Portman also wore it for a cover of *Harper's Bazaar* in November 2006.

- *HIGH SOCIETY:* Recently engaged to Prince Rainier of Monaco, leading lady Grace Kelly wore her actual engagement ring for her character's engagement ring. Set in the decadent, lavish world of Newport, Rhode Island, the movie was to be her last before she retired from acting and became a princess. Interestingly, MGM studio's head designer, Helen Rose, created not only Grace Kelly's stunning wardrobe for the film, but also the actress's real-life wedding gown.

- *CLUELESS:* "You're a virgin who can't drive . . ." My most overused quotation ever! I must have seen this movie twenty times and it never gets old. Alaïa mini-dresses, matchy-matchy suits, knee-length socks, and walk-in, computer-enhanced wardrobes—we all just wanted to be Cher and Dionne during high school.

- *PRETTY WOMAN:* I watched this movie (again) the night before moving to Los Angeles, five years ago. It got me extremely excited to board my plane! Word has it Julia Roberts kept the brown-and-cream tea dress she wore to the polo, and still tries it on now and again.

- *LA DOLCE VITA:* Fellini's three-hour tale of decadence and excess is truly iconic, and creates a real contrast to my other favorite movie set in Rome, *Roman Holiday*. Anita Ekberg emerging from the Trevi Fountain in a black dress is one of the most memorable scenes in film history. Fellini claimed that Balenciaga's sack dress, with its dramatic silhouette—and billowing in the wind like Anita's black ball gown—inspired the scene.

- *LOVE STORY:* Keep the tissues handy. Retro Manhattan, a heart-wrenching storyline, and last but not least, Ali MacGraw's preppy wardrobe, which Calvin Klein called "great American style," are all reasons to rent this one.

- *BELLE DE JOUR:* Catherine Deneuve epitomizes the erotically charged, icy femme fatale. A sexually frustrated housewife who turns to prostitution for satisfaction, her wardrobe (designed by Yves Saint Laurent) is '60s-prim with a very seductive and powerful undertone—high-waisted pencil skirts, silk bow blouses, and killer patent stilettos.

- *THE GREAT GATSBY* (both versions!): The 1974 film perfectly captured the flapper style of the Jazz Age, with the character Daisy (played by a secretly pregnant Mia Farrow) dressed almost exclusively in white. The film went on to win the Oscar for Best Costume Design. Baz Luhrmann's 2013 version is awesome, too: check out Prada's flapper dresses and headpieces on Carey Mulligan. Gorgeous.

- *DESPERATELY SEEKING SUSAN:* I mean, you just have to try out '80s fingerless lace gloves and fishnet stockings after watching Madonna rock them out in this fashion-pioneering movie! And here's a bit of trivia: the thrift store where the two Susans go shopping actually exists. It's called Love Saves the Day and is in Greenwich Village in New York City.

- *ANNIE HALL:* Diane Keaton styled a bunch of her looks for this Woody Allen flick, using clothes from her own closet. Magazines and runway shows caught on to her androgynous, loose tailoring, ties, and fedoras, and copied the look in a big way.

A Final Word
...and More

I HOPE YOU'VE FOUND THIS BOOK AS ENJOYABLE to read, as it was for me to write. While I hope the tips and anecdotes have amused and inspired you, if there's one thing I hope you walk away with, it's a newfound confidence in yourself. Before I say good-bye, I want to share the most important part of the book: how to be kind to yourself. How often do you put yourself first? Inwardly congratulate yourself? Approve of yourself? And dare I say it, *love* yourself?

It might sound simple, but we women are a lot harder on ourselves throughout life than we should be. We multitask, we're pulled in a million different directions, we often look after everybody else except ourselves, and to top it all off, we look in the mirror and more often cringe rather than celebrate. Flicking through a magazine recently, I was moved by a quote by the actress Emma Stone. She said, "I remind myself to be kind to myself, and as slightly ridiculous as it may sound, to treat myself in the same gentle way I'd want to treat a daughter of mine." For some reason, her words hit me like a bolt of lightning, and stuck with me. A yoga teacher once said to me at the end of our practice: "Think of one word that you wish there was more of in the world. Compassion, kindness, warmth, peace?" I thought of kindness. Then she said, "Now direct that word at yourself for the rest of the day." What a powerful and loving idea.

HOW TO BE KIND TO YOURSELF

Focus on your strengths, not your weaknesses. Just like at the start of this book, when I advised you to look in the mirror and pick out your favorite body parts, and when I later told you to toot your own horn at work, the same goes for your personality. Think you're quiet? See it as pensive and thoughtful. Think you're pushy? See it as ambitious and organized. Think you're too loud? Actually, you're vivacious and fun—the life and soul of the party. Switch up your perspective: quit criticizing what you *aren't*, and start seeing what you *are*.

Steal three to five minutes per day of *you* time, to engage in the moment. This might not sound like much time, but trust me, it will make a world of difference to your mindfulness and clarity. It might be when you wake up, before the rest of the family starts demanding your attention, it could be walking the dog after work, or even during your commute. Push busy thoughts aside and slow the busy brain-whirring (this takes practice, and is the basis for meditation). Even if we're not checking e-mails and answering texts, we tend to be making mental lists of what's next. So press PAUSE; breathe slowly in through your nose and out through your mouth. Allow your diaphragm to expand all the way to the back of your rib cage. Breathing evenly fills the brain with optimum levels of oxygen and makes the neurological system fire at its best. It also levels out our stress hormone, cortisol, and boosts happy chemicals, such as serotonin and dopamine. Let your mind peacefully get ready for, or wrap up, the day.

You are the sum of the ten most present people in your life. So think hard about with whom you share your precious time, thoughts, and energy. Okay, you can't pick your boss, but your friends, fitness instructor, pastor, assistant, and even the chick who does your nails every week—are people you can choose. Surround yourself with kind, inspiring people, who bestow confidence and happiness.

Buy yourself a beautiful bunch of flowers, and arrange them in a vase in your bedroom. There's something extra luxurious about buying yourself flowers, for absolutely no other reason than just to treat yourself. And I love waking up and seeing my favorite blooms in the morning. It's also well known that plants and blooms lift the spirits. Speaking of lifting your spirits—pick your colors carefully. Yellow is the happiest color. Yellow stimulates mental processes, encourages communication, and is the symbol for liberalism in many countries. The most calming color? Pink. One shade known as "drunk-tank pink" is sometimes used in prisons to calm inmates, and sports teams sometimes paint the opposing team's locker room pink to keep the players passive and less energetic! But don't forget to add lots of foliage: green is proven to help us feel refreshed and restored.

Arm yourself against negativity by practicing forgiveness. I get wound up easily, and I'm also very sensitive: two personality traits that when combined, make me super susceptible to getting upset easily. I find it difficult to ignore or rise above any drama or confrontation that unfolds around me. But an equally Type A girlfriend recently joked that her new tactic for those with road rage, was to simply smile and wave at the furious person cutting you up on the street. Or to maintain total friendliness toward the nasty waiter, wishing them well in your head and forgiving them. The next day, I employed her idea. A young guy completely cut me up on Sunset Boulevard, honked his horn, and gesticulated out of his window. Nice. Remembering her words, I smiled, waved (probably a little over-enthusiasti-

cally!), and slowly drove off. The guy just dropped his hand. He seemed a mix of flawed and confused, and I laughed all the way home. The point is, see the best in everybody. Drop your ego, inwardly forgive people who act like idiots, and you'll be gobsmacked at how much calmer and at peace you feel with yourself. Letting go of things that could potentially irritate you is unbelievably empowering.

Let go of the quest for constant self-improvement, and give yourself a break. Sometimes it's fine to ignore that nagging voice in your head that says you really should hit the gym, you shouldn't order the apple pie, you should have finished that work project by now, you should look better in that dress. We women constantly overload and pressure ourselves. Once in a while, just stop. Treat yourself. Do what makes you *happy* right then and there. If that means skipping the treadmill, ordering the naughtiest option on the menu, drinking too much wine at dinner, or staying in bed watching TV reruns all day on Sunday, so be it.

Never stop learning. As Plutarch wisely said, "the mind is not a vessel to be filled, but a fire to be kindled." So invest in the things that help you grow, to be the best, the smartest version of you. Join the library or a film society, attend a conference, take an evening class, book a trip. Enrich your mind.

THOUGHTS TO BE INSPIRED BY

Following are the quotes I find inspiring, funny, uplifting, and empowering. I hope you'll take them with you through life, long after the final pages of this book. Enjoy!

"Whatever you can do, or dream you can do, begin it. Boldness has genius, power, and magic in it!"
—JOHANN WOLFGANG VON GOETHE

"Ever notice that 'what the hell' is always the right decision?"
—MARILYN MONROE

"I've learned that people will forget what you said, people will forget what you did, but people will never forget how you made them feel."
—MAYA ANGELOU

"I believe in pink. I believe that laughing is the best calorie-burner. I believe in kissing, kissing a lot."
—AUDREY HEPBURN

"Clothes make the man. Naked people have little or no influence on society."
—MARK TWAIN

"Laughter is the closest distance between two people."
—VICTOR BORGE

"We are all in the gutter, but some of us are looking at the stars."
—OSCAR WILDE

"Dress shabbily and they remember the dress; dress impeccably and they remember the woman."
—COCO CHANEL

"People can succeed at almost anything for which they have unlimited enthusiasm."
—CHARLES SCHWAB

"When the pond is still, the reflection is clear."
—UNKNOWN

"Cherish all your happy moments: they make a fine cushion for old age."
—CHRISTOPHER MORLEY

"Those who bring sunshine to the lives of others cannot keep it from themselves." —J. M. BARRIE

"Put your trust in God, my boys, and keep your powder dry." —OLIVER CROMWELL

"Don't let your sorrow come higher than your knees."
—SWEDISH PROVERB

"Every man is the arbiter of his own virtues; whether or not you consider it courageous is more important than the act itself." —WILLIAM FAULKNER

"Dreams nourish the soul, just as food nourishes the body. The pleasure of the search and of adventure feed our dreams." —PAULO COELHO

Index

A

accessories, up-styling with, 72–80

afternoon tea, 273–277

alcohol, 127

angora, caring for, 118

Annie Hall, 291

antiques, 245–246

apple body type, 21

apple cider vinegar, 136

at-home face mask, 139–140

B

balconette bras, 111

bathrooms, 232–240, 251–252

baths, 236–240

bean puree, 259

beanies, 93

beauty juice, 135

beauty products
    for hair removal, 150–153
    must-haves, 155–156
    for self-tan, 153–155
    what to avoid, 145–146
    what to look for, 147, 149
    See also hair; makeup

bedding, 229–231, 253

bedrooms, 220–231, 254

Belle de Jour, 291

berets, 93

black hair, caring for, 167

black tie, 51

bloating, facial, 128–129

blushes, 180–183

boaters, 91

body brushing, 142

body image, 14–15

body types, 19–22

bowlers, 93

bras
    buying, 110–111
    fitting, 109–110
    measuring for, 108–109
    types of, 111

breakfast, 262

Breakfast at Tiffany's, 290

brides, 53–55

bronzers, 180–183

brushes, 178–179

budget tips, 278–289

C

Cacao Coconut Balls, 258

career tips, 43–46

cashmere, caring for, 117–118

cat eye, 195–196

cellulite, 141–143

changing rooms, 31

chokers, 79

chypre fragrances, 211

citrus fragrances, 211

cleaning, natural alternatives for,
    251–254

cloche hats, 93

closets
    cleaning, 27
    organizing, 27, 29–30

clothes
    caring for, 113–121
    changing, 25
    getting rid of, 24
    putting looks together, 26
    storing, 27, 29
    trying on, 31
    vintage, 94–101
    See also dressing

Clueless, 290

cocktails, 256–257

coconut
    exfoliation with, 137
    recipes with, 258

Coconut Cashew Shake, 258

color
    effects of, 295
    for first date, 48
    hair, 160–161
    for job interviews, 38–39
    for lips, 188–189
    for makeup, 173
    selecting color schemes, 241–244

column body type, 22

concealer, 175–178

conditioner, 164

confidence, 14–15

contouring, 184–185

convertible bras, 111

Coronation Chicken, 261

cooking, 254–262

Cream Cheese Frittata, Parsley and, 261

cucumber peel, 137–138

curling lashes, 199

cybershopping, 97–99, 103, 104

D

dates, first, 47–50

decorating
    about, 218
    bathrooms, 233–236

bedrooms, 223–226
    space issues and, 249
    tips for, 250

depilatory creams, 152

Desperately Seeking Susan, 291

desserts, 258

diamonds, 74–76

dinner, 259

Dolce Vita, La, 291

dress codes, for weddings, 51

dresses, caring for, 120

dressing
    as a bride, 53–55
    for a first date, 47–50
    in the morning, 36
    for a wedding, 50–52
    for work, 37–40
    See also clothes

dry shampoo, 169

Duigan, James, 127, 286

E

earrings, 79

electrolysis, 150

exercise, 126, 278–279

exfoliation
    with coconut, 137
    of lips, 192
    self-tanning and, 153

eye circles, 176

eye shadow, 197–198

eyebrows
    makeup for, 201–204
    tweezing, 152

eyeliner, 194–195

eyes, makeup for, 194–200

F

face
    at-home mask, 139–140
    massage for, 128–129, 282
    puffiness in, 128–129
    washing, 140–141

false lashes, 200

fashion, 14–15

fedoras, 92

Festive Mulled Wine, 256

fish recipe, 259

floral fragrances, 211

flowers, 226–228, 294–295

food/nutrition, 126–127, 141–142, 158, 160, 206, 286, 288

forgiveness, 295

fougère fragrances, 210–211

foundation, 173–174

Frittata, Parsley and Cream Cheese, 261

G

gifts, 273

glass ceiling, smashing, 43

glitter, 198

Great Gatsby, The, 291

H

hair
  about, 157
  accessorizing, 170
  black, 167
  color, 160–161
  conditioning, 165
  cutting, 163–164
  drying, 168
  feeding, 158, 160
  products for, 162
  shine and, 166
  styling, 169
  washing, 164

hair removal, 150–153

handbags
  about, 81
  caring for, 120–121
  choosing, 82–83
  glossary of, 84–85

hands, 149

hats
  about, 89
  caring for, 120
  summer, 90–91
  at weddings, 52
  winter, 92–93

heels
  for dates, 49
  walking in, 68

High Society, 290

highlighter, 176

home, shopping for, 219

hosting, 263–276

hourglass body type, 20

hydration, 129, 136

I

ingrown hair, 153

inspirational thoughts, 297

interviews, 38–39, 42

J

jeans
  caring for, 60
  finding perfect, 55–60
  styling, 58
  types of, 56

jewelry
  buying, 80
  caring for, 77
  trends in, 79

juices for nourishing, 132, 134–135

K

kindness, 293–295

kitchens, 253, 254–262

L

lamb's wool, caring for, 118

laser hair removal, 150

lashes
  curling, 199
  false, 200

laundry, 115

Lean In (Sandberg), 43

leather, caring for, 117

lighting, 221, 233, 270

lingerie, 107–108. *See also* underwear

lip liners, 190

lipstick, 186–194

living rooms, 240–249, 252

Louboutin, Christian, 69

Louise's Mezcal Kicker, 257

Love Story, 291

lunches, 260–261

M

makeup
  about, 170, 172
  blush and bronzes, 180–183
  brushes, 178–179
  concealer, 175–178
  contouring, 184–185
  for dates, 49–50
  for eyebrows, 201–204
  for eyes, 194–200
  foundation, 173–174
  for lips, 186–194

manicures, 206–207

manuka honey, 136

mascara, 196, 199

massage, for face, 128–129, 282

mentors, 45

merino, caring for, 118

Mezcal Kicker, Louise's, 257

milk baths, 138, 239

minimizer bras, 111

mirrors, 27

mohair, caring for, 118

monograms, 235–236

moths, 30, 116

movies, 290–291

My Mom's Coronation Chicken, 261

N

nails, 205–208

natural skin remedies, 136–140

networking, 45

O

oils, good, 149

Oriental fragrances, 210

ozonic fragrances, 211

P

packing, 62

panama hats, 91

Parsley and Cream Cheese
    Frittata, 262

parties, hosting, 263–276

pear body type, 21–22

Pear Prosecco Cocktail, 256

pearls, 79

pedicures, 208

perfume, 209–215

personalization, 247–248

pillbox hats, 91

pimples, hiding, 176, 177

plants, 250, 286, 294–295

playlists, 229, 267

plucking/tweezing, 152, 203

plunge bras, 111

pockmarks, 177

pork pie hats, 92

Pretty Woman, 291

Prosecco Cocktail, Pear, 256

push-up bras, 111

R

Rachel's Turkey Burgers, 260

recipes, 256–262

rejuvenating juice, 134

retinol, 149

rose petal bath, 239

S

sales, 102–105

salts, bath, 239–240

Sandberg, Sheryl, 43

scalp, 157–158

scars, covering, 176, 177

scarves, 86–89

scents
    in bathroom, 232
    in bedrooms, 228–229
    for contentment, 282
    perfume, 209–215

self-tanning, 153–155

sensitive skin, 146, 147

shampoo, 164
    dry, 169

shapewear, 32, 112

shaving, 151

shoes
    about, 65, 67
    for brides, 53–54
    caring for, 71, 121
    for dates, 49
    red, 68–69
    shopping for, 70
    slimming tips and, 33
    storing, 29–30
    for travel, 60–61
    walking in heels, 68

shopping
    cybershopping, 97–99, 103, 104
    for home, 219
    tips for, 31–32, 101–105

skin
 beauty products for, 147
 cellulite, 141–143
 juices for nourishing, 132
 natural remedies for, 135–140
 sensitive, 146, 147
 smoothie for, 130–131
 stretch marks, 143–144
 tips for, 125–135
 washing face, 140–141

sleep, 126, 280

slimming tips, 32–33

smoothie, skin-brightening,
 130–131

space, decorating and, 249

sports bras, 111

stains, treating, 114

Stephanie's Double Date Dish, 259

storage, 246

strapless bras, 111

stretch marks, 143–144

style
 discovering personal, 16–18
 as self-expression, 18

suede, caring for, 117

sugar, 126–127

suits, 39–40

sunhats, 90

swimwear, 63–64

T

tattoos
 covering, 176
 eyebrow, 204

tea parties, 273–276

technology
 in bedroom, 222
 contentment and, 280–281

texture, 33, 244

threading, 203

tights, caring for, 120

top heavy body type, 20

traveling, 60–62

trilby hats, 93

T-shirt bras, 111

Turkey Burgers, Rachel's, 260

TVs, 222

tweezing/plucking, 152, 203

U

underwear
 about, 106–107
 choosing, 112
 lingerie, 107–108
 shapewear, 32, 112
 See also bras

V

veins, covering, 176

vintage clothing, 94–101

vintage stores, 99

visors, 91

Vitamix, 132

W

waxing, 151, 203

weddings, 50–55

white tie, 51

Wine, Festive Mulled, 256

wireless bras, 111

work life, 37–46

Y

yogurt, 138–139

Acknowledgments

I feel a huge amount of gratitude to my followers on social media and the viewers of my shows, in particular the fans of *Plain Jane* and *Style By Jury*. You guys are so inquisitive, fun and loyal to the core. You're the reason I wrote this book—thank you for being awesome!

Thank you to my big sisters, Caroline and Juliette, for always being there for me with hugs, tea, words of wisdom, and the odd judo chop.

Thank you to Kirsty, for whipping me away from an office job seven years ago and making my dreams come true. To Ennis, the sweetest, funniest, most supportive Turkish man I ever met. To Pearl, Jen, Ashley, Jonathan, and Katie, the dream team that believes in me and hustles on my behalf 24/7 with smiles on their faces!

Thank you Erin Cox, for so passionately "getting" this book and selling it many years after I had the idea. To Cindy De La Hoz and Susan Van Horn for their incredible support and understanding, especially when it came to covers!

I also want to shout out my wonderful friends for helping me, whether they realized it or not, with this book. Thank you to the bestos: Steph, Suza, and T, this is my epitome of "bower!" Rachel, my sista from another mista, who has been by my side through thick and thin. Anita and Tom, my incredible L.A. family, who make me laugh till I cry.

To Granny, for still telling me filthy jokes with a twinkle in her eye, aged ninety-three. Mum and Dad, for unwavering love and support, and for becoming two of my best mates.

And finally, to Mackenzie, for always listening and caring, for giving me surprisingly apt advice about the world of fashion, for making me laugh when all I want to do is tear my hair out, and for taking me to play *Pacman* on Valentine's Day. My partner in crime, my mate, my director (ha!) and my love.